Classic
ADVENTURE STORIES

Classic
ADVENTURE STORIES

Twenty-one tales of people pushed to the limit

EDITED *by*

STEPHEN BRENNAN

THE LYONS PRESS
GUILFORD, CONNECTICUT
AN IMPRINT OF THE GLOBE PEQUOT PRESS

The Lyons Press is an imprint of The Globe Pequot Press

10   9   8   7   6   5   4   3   2   1

Printed in the United States of America

Designed by Claire Zoghb

ISBN 1-59228-182-6

Library of Congress Cataloging-in-Publication data is
available on file.

For Lara

Contents

Introduction

Why does a man desire to know
of sufferings he would himself by
no means suffer?

—*St. Augustine*

Why indeed? And yet it's a fair bet the first stories people told one another were adventure stories. This makes perfect sense. Gathered about the primordial campfire, at ease at last after a long day of risks, dangers, privations, and facing the terrors of the dark night to come, people solaced one another with tales of daring exploits, sufferings set at nought, villains outfaced, monsters slain. We do this still, and for the same reasons. The appeal of adventure is universal, in that every one of us has known adventure of one kind or another. It may have involved extreme physical peril, or only, but never merely, our sense of ourselves. Most often it is a testing, a flying in the face of fate, a matching of wit and skill and strength against the odds, gravity defied. Adventure is first a matter of risk, something at-venture. We say *per adventure*, when we mean *by chance*—chance being a question of luck, or the lack of it. If the crocs get you, or you fall off the mountain, the coroner brings in a verdict of death by *misadventure*.

Some adventures we seek after and carefully plan. We plot routes, arrange for mounts, engage guides, cache supplies. This may be regarded as risk-management, and would seem counter-intuitive, too much a hedging of bets against the very risk you are seeking. But just as a matter of practicality, if you aim to chase whales you'll need a boat. You can't possibly hunt musk-oxen at the Pole unless you can get to the Pole, and, presumably, home again with your grisly trophy.

Sometimes you are unaware an adventure has commenced, then suddenly you're in it—in it over your boots—and just as often this pleases you. Witness young Marlow in Conrad's "Youth." "And there was somewhere in me the thought: By Jove! this is the deuce of an adventure—something you read about." These adventures come unbidden, and like greatness are thrust upon us. They have an out-sized, epic quality about them; desperate circumstances demand heroic efforts. Heroes have adventures, but does adventure make you a hero? I think it does, and perhaps something more. Note the Greeks had no god of adventure, instead the gods themselves had adventures, scores of them.

An adventure may fall like a bolt from the sky and be over in a moment, or it may involve long periods of back-breaking, heart-shattering, mind-numbing labor. Adventure may even be dull, but an adventure story never is. The good ones take you firmly by your front button and lead you on. In a little while you are bound hand and foot in the skein of the tale.

Must the account be true? Well, yes and no. A wholly invented tale may bespeak a truth at least as profound as a *true* narrative. And no memoir is ever more than mostly true. On one hand it is nearly impossible to tell your own story truthfully, though you may try; but even in the shaping of the tale, the little elves of fiction have come in the night and done their bit. By the same token, since we can't help telling stories on ourselves, even our wildest fantasy is shot through with the truth, as we know it.

One of the best known adventure stories comes from the Old Testament. In "Jonah" (the only outright comedy I know of in the Bible) we apprehend many of the themes that make a classic adventure. Jonah hears the word of God and he doesn't like it. He seeks escape by running away to sea. Sound familiar? He makes his way to the coast and books passage aboard a ship bound for a far away land, exotic Tarshish. At sea a great tempest arises. The typhoon, the tempest, the perfect storm are staples of classic adventure. The ship looks to founder as the sailors battle the sea. They struggle at the oars, they lighten load by throwing cargo over the side. Eventually they throw Jonah too. The sea calms, perhaps all will be well, perhaps not. Can Jonah cope? Can Jonah swim? Then catastrophe strikes, upping the ante here (a technique tried and true) and Jonah is swallowed by a great fish. He survives, in a fish, for three days. One requirement of the classic adventure story is that the hero survive. Were he to perish, it would be a tragedy. Within the fish, Jonah has an epiphany, an illumination. He takes action: He cries out to the Lord, and that is the thing that saves him. In the best adventure stories there comes a moment when the hero, hard pressed, comes up against the thing that would kill him. It may be a sheet of ice or a savage beast, a sworn enemy or just a figure of his own imagination. How he meets this peril will determine his fate. Outside the fish, again on dry land, Jonah has become a wiser man. He goes to the city of his enemy, there to preach and try to understand the will of God. What began as an escape has now become a search. We all feel somehow that to know adventure is a path to wisdom. At story's end there is the leaven of humor, adventure's yeast, as the Lord makes a smart crack about the Ninevites and their cattle.

My aim in this collection is to give a sampling of different kinds of adventure stories: different heroes, humors, settings, circumstances, different points of view. The order of the stories is roughly chronological, but I suggest the reader adopt my own practice with any anthology. Turn first to the Contents page, and in your reading, order the tales for yourself. Read first the authors you know, or better yet, those you have never heard of. Set Homer's "Odyssey" against Herman Melville's "The First Lowering." Cruise the South Atlantic with Richard Henry Dana, or try with Marlow to get yourself down east in Conrad's "Youth," or up north with Frederic Remington in "The Strange Days That Came to Jimmie Friday." If hunting stirs your blood, stalk the lion with Alfred H. Miles; or should you prefer smaller prey, join W. H. Hudson in "Wildfowling Adventures." Perhaps you are of a swashbuckling persuasion; very well, you have "The Forcing of the Trap" by Anthony Hope, and "How the Brigadier Slew the Fox" by Arthur Conan Doyle. If sparse, hard-bitten realism is your metier, read "The Road Home" by Peter Collinson (Dashiell Hammett).

My own guilty secret is this: I read classic adventure for the *how-to* stuff: how to plan an exploit, sail a ship, pack a kit; how to break a castle, face down an arch villain, save a king. Tom Sawyer has much to say on the subject of how to live a pirate's life, and Tom knows what he's talking about. Should my estate be threatened by a holocaust of ants, Carl Stephenson's "Leiningen Versus the Ants" offers a lot of sound advice. "The Venturers" by O'Henry advances as good a reason as any for *not* running away to sea and leaving your domestic affairs to sort themselves out in your absence. If I am ever be-reefed on a lea shore, my vessel breaking up beneath my feet, I will have some idea as to how I might get my crew safely ashore thanks to "Shipwreck" by Captain James Riley.

Classic adventure stories mix locale, mystery, danger, and romance. They grip!—which is, after all, the point. Every great adventure story comes with its own needle, and the juiced reader reels. Who's at risk? The reader is, you are. Will you survive? How will you cope? Read on.

—Stephen Vincent Brennan

Classic

ADVENTURE STORIES

Jonah

[KING JAMES BIBLE]

JONAH, CHAPTER I

1: Now the word of the LORD came unto Jonah the son of Amittai, saying,

2: Arise, go to Nineveh, that great city, and cry against it; for their wickedness is come up before me.

3: But Jonah rose up to flee unto Tarshish from the presence of the LORD, and went down to Joppa; and he found a ship going to Tarshish: so he paid the fare thereof, and went down into it, to go with them unto Tarshish from the presence of the LORD.

4: But the LORD sent out a great wind into the sea, and there was a mighty tempest in the sea, so that the ship was like to be broken.

5: Then the mariners were afraid, and cried every man unto his god, and cast forth the wares that were in the ship into the sea, to lighten it of them. But Jonah was gone down into the sides of the ship; and he lay, and was fast asleep.

6: So the shipmaster came to him, and said unto him, What meanest thou, O sleeper? arise, call upon thy God, if so be that God will think upon us, that we perish not.

7: And they said every one to his fellow, Come, and let us cast lots, that we may know for whose cause this evil is upon us. So they cast lots, and the lot fell upon Jonah.

8: Then said they unto him, Tell us, we pray thee, for whose cause this evil is upon us; What is thine occupation? and whence comest thou? what is thy country? and of what people art thou?

9: And he said unto them, I am a Hebrew; and I fear the LORD, the God of heaven, which hath made the sea and the dry land.

10: Then were the men exceedingly afraid, and said unto him, Why hast thou done this? For the men knew that he fled from the presence of the LORD, because he had told them.

11: Then said they unto him, What shall we do unto thee, that the sea may be calm unto us? for the sea wrought, and was tempestuous.

12: And he said unto them, Take me up, and cast me forth into the sea; so shall the sea be calm unto you: for I know that for my sake this great tempest is upon you.

13: Nevertheless the men rowed hard to bring it to the land; but they could not: for the sea wrought, and was tempestuous against them.

14: Wherefore they cried unto the LORD, and said, We beseech thee, O LORD, we beseech thee, let us not perish for this man's life, and lay not upon us innocent blood: for thou, O LORD, hast done as it pleased thee.

15: So they took up Jonah, and cast him forth into the sea: and the sea ceased from her raging.

16: Then the men feared the LORD exceedingly, and offered a sacrifice unto the LORD, and made vows.

17: Now the LORD had prepared a great fish to swallow up Jonah. And Jonah was in the belly of the fish three days and three nights.

JONAH, CHAPTER 2

1: Then Jonah prayed unto the LORD his God out of the fish's belly,

2: And said, I cried by reason of mine affliction unto the LORD, and he heard me; out of the belly of hell cried I, and thou heardest my voice.

3: For thou hadst cast me into the deep, in the midst of the seas; and the floods compassed me about: all thy billows and thy waves passed over me.

4: Then I said, I am cast out of thy sight; yet I will look again toward thy holy temple.

5: The waters compassed me about, even to the soul: the depth closed me round about, the weeds were wrapped about my head.

6: I went down to the bottoms of the mountains; the earth with her bars was about me for ever: yet hast thou brought up my life from corruption, O LORD my God.

7: When my soul fainted within me I remembered the LORD: and my prayer came in unto thee, into thine holy temple.

8: They that observe lying vanities forsake their own mercy.

9: But I will sacrifice unto thee with the voice of thanksgiving; I will pay that that I have vowed. Salvation is of the LORD.

10: And the LORD spake unto the fish, and it vomited out Jonah upon the dry land.

JONAH, CHAPTER 3

1: And the word of the LORD came unto Jonah the second time, saying,

2: Arise, go unto Nineveh, that great city, and preach unto it the preaching that I bid thee.

3: So Jonah arose, and went unto Nineveh, according to the word of the LORD. Now Nineveh was an exceeding great city of three days' journey.

4: And Jonah began to enter into the city a day's journey, and he cried, and said, Yet forty days, and Nineveh shall be overthrown.

5: So the people of Nineveh believed God, and proclaimed a fast, and put on sackcloth, from the greatest of them even to the least of them.

6: For word came unto the king of Nineveh, and he arose from his throne, and he laid his robe from him, and covered him with sackcloth, and sat in ashes.

7: And he caused it to be proclaimed and published through Nineveh by the decree of the king and his nobles, saying, Let neither man nor beast, herd nor flock, taste any thing: let them not feed, nor drink water:

8: But let man and beast be covered with sackcloth, and cry mightily unto God: yea, let them turn every one from his evil way, and from the violence that is in their hands.

9: Who can tell if God will turn and repent, and turn away from his fierce anger, that we perish not?

10: And God saw their works, that they turned from their evil way; and God repented of the evil, that he had said that he would do unto them; and he did it not.

Jonah, chapter 4

1: But it displeased Jonah exceedingly, and he was very angry.

2: And he prayed unto the LORD, and said, I pray thee, O LORD, was not this my saying, when I was yet in my country? Therefore I fled before unto

Tarshish: for I knew that thou art a gracious God, and merciful, slow to anger, and of great kindness, and repentest thee of the evil.

3: Therefore now, O LORD, take, I beseech thee, my life from me; for it is better for me to die than to live.

4: Then said the LORD, Doest thou well to be angry?

5: So Jonah went out of the city, and sat on the east side of the city, and there made him a booth, and sat under it in the shadow, till he might see what would become of the city.

6: And the LORD God prepared a gourd, and made it to come up over Jonah, that it might be a shadow over his head, to deliver him from his grief. So Jonah was exceeding glad of the gourd.

7: But God prepared a worm when the morning rose the next day, and it smote the gourd that it withered.

8: And it came to pass, when the sun did arise, that God prepared a vehement east wind; and the sun beat upon the head of Jonah, that he fainted, and wished in himself to die, and said, It is better for me to die than to live.

9: And God said to Jonah, Doest thou well to be angry for the gourd? And he said, I do well to be angry, even unto death.

10: Then said the LORD, Thou hast had pity on the gourd, for which thou hast not laboured, neither

madest it grow; which came up in a night, and per-
ished in a night:

11: And should not I spare Nineveh, that great city,
wherein are more than sixscore thousand persons
that cannot discern between their right hand and
their left hand; and also much cattle?

Book XII of The Odyssey

[**HOMER**]

"After we were clear of the river Oceanus, and had got out into the open sea, we went on till we reached the Aeaean island where there is dawn and sunrise as in other places. We then drew our ship on to the sands and got out of her on to the shore, where we went to sleep and waited till day should break.

"Then, when the child of morning, rosy-fingered Dawn, appeared, I sent some men to Circe's house to fetch the body of Elpenor. We cut firewood from a wood where the headland jutted out into the sea, and after we had wept over him and lamented him we performed his funeral rites. When his body and armor had been burned to ashes, we raised a cairn, set a stone over it, and at the top of the cairn we fixed the oar that he had been used to row with.

"While we were doing all this, Circe, who knew that we had got back from the house of Hades, dressed herself and came to us as fast as she could; and her maidservants came with her bringing us bread, meat, and wine. Then she stood in the midst of us and said, 'You have done a bold thing in going down alive to the house of Hades, and you will have died twice, to other people's once. Now, then, stay here for the rest of the day, feast your fill, and go on with your voyage at daybreak tomorrow morning. In the meantime I will tell Odysseus about your course, and will explain everything to him so as to prevent your suffering from misadventure either by land or sea.'

"We agreed to do as she had said, and feasted through the livelong day to the going down of the sun, but when the sun had set and it came on dark, the men laid themselves down to sleep by the stern cables of the ship. Then Circe took me by the hand and bade me be seated away from the others, while she reclined by my side and asked me all about our adventures.

"'So far so good,' said she, when I had ended my story, 'and now pay attention to what I am about to tell you—heaven itself, indeed, will recall it to your recollection. First you will come to the Sirens who enchant all who come near them. If anyone unwarily draws in too close and hears the singing of the Sirens, his wife and children will never welcome him home again, for they sit in a green field and warble him to death with the sweetness of their song. There is a great heap of dead men's bones lying all around, with the flesh still rotting off them. Therefore pass these Sirens by, and stop your men's ears with wax that none of them may hear; but if you like you can listen yourself, for you may get the men to bind you as you stand upright on a cross-piece halfway up the mast, and they must lash the rope's ends to the mast itself, that you may have the pleasure of listening. If you beg and pray the men to unloose you, then they must bind you faster.

"'When your crew have taken you past these Sirens, I cannot give you coherent directions as to which of two courses you are to take; I will lay the two alternatives before you, and you must consider them for yourself. One the one hand there are some overhanging rocks against which the deep blue waves of Amphitrite beat with terrific fury; the blessed gods call these rocks the Wanderers. Here not even a bird may pass, no, not even the timid doves that bring ambrosia to Father Zeus, but the sheer rock always carries off one of them, and Father Zeus has to send another to make up their number. No ship that ever yet came to these rocks has got away again, but the waves and whirlwinds of fire are freighted with wreckage and with the bodies of dead men. The only vessel that ever sailed and got through was the famous Argo on her way from the house of Aeetes, and she too would have gone against these great rocks, only that Hera piloted her past them for the love she bore to Jason.

"'Of these two rocks the one reaches heaven and its peak is lost in a dark cloud. This never leaves it, so that the top is never clear not even in summer and early autumn. No man, though he had twenty hands and twenty feet, could get a foothold on it and climb it, for it runs sheer up, as smooth as though it had been polished. In the middle of it there is a large cavern, looking west and turned towards Erebus; you must take your ship this way, but the cave is so high up that not even the stoutest archer could send an arrow into it. Inside it Scylla sits and yelps with a voice that you might take to be that of a young hound, but in truth she is a dreadful monster and no one—not even a god—could face her without being terror-struck. She has twelve misshapen feet, and six necks of the most prodigious length; and at the end of each neck she has a fright-ful head with three rows of teeth in each, all set very close together, so that they would crunch any-one to death in a moment. She sits deep within her shady cell thrusting out her heads and peering all round the rock, fishing for dolphins or dogfish or any larger monster that she can catch of the thou-sands with which Amphitrite teems. No ship ever yet got past her without losing some men, for she shoots out all her heads at one, and carries of a man in each mouth.

"'You will find the other rock lies lower, but they are so close together that there is not more than a bow-shot between them. A large fig tree in full leaf grows upon it, and under it lies the sucking whirlpool of Charybdis. Three times in the day does she vomit forth her waters, and three times she sucks them down again. See that you be not there when she is sucking, for if you are, Poseidon himself could not save you; you must hug the Scylla side and drive your ship by as fast as you can, for you had better lose six men than your whole crew.'

"'Is there no way,' said I, 'of escaping Charybdis, and at the same time keeping Scylla off when she is trying to harm my men?'

"'You daredevil,' replied the goddess, 'you are always wanting to fight somebody or something; you will not let yourself be beaten even by the immortals. For Scylla is not mortal; moreover, she is savage, extreme, rude, cruel and invincible. There is no help for it; your best chance will be to get by her as fast as ever you can, for if you dawdle about her rock while you are putting on your armor, she may catch you with a second cast of her six heads, and snap up another half dozen of your men. So drive your ship past her at full speed, and roar out lustily to Crataiis who is Scylla's dam, bad luck to her; she will then stop her from making a second raid upon you.

"'You will now come to the Thrinacian island, and here you will see many herds of cattle and flocks of sheep belonging to the sun-god—seven herds of cattle and seven flocks of sheep, with fifty head in each flock. They do not breed, nor do they become fewer in number, and they are tended by the goddesses Phaethusa and Lampetie, who are children of the sun-god Hyperion by Neaera. Their mother, when she had borne them and had done suckling them, sent them to the Thrinacian island, which was a long way off, to live there and look after their father's flocks and herds. If you leave these flocks unharmed, and think of nothing but getting home, you may yet after much hardship reach Ithaca. But if you harm them, then I forewarn you of the destruction both of your ship and of your comrades; and even though you may yourself escape, you will return late, in bad plight, after losing all your men.'

"Here she ended, and dawn enthroned in gold began to show in heaven, whereon she returned inland. I then went on board and told my men to loose the ship from her moorings; so they at once got into her, took their places, and began to smite the gray sea with their oars. Presently the great and cunning goddess Circe befriended us with a fair wind that blew dead aft, and stayed steadily with us, keeping our sails well filled, so we did whatever wanted doing to the ship's gear, and let her go as wind and helmsman headed her.

"Then, being much troubled in mind, I said to my men, 'My friends, it is not right that one or two of us alone should know the prophecies that Circe has made me, I will therefore tell you about them, so that whether we live or die we may do so with our eyes open. First she said we were to keep clear of the Sirens, who sit and sing most beautifully in a field of flowers; but she said I might hear them myself so long as no one else did. Therefore, take me and bind me to the crosspiece halfway up the mast; bind me as I stand upright, with a bond so fast that I cannot possibly break away, and lash the rope's ends to the mast itself. If I beg and pray you to set me free, then bind me more tightly still.'

"I had hardly finished telling everything to the men before we reached the island of the two Sirens, for the wind had been very favorable. Then all of a sudden it fell dead calm; there was not a breath of wind or a ripple upon the water, so the men furled the sails and stowed them; then taking to their oars they whitened the water with the foam they raised in rowing. Meanwhile I took a large wheel of wax and cut it up small with my sword. Then I kneaded the wax in my strong hands till it became soft, which it soon did between the kneading and the rays of the sun-god son of Hyperion. Then I stopped the ears of all my men, and they bound me hands and feet to the mast as I stood upright on the crosspiece; but they went on rowing themselves. When we had got within earshot of the land, and the ship was going at a good rate, the Sirens saw that we were getting in shore and began with their singing.

"'Come here,' they sang, 'renowned Odysseus, honor to the Achaean name, and listen to our two voices. No one ever sailed past us without staying to hear the enchanting sweetness of our song—and he who listens will go on his way not only charmed, but wiser, for we know all the ills that the gods laid upon the Argives and Trojans before Troy, and can tell you everything that is going to happen over the whole world.'

"They sang these words most musically, and as I longed to hear them further I made signs by frowning to my men that they should set me free; but they quickened their stroke, and Eurylochus and Perimedes bound me with still stronger bonds till we had got out of hearing of the Sirens' voices. Then my men took the wax from their ears and unbound me.

"Immediately after we had got past the island I saw a great wave from which spray was rising, and I heard a loud roaring sound. The men were so frightened that they loosed hold of their oars, for the whole sea resounded with the rushing of the waters, but the ship stayed where it was, for the men had left off rowing. I went round, therefore, and exhorted them man by man not to lose heart.

"'My friends,' said I, 'this is not the first time that we have been in danger, and we are in nothing like so bad a case as when the Cyclops shut us up in his cave; nevertheless, my courage and wise counsel saved us then, and we shall live to look back on all this as well.

Now, therefore, let us all do as I say, trust in Zeus and row on with might and main. As for you, coxswain, these are your orders—attend to them, for the ship is in your hands: turn her head away from these steaming rapid and hug the rock, or she will give you the slip and be over yonder before you know where you are, and you will be the death of us.'

"So they did as I told them; but I said nothing about the awful monster Scylla, for I knew the men would not go on rowing if I did, but would huddle together in the hold. In one thing only did I disobey Circe's strict instructions—I put on my armor. Then seizing two strong spears I took my stand on the ship's bows, for it was there that I expected first to see the monster of the rock, who was to do my men so much harm; but I could not make her out anywhere, though I strained my eyes with looking the gloomy rock all over and over.

"Then we entered the Straits[1] in great fear of mind, for on the one hand was Scylla, and on the other dread Charybdis kept sucking up the salt water. As she vomited it up, it was like the water in a cauldron when it is boiling over upon a great fire, and the spray reached the top of the rocks on either side. When she began to suck again, we could see the water all inside whirling round and round, and it made a deafening sound as it broke against the rocks. We could see the bottom of the whirlpool all black with sand and mud, and the men were at their wits ends for fear. While we were taken up with this, and were expecting each moment to be our last, Scylla pounced suddenly upon us and snatched up my six best men. I was looking at once after both ship and men, and in a moment I saw their hands and feet ever so high above me, struggling in the air as Scylla was carrying them off, and I heard them call out my name in one last despairing cry. As a fisherman, seated, spear in hand, upon some jutting rock,[2] throws bait into the water to deceive the poor little fishes, and spears them with the ox's horn with which his spear is shod, throwing them gasping onto the land as he catches them one by one—even so did Scylla land these panting creatures on her rock and munch them up at the mouth of her den, while they screamed and stretched out their hands to me in their mortal agony. This was the most sickening sight that I saw throughout all my voyages.

"When we had passed the [Wandering] rocks, with Scylla and terrible Charybdis, we reached the noble island of the sun-god, where were the goodly cattle and sheep belonging to the sun Hyperion. While still at sea in my ship I could hear the cattle lowing as they came home to the yards, and the sheep bleating. Then I remembered what the blind Theban prophet Teiresias had told me, and how carefully Aeaean Circe had warned me to shun the island of the blessed sun-god. So being much troubled, I said to the men, 'My men,

I know you are hard pressed, but listen while I tell you the prophecy that Teiresias made me, and how carefully Aeaean Circe warned me to shun the island of the blessed sun-god, for it was here, she said, that our worst danger would lie. Head the ship, therefore, away from the island.'

"The men were in despair at this, and Eurylochus at once gave me an insolent answer. 'Odysseus,' said he, 'you are cruel. You are very strong yourself and never get worn out; you seem to be made of iron, and now, though your men are exhausted with toil and want of sleep, you will not let them land and cook themselves a good supper upon this island, but bid them put out to sea and go faring fruitlessly on through the watches of the flying night. It is by night that the winds blow hardest and do so much damage. How can we escape should one of those sudden squalls spring up from southwest or west, which so often wreck a vessel when our lords the gods are unpropitious? Now, therefore, let us obey the behests of night and prepare our supper here hard by the ship; tomorrow morning we will go on board again and put out to sea.'

"Thus spoke Eurylochus, and the men approved his words. I saw that heaven meant us a mischief and said, 'You force me to yield, for you are many against one, but at any rate each one of you must take his solemn oath that if he meet with a herd of cattle or a large flock of sheep, he will not be so mad as to kill a single head of either, but will be satisfied with the food that Circe has given us.'

"They all swore as I bade them, and when they had completed their oath we made the ship fast in a harbor that was near a stream of fresh water, and the men went ashore and cooked their suppers. As soon as they had had enough to eat and drink, they began talking about their poor comrades whom Scylla had snatched up and eaten; this set them weeping, and they went on crying till they fell off into a sound sleep.

"In the third watch of the night when the stars had shifted their places, Zeus raised a great gale of wind that blew a hurricane so that land and sea were covered with thick clouds, and night sprang forth out of the heavens. When the child of morning, rosy-fingered Dawn, appeared, we brought the ship to land and drew her into a cave wherein the sea-nymphs hold their courts and dances, and I called the men together in council.

"'My friends,' said I, 'we have meat and drink in the ship, let us mind, therefore, and not touch the cattle, or we shall suffer for it; for these cattle and sheep belong to the mighty sun, who sees and gives ear to everything.' And again they promised that they would obey.

"For a whole month the wind blew steadily from the south, and there was no other wind, but only south and east.[3] As long as corn and wine held out the men did not touch the cattle when they were hungry. When, however, they had eaten all there was in the ship, they were forced to go further afield, fishing with hook and line, catching birds, and taking whatever they could lay their hands on, for they were starving. One day, therefore, I went up inland that I might pray heaven to show me some means of getting away. When I had gone far enough to be clear of all my men, and had found a place that was well sheltered from the wind, I washed my hands and prayed to all the gods in Olympus till by and by they sent me off into a sweet sleep.

"Meanwhile Eurylochus had been giving evil counsel to the men. 'Listen to me,' said he, 'my poor comrades. All deaths are bad enough, but there is none so bad as famine. Why should not we drive in the best of these cows and offer them in sacrifice to the immortal gods? If we ever get back to Ithaca, we can build a fine temple to the sun-god and enrich it with every kind of ornament. If, however, he is determined to sink our ship out of revenge for these horned cattle, and the other gods are of the same mind, I for one would rather drink salt water once for all and have done with it than be starved to death by inches in such a desert island as this is.'

"Thus spoke Eurylochus, and the men approved his words. Now the cattle, so fair and goodly, were feeding not far from the ship; the men, therefore, drove in the best of them, and they all stood round them saying their prayers, and using young oak-shoots instead of barley meal, for there was no barley left. When they had done praying they killed the cows and dressed their carcasses; they cut out the thighbones, wrapped them round in two layers of fat, and set some pieces of raw meat on the top of them. They had no wine with which to make drink offerings over the sacrifice while it was cooking, so they kept pouring on a little water from time to time while the inward meats were being grilled. Then, when the thighbones were burned and they had tasted the inward meats, they cut the rest up small and put the pieces upon the spits.

"By this time my deep sleep had left me, and I turned back to the ship and to the seashore. As I drew near I began to smell hot roast meat, so I groaned out a prayer to the immortal gods. 'Father Zeus,' I exclaimed, 'and all you other gods who live in ever-lasting bliss, you have done me a cruel mischief by the sleep into which you have sent me. See what fine work these men of mine have been making in my absence.'

"Meanwhile Lampetie went straight off to the sun and told him we had been killing his cows, whereon he flew into a great rage, and said to the immortals, 'Father Zeus, and all you other gods who live in everlasting bliss, I must have vengeance on the crew of Odysseus' ship. They have had the insolence to kill my cows, which were the one thing I loved to look upon, whether I was going up heaven or down again. If they do not square accounts with me about my cows, I will go down to Hades and shine there among the dead.'

"'Sun,' said Zeus, 'go on shining upon us gods and upon mankind over the fruitful earth. I will shiver their ship into little pieces with a bolt of white lightning as soon as they get out to sea.'

"I was told all this by Calypso, who said she had heard it from the mouth of Hermes.

"As soon as I got down to my ship and to the seashore, I rebuked each one of the men separately, but we could see no way out of it, for the cows were dead already. And indeed the gods began at once to show signs and wonders among us, for the hides of the cattle crawled about, and the joints upon the spits began to low like cows, and the meat, whether cooked or raw, kept on making a noise just as cows do.

"For six days my men kept driving in the best cows and feasting upon them, but when Zeus the son of Cronus had added a seventh day, the fury of the gale abated; we therefore went on board, raised our masts, spread sail, and put out to sea. As soon as we were well away from the island, and could see nothing but sky and sea, the son of Cronus raised a black cloud over our ship, and the sea grew dark beneath it. We did not get on much further, for in another moment we were caught by a terrific squall from the west that snapped the forestays of the mast so that it fell aft, while all the ship's gear tumbled about at the bottom of the vessel. The mast fell upon the head of the helmsman in the ship's stern, so that the bones of his head were crushed to pieces, and he fell overboard as though he were diving, with no more life left in him.

"Then Zeus let fly with his thunderbolts, and the ship went round and round, and was filled with fire and brimstone as the lightning struck it. The men all fell into the sea; they were carried about in the water round the ship, looking like so many sea gulls, but the god presently deprived them of all chance of getting home again.

"I stuck to the ship till the sea knocked her sides from her keel (which drifted about by itself) and struck the mast out of her in the direction of the keel; but there was a backstay of stout ox-thong still hanging about it, and with this I lashed the mast and keel together, and getting astride of them was carried wherever the winds chose to take me.

"The gale from the west had now spent its force, and the wind got into the south again, which frightened me lest I should be taken back to the terrible whirlpool of Charybdis. This indeed was what actually happened, for I was borne along by the waves all night, and by sunrise had reached the rock of Scylla, and the whirlpool. She was then sucking down the salt sea water, but I was carried aloft toward the fig tree, which I caught hold of and clung on to like a bat. I could not plant my feet anywhere so as to stand securely, for the roots were a long way off and the boughs that overshadowed the whole pool were too high, too vast, and too far apart for me to reach them; so I hung patiently on, waiting till the pool should discharge my mast and raft again—and a very long while it seemed. A juryman is not more glad to get home to supper, after having been long detained in court by troublesome cases, then I was to see my raft beginning to work its way out of the whirlpool again. At last I let go with my hands and feet, and fell heavily into the sea, hard by my raft on to which I then got, and began to row with my hands. As for Scylla, the father of gods and men would not let her get further sight of me—otherwise I should have certainly been lost.

"Hence I was carried along for nine days till on the tenth night the gods stranded me on the Ogygian island, where dwells the great and powerful goddess Calypso. She took me in and was kind to me, but I need say no more about this, for I told you and your noble wife all about it yesterday, and I hate saying the same thing over and over again."

---

[1] These straits are generally understood to be the Straits of Messina.

[2] In the islands of Favorgnana and Marettimo off Sicily I have seen men fish exactly as here described. They chew bread into a paste and throw it into the sea to attract the fish, which they then spear. No line is used. (B.)

[3] The writer evidently regards Odysseus as on a coast that looked east at no great distance south of the Straits of Messina somewhere, say, near Tauromenium, now Taormina. (B.)

Shipwreck

[CAPTAIN JAMES RILEY]

We set sail from the bay of Gibraltar on the 23rd of August, 1815, intending to go by way of the Cape de Verd Islands, to complete the lading of the vessel with salt. We passed Cape Spartel on the morning of the 24th, giving it a birth of from ten to twelve leagues, and steered off to the W.S.W. I intended to make the Canary Islands, and pass between Teneriffe and Palma, having a fair wind; but it being very thick and foggy weather, though we got two observations at noon, neither could be much depended upon. On account of the fog, we saw no land, and found, by good meridian altitudes on the 28th, that we were in the latitude of 27.30.N. having differed our latitude by the force of current, one hundred and twenty miles; thus passing the Canaries without seeing any of them. I concluded we must have passed through

the intended passage without discovering the land
on either side, particularly, as it was in the night,
which was very dark, and black as pitch; nor could I
believe otherwise from having had a fair wind all the
way, and having steered one course ever since we
took our departure from Cape Spartel. Soon after
we got an observation on the 28th, it became as
thick as ever, and the darkness seemed (if possible) to
increase. Towards evening I got up my reckoning,
and examined it all over, to be sure that I had committed no error, and caused the mates to do the same
with theirs. Having thus ascertained that I was correct in calculation, I altered our course to S.W.
which ought to have carried us nearly on the course
I wished to steer, that is, for the easternmost of the
Cape de Verds; but finding the weather becoming
more foggy towards night, it being so thick that we
could scarcely see the end of the jib-boom, I
rounded the vessel to, and sounded with one hundred and twenty fathoms of line, but found no bottom, and continued on our course, still reflecting on
what should be the cause of our not seeing land, (as
I never had passed near the Canaries before without
seeing them, even in thick weather or in the night.)
I came to a determination to haul off to the N.W. by
the wind at 10 P.M. as I should then be by the log
only thirty miles north of Cape Bajador. I concluded on this at nine, and thought my fears had
never before so much prevailed over my judgement

and my reckoning. I ordered the light sails to be handed, and the steering sail booms to be rigged in snug, which was done as fast as it could be by one watch, under the immediate direction of Mr. Savage.

We had just got the men stationed at the braces for hauling off, as the man at helm cried "ten o'clock." Our try-sail boom was on the starboard side, but ready for jibing; the helm was put to port, dreaming of no danger near. I had been on deck all the evening myself; the vessel was running at the rate of nine or ten knots, with a very strong breeze, and high sea, when the main boom was jibed over, and I at that instant heard a roaring; the yards were braced up—all hands were called. I imagined at first it was a squall, and was near ordering the sails to be lowered down; but I then discovered breakers foaming at a most dreadful rate under our lee. Hope for a moment flattered me that we could fetch off still, as there were no breakers in view ahead: the anchors were made ready; but these hopes vanished in an instant, as the vessel was carried by a current and a sea directly towards the breakers, and she struck! We let go the best bower anchor; all sails were taken in as fast as possible: surge after surge came thundering on, and drove her in spite of anchors, partly with her head on shore. She struck with such violence as to start every man from the deck. Knowing there was no possibility of saving her, and that she must very soon bilge and fill with water, I ordered all the provisions we could get at to be brought on deck, in hopes of saving some, and as much water to be drawn from the large casks as possible. We started several quarter casks of wine, and filled them with water. Every man worked as if his life depended upon his present exertions; all were obedient to every order I gave, and seemed perfectly calm;—The vessel was stout and high, as she was only in ballast trim;—The sea combed over her stern and swept her decks; but we managed to get the small boat in on deck, to sling her and keep her from staving. We cut away the bulwark on the larboard side so as to prevent the boats from staving when we should get them out; cleared away the long boat and hung her in tackles, the vessel continuing to strike very heavy, and filling fast. We however, had secured five or six barrels or water, and as many of wine,— three barrels of bread, and three or four salted provisions. I had as yet been so busily employed, that no pains had been taken to ascertain what distance we were from the land, nor had any of us yet seen it; and in the meantime all the clothing, chests, trunks, &c. were got up, and the books, charts, and sea instruments, were stowed in them, in the hope of their being useful to us in future.

The vessel being now nearly full of water, the surf making a fair breach over her, and fearing she would go to pieces, I prepared a rope, and put it in the small boat, having got a glimpse of the shore, at no great distance, and taking Porter with me, we were lowered down on the larboard or lee side of the vessel, where she broke the violence of the sea, and made it comparatively smooth; we shoved off, but on clearing away from the bow of the vessel, the boat was overwhelmed with a surf, and we were plunged into the foaming surges: we were driven along by the current, aided by what seamen call the undertow, (or recoil of the sea) to the distance of three hundred yards to the westward, covered nearly all the time by the billows, which, following each other in quick succession, scarcely gave us time to catch a breath before we were again literally swallowed by them, till at length we were thrown, together with our boat, upon a sandy beach. After taking breath a little, and ridding our stomachs of the salt water that had forced its way into them, my first care was to turn the water out of the boat, and haul her up out of the reach of the surf. We found the rope that was made fast to her still remaining; this we carried up along the beach, directly to leeward of the wreck, where we fastened it to sticks about the thickness of handspikes, that had drifted on the shore from the vessel, and which we drove into the sand by the help of other pieces of wood. Before leaving the vessel, I had directed that all the chests, trunks, and everything that would float, should be hove overboard: this all hands were busied in doing. The vessel lay about one hundred fathoms from the beach, at high tide. In order to save the crew, a hawser was made fast to the rope we had on shore, one end of which we hauled to us, and made it fast to a number of sticks we had driven into the sand for the purpose. It was then tautened on board the wreck, and made fast. This being done, the long-boat (in order to save the provisions already in her) was lowered down, and two hands steadied her by ropes fastened to the rings in her stem and stern posts over the hawser, so as to slide, keeping her bow to the surf. In this manner they reached the beach, carried on the top of a heavy wave. The boat was stove by the violence of the shock against the beach; but by great exertions we saved the three barrels of bread in her before they were much damaged; and two barrels of salted provisions were also saved. We were now, four of us, on shore, and busied in picking up the clothing and other things which drifted from the vessel, and carrying them up out of the surf. It was by this time daylight, and high water; the vessel careened deep off shore, and I made signs to have the masts cut away, in the hope of easing her, that she might not go to pieces. They were accordingly cut away, and fell on her starboard side, making a better lee for a boat alongside the wreck, as they projected considerably beyond her bows. The masts and rigging being gone, the sea breaking very high over the wreck, and nothing left to hold on by, the mates and six men still on board, though secured, as well as they could be, on the bowsprit and in the larboard fore-channels, were yet in imminent dangers of being washed off by every surge. The long-boat was stove, and it being impossible for the small one to live, my great object was now to save the lives of the crew by means of the hawser. I therefore made signs to them to come, one by one, on the hawser, which had been stretched taut for that purpose. John Hogan ventured first, and having pulled off his jacket, took to the hawser, and made for the shore. When he had got clear of the immediate lee of the wreck, every surf buried him, combing many feet above his head; but he still held fast to the rope with a death-like grasp, and as soon as the surf was passed, proceeded on towards the shore, until another surf, more powerful than the former, unclenched his hands, and threw him within our reach; when we laid hold of him and dragged him to the beach; we then rolled him on the sand, until he discharged the salt water from his stomach, and revived. I kept in the water up to my chin, steadying myself by the hawser, while the surf passed over me, to catch the others as they approached, and thus, with the assistance of those already on shore, was enabled to save all the rest from a watery grave.

Ice Again

[RICHARD HENRY DANA]

In our first attempt to double the Cape, when we came up to the latitude of it, we were nearly seventeen hundred miles to the westward, but, in running for the straits of Magellan, we stood so far to the eastward, that we made our second attempt at a distance of not more than four or five hundred miles; and we had great hopes, by this means, to run clear of the ice; thinking that the easterly gales, which had prevailed for a long time, would have driven it to the westward. With the wind about two points free, the yards braced in a little, and two close-reefed topsails and a reefed foresail on the ship, we made great way toward the southward; and, almost every watch, when we came on deck, the air seemed to grow colder, and the sea to run higher. Still, we saw no ice, and had great hopes of going clear of it altogether, when, one afternoon, about three o'clock, while we were taking a *siesta* during our watch below, "All hands!" was called in a loud and fearful voice. "Tumble up here, men!—tumble up!—don't stop for your clothes—before we're upon it!" We sprang out of our berths and hurried upon deck. The loud, sharp voice of the captain was heard giving orders, as though for life or death, and we ran aft to the braces, not waiting to look ahead, for not a moment was to be lost. The helm was hard up, the after yards shaking, and the ship in the act of wearing. Slowly, with the stiff ropes and iced rigging, we swung the yards round, everything coming hard, and with a creaking and rending sound, like pulling up a plank which has been frozen into the ice. The ship wore round fairly, the yards were steadied, and we stood off on the other tack, leaving behind us, directly under our larboard quarter, a large ice island, peering out of the mist, and reaching high above our tops, while astern; and on either side of the island, large tracts of field-ice were dimly seen, heaving and rolling in the sea. We were now safe, and standing to the northward; but, in a few minutes more, had it not been for the sharp look-out of the watch, we should have been fairly upon the ice, and left our ship's old bones adrift in the Southern ocean. After standing to the northward a few hours, we wore ship, and, the wind having hauled, we stood to the southward and eastward. All night long, a bright look-out was kept from every part of the deck; and whenever ice was seen on the one bow or the other, the helm was shifted and the yards braced, and by quick working of the ship she was kept clear. The accustomed cry of "Ice ahead!"—"ice on the lee bow!"—"Another island!" in the same tones, and with the same orders following them, seemed to bring us directly back to our old position of the week before. During our watch on deck, which was from twelve to four, the wind came out ahead, with a pelting storm of hail and sleet, and we lay hove-to, under a close-reefed main topsail, the whole watch. During the next watch it fell calm, with a drenching rain, until day-break, when the wind came out to the westward, and the weather cleared up, and showed us the whole ocean, in the course which we should have steered, had it not been for the head wind and calm, completely blocked up with ice. Here then our progress was stopped, and we wore ship, and once more stood to the northward and eastward; not for the straits of Magellan, but to make another attempt to double the Cape, still farther to the eastward; for the captain was determined to get round if perseverance could do it; and the third time, he said, never failed.

With a fair wind we soon ran clear of the field-ice, and by noon had only the stray islands floating far and near upon the ocean. The sun was out bright, the sea of a deep blue, fringed with the white foam of the waves which ran high before a strong south-wester; our solitary ship tore on through the water, as though glad to be out of her confinement; and the ice islands lay scattered upon the ocean here and there, of various sizes and shapes, reflecting the bright rays of the sun, and drifting slowly northward before the gale. It was a contrast to much that we had lately seen, and a spectacle not only of beauty, but of life; for it required but little fancy to imagine these islands to be animate masses which had broken loose from the "thrilling regions of thick-ribbed ice," and were working their way, by wind and current, some alone, and some in fleets, to milder climes. No pencil has ever yet given anything like the true effect of an iceberg. In a picture, they are huge, uncouth masses, stuck in the sea, while their chief beauty and grandeur,—their slow, stately motion; the whirling of the snow about their summits, and the fearful groaning and cracking of their parts,—the picture cannot give. This is the large iceberg; while the small and distant islands, floating on the smooth sea, in the light of a clear day, look like little floating fairy isles of sapphire.

From a north-east course we gradually hauled to the eastward, and after sailing about two hundred miles, which brought us as near to the western coast of Terra del Fuego as was safe, and having lost sight of the ice altogether,—for the third time we put the ship's head to the southward, to try the passage of the Cape. The weather continued clear and cold, with a strong gale from the westward, and we were fast getting up with the latitude of the Cape, with a prospect of soon being round. One fine afternoon, a man who had gone into the fore-top to shift the rolling tackles, sung out, at the top of his voice, and with evident glee,—"Sail ho!" Neither land nor sail had we seen since leaving San Diego; and any one who has traversed the length of a whole ocean alone, can imagine what an excitement such an announcement produced on board. "Sail ho!" shouted the cook, jumping out of his galley; "Sail ho!" shouted a man, throwing back the slide of the scuttle, to the watch below, who were soon out of their berths and on deck; and "Sail ho!" shouted the captain down the companionway to the passenger in the cabin. Beside the pleasure of seeing a ship and human beings in so desolate a place, it was important for us to speak a vessel, to learn whether there was ice to the eastward, and to ascertain the longitude; for we had no chronometer, and had been drifting about so long that we had nearly lost our reckoning, and opportunities for lunar observations are not frequent or sure in such a place as Cape Horn. For these various reasons, the excitement in our little community was running high, and conjectures were made and everything thought of for which the captain would hail, when the man aloft sung out— "Another sail, large on the weather bow!" this was a little odd, but so much the better, and did not shake our faith in their being sails. At length the man in the top hailed, and said he believed it was land, after all. "Land in your eye!" said the mate, who was looking through the telescope; "they are ice islands, if I can see a hole through a ladder;" and a few moments showed the mate to be right; and all our expectations fled; and instead of what we most wished to see, we had what we most dreaded, and what we hoped we had seen the last of. We soon, however, left these astern, having passed within about two miles of them; and at sundown the horizon was clear in all directions.

Having a fine wind, we were soon up with and passed the latitude of the Cape, and having stood far enough to the southward to give it a wide berth, we began to stand to the eastward, with a good prospect of being round and steering to the northward on the other side, in a very few days. But ill luck seemed to have lighted upon us. Not four hours had we been standing on in this course, before it fell dead calm; and in half an hour it clouded up; a few straggling blasts, with spits of snow and sleet, came from the eastward; and in an hour more, we lay hove-to under a close-reefed main topsail, drifting bodily off to leeward before the fiercest storm that we had yet felt, blowing dead ahead, from the eastward. It seemed as though the genius of the place had been roused at finding that we had nearly slipped through his fingers, and had come down upon us with tenfold fury. The sailors said that every blast, as it shook the shrouds, and whistled through the rigging, said to the old ship, "No, you don't!"—"No, you don't!"

For eight days we lay drifting about in this manner. Sometimes,—generally towards noon,—it fell calm; once or twice a round copper ball showed itself for a few moments in the place where the sun ought to have been; and a puff or two came from the westward, giving some hope that a fair wind had come at last. During the first two days, we made sail for these puffs, shaking the reefs out of the topsails and boarding the tacks of the courses; but finding that it only made work for us when the gale set in again, it was soon given up, and we lay-to under our close-reefs. We had less snow and hail than when we were farther to the westward, but we had an abundance of what is worse to a sailor in cold weather— drenching rain. Snow is blinding, and very bad when coming upon a coast, but, for genuine discomfort, give me rain with freezing weather. A snowstorm is exciting, and it does not wet through the clothes (which is important to a sailor); but a constant rain there is no escaping from. It wets to the skin, and makes all protection vain. We had long ago run through all our dry clothes, and as sailors have no other way of drying them than by the sun, we had nothing to do but to put on those which were the least wet. At the end of each watch, when we came below, we took off our clothes and wrung them out; two taking hold of a pair of trowsers,—

one at each end,—and jackets in the same way. Stockings, mittens, and all, were wrung out also and then hung up to drain and chafe dry against the bulkheads. Then, feeling of all our clothes, we picked out those which were the least wet, and put them on, so as to be ready for a call, and turned-in, covered ourselves up with blankets, and slept until three knocks on the scuttle and the dismal sound of "All starbowlines ahoy! Eight bells, there below! Do you hear the news?" drawled out from on deck, and the sulky answer of "Aye, aye!" from below, sent us up again.

On deck, all was as dark as a pocket, and either a dead calm, with the rain pouring steadily down, or, more generally, a violent gale dead ahead, with rain pelting horizontally, and occasional variations of hail and sleet;—decks afloat with water swashing from side to side, and constantly wet feet; for boots could not be wrung out like drawers, and no composition could stand the constant soaking. In fact, wet and cold feet are inevitable in such weather, and are not the least of those little items which go to make up the grant total of the discomforts of a winter passage round the Cape. Few words were spoken between the watches as they shifted, the wheel was relieved, the mate took his place on the quarter-deck, the lookouts in the bows; and each man had his narrow space to walk fore and aft in, or, rather, to swing himself forward and back in, from one belaying pin

to another,—for the decks were too slippery with
ice and water to allow of much walking. To make a
walk, which is absolutely necessary to pass away the
time, one of us hit upon the expedient of sanding
the deck; and afterwards, whenever the rain was not
so violent as to wash it off, the weatherside of the
quarter-deck, and a part of the waist and forecastle
were sprinkled with the sand which we had on
board for holystoning; and thus we made a good
promenade, where we walked fore and aft, two and
two, hour after hour, in our long, dull, and comfort-
less watches. The bells seemed to be an hour or two
apart, instead of half an hour, and an age to elapse
before the welcome sound of eight bells. The sole
object was to make the time pass on. Any change
was sought for, which would break the monotony of
the time; and even the two hours' trick at the wheel,
which came round to each of us in turn, once in
every other watch, was looked upon as a relief. Even
the never-failing resource of long yarns, which eke
out many a watch, seemed to have failed us now; for
we had been so long together that we had heard
each other's stories told over and over again, till we
had them by heart; each one new the whole history
of the others, and we were fairly and literally talked
out. Singing and joking we were in no humor for,
and, in fact, any sound of mirth or laughter would
have struck strangely upon our ears, and would not
have been tolerated, any more than whistling, or a

wind instrument. The last resort, that of speculating upon the future, seemed now to fail us, for our discouraging situation, and the danger we were really in, (as we expected every day to find ourselves drifted back among the ice) "clapped a stopper" upon all that. From saying—"*when* we get home"— we began insensibly to alter it to—"*if* we get home"—and at last the subject was dropped by a tacit consent.

In this state of things, a new light was struck out, and a new field opened, by a change in the watch. One of our watch was laid up for two or three days by a bad hand, (for in cold weather the least cut or bruise ripens into a sore,) and his place was supplied by the carpenter. This was a windfall, and there was quite a contest, who should have the carpenter to walk with him. As "Chips" was a man of some little education, and he and I had had a good deal of intercourse with each other, he fell in with me in my walk. He was a Fin, but spoke English very well, and gave me long accounts of his country;—the customs, the trade, the towns, what little he knew of the government, (I found he was no friend of Russia,) his voyages, his first arrival in America, his marriage and courtship;—he had married a countrywoman of his, a dress-maker, whom he met with in Boston. I had very little to tell him of my quiet, sedentary life at home; and, in spite of our best efforts, which had protracted these yarns through five or six watches, we fairly talked one another out, and I turned him over to another man in the watch, and put myself upon my own resources.

I commenced a deliberate system of time-killing, which united some profit with a cheering up of the heavy hours. As soon as I came on deck, and took my place and regular walk, I began with repeating over to myself a string of matters which I had in my memory, in regular order. First, the multiplication table and the tables of weights and measures; then the states of the Union, with their capitals; the counties of England, with their shire towns; the kings of England in their order; and a large part of the peerage, which I committed from an almanac that we had on board; and then the Kanaka numerals. This carried me through my facts, and, being repeated deliberately, with long intervals, often eked out the two first bells. Then came the ten commandments; the thirty-ninth chapter of Job, and a few other passages from Scripture. The next in the order, that I never varied from, came Cowper's "Castaway," which was a great favorite with me; the solemn measure and gloomy character of which, as well as the incident that it was founded upon, made it well suited to a lonely watch at sea. Then his lines to Mary, his address to the jackdaw, and a short extract from "Table Talk;" (I abounded in Cowper, for I happened to have a volume of his poems in my chest;) "Ille et nefasto" from Horace, and Goethe's

"Erl King." After I had got through these, I allowed myself a more general range among everything that I could remember, both in prose and verse. In this way, with an occasional break by relieving the wheel, heaving the log, and going to the scuttlebutt for a drink of water, the longest watch was passed away; and I was so regular in my silent recitations, that if there was no interruption by ship's duty, I could tell very nearly the number of bells by my progress.

Our watches below were no more varied than the watch on deck. All washing, sewing, and reading was given up; and we did nothing but eat, sleep, and stand our watch, leading what might be called a Cape Horn life. The forecastle was too uncomfortable to sit up in; and whenever we were below, we were in our berths. To prevent the rain, and the sea-water which broke over the bows, from washing down, we were obliged to keep the scuttle closed, so that the forecastle was nearly air-tight. In this little, wet, leaky hole, we were all quartered, in an atmosphere so bad that our lamp, which swung in the middle from the beams, sometimes actually burned blue, with a large circle of foul air about it. Still, I was never in better health than after three weeks of this life. I gained a great deal of flesh, and we all ate like horses. At every watch, when we came below, before turning-in, the bread barge and beef kid were overhauled. Each man drank his quart of hot tea night and morning; and glad enough we were to get it, for no nectar and ambrosia were sweeter to the lazy immortals, than was a pot of hot tea, a hard biscuit, and a slice of cold salt beef, to us after a watch on deck. To be sure, we were mere animals, and had this life lasted a year instead of a month, we should have been little better than the ropes in the ship. Not a razor, nor a brush, nor a drop of water, except the rain and the spray, had come near us all the time; for we were on an allowance of fresh water; and who would strip and wash himself in salt water on deck, in the snow and ice, with the thermometer at zero?

After about eight days of constant easterly gales, the wind hauled occasionally a little to the south-ward, and blew hard, which, as we were well to the southward, allowed us to brace in a little and stand on, under all the sail we could carry. These turns lasted but a short while, and sooner or later it set in again from the old quarter; yet at each time we made something, and were gradually edging along to the eastward. One night, after one of these shifts of the wind, and when all hands had been up a great part of the time, our watch was left on deck, with the main-sail hanging in the buntlines, ready to be set if neces-sary. It came on to blow worse and worse, with hail and snow beating like so many furies upon the ship, it being as dark and thick as night could make it. The mainsail was blowing and slatting with a noise like thunder, when the captain came on deck, and ordered it to be furled. The mate was about to call

all hands, when the captain stopped him, and said that the men would be beaten out if they were called up so often; that as our watch must stay on deck, it might as well be doing that as anything else. Accordingly, we went upon the yard; and never shall I forget that piece of work. Our watch had been so reduced by sickness, and by some having been left in California, that, with one man at the wheel, we had only the third mate and three beside myself to go aloft; so that, at most, we could only attempt to furl one yard-arm at a time. We manned the weather yard-arm, and set to work to make a furl of it. Our lower masts being short, and our yards very square, the sail had a head of nearly fifty feet, and a short leach, made still shorter by the deep reef which was in it, which brought the clue away out on the quarters of the yard, and made a bunt nearly as square as the mizen royal-yard. Beside this difficulty, the yard over which we lay was cased with ice, the gaskets and rope of the foot and leach of the sail as stiff and hard as a piece of suction-hose, and the sail itself about as pliable as though it had been made of sheets of sheathing copper. It blew a perfect hurricane, with alternate blasts of snow, hail, and rain. We had to *fist* the sail with bare hands. No one could trust himself to mittens, for if he slipped, he was a gone man. All the boats were hoisted in on deck, and there was nothing to be lowered for him. We had need of every finger God had given us. Several times we got the sail upon the yard, but it blew away again before we could secure it. It required men to lie over the yard to pass each turn of the gaskets, and when they were passed, it was almost impossible to knot them so that they would hold. Frequently we were obliged to leave off altogether and take to beating our hands upon the sail, to keep them from freezing. After some time,— which seemed forever,—we got the weather side stowed after a fashion, and went over to leeward for another trial. This was still worse, for the body of the sail had been blown over to leeward, and as the yard was a-cock-bill by the lying over of the vessel, we had to light it all up to windward. When the yard-arms were furled, the bunt was all adrift again, which made more work for us. We got all secure at last, but we had been nearly an hour and a half upon the yard, and it seemed an age. It had just struck five bells when we went up, and eight were struck soon after we came down. This may seem slow work, but considering the state of everything, and that we had only five men to a sail with just half as many square yards of canvas in it as the mainsail of the *Independence,* sixty-gun ship, which musters seven hundred men at her quarters, it is not wonderful that we were no quicker about it. We were glad enough to get on deck, and still more, to go below. The oldest sailor in the watch said, as he went down,—"I shall never forget that main yard;—it beats all my going a fishing. Fun is fun, but furling one yard-arm of a course, at a time, off Cape Horn, is no better than man-killing."

During the greater part of the next two days, the wind was pretty steady from the southward. We had evidently made great progress, and had good hope of being soon up with the Cape, if we were not there already. We could put but little confidence in our reckoning, as there had been no opportunities for an observation, and we had drifted too much to allow of our dead reckoning being anywhere near the mark. If it would clear off enough to give a chance for an observation, or if we could make land, we should know where we were; and upon these, and the chances of falling in with a sail from the eastward, we depended almost entirely.

Friday, July 22d. This day we had a steady gale from the southward, and stood on under close sail, with the yards eased a little by the weather braces, the clouds lifting a little, and showing signs of breaking away. In the afternoon, I was below with Mr. H——, the third mate, and two others, filling the bread locker in the steerage from the casks, when a bright gleam of sunshine broke out and shone down the companionway and through the sky-light, lighting up everything below, and sending a warm glow through the heart of every one. It was a sight we had not seen for weeks,—an omen, a god-send. Even the roughest and hardest face acknowledged its influence. Just at that moment we heard a loud shout from all parts of the deck, and the mate called out down the companionway to the captain, who was sitting in the cabin. What he said, we could not distinguish, but the captain kicked over his chair, and was on deck at one jump. We could not tell what it was; and, anxious as we were to know, the discipline of the ship would not allow of our leaving our places. Yet, as we were not called, we knew there was no danger. We hurried to get through with our job, when, seeing the steward's black face peering out of the panty, Mr. H— hailed him, to know what was the matter. "Lan' o, to be sure, sir! No you hear 'em sing out, 'Lan' o?' De cap'em say 'im Cape Horn!"

This gave us a new start, and we were soon through our work, and on deck; and there lay the land, fair upon the larboard beam, and slowly edging away upon the quarter. All hands were busy looking at it,—the captain and mates from the quarter-deck, the cook from his galley, and the sailors from the forecastle; and even Mr. N., the passenger, who had kept in his shell for nearly a month, and hardly been seen by anybody, and who we had almost forgotten was on board, came out like a butterfly, and was hopping round as bright as a bird.

The land was the island of Staten Land, just to the eastward of Cape Horn; and a more desolate-looking spot I never wish to set eyes upon;—bare, broken, and girt with rocks and ice, with here and there, between the rocks and broken hillocks, a little stunted vegetation of shrubs. It was a place well suited to stand at the junction of the two oceans, beyond the reach of human cultivation, and encounter the blasts and snows of a perpetual winter. Yet, dismal as it was, it was a pleasant sight to us; not only as being the first land we had seen, but because it told us that we had passed the Cape,—were in the Atlantic,—and that, with twenty-four hours of this breeze, might bid defiance to the Southern ocean. It told us, too, our latitude and longitude better than any observation; and the captain now knew where we were, as well as if we were off the end of Long wharf.

In the general joy, Mr. N. said he should like to go ashore upon the island and examine a spot which probably no human being had ever set foot upon; but the captain intimated that he would see the island—specimens and all,—in—another place, before he would get out a boat or delay the ship one moment for him.

We left the land gradually astern; and at sundown had the Atlantic ocean clear before us.

The First Lowering

[HERMAN MELVILLE]

The phantoms, for so they then seemed, were flitting on the other side of the deck, with a noiseless celerity, were casting loose the tackles and bands of the boat which swung there. This boat had always been deemed one of the spare boats, though technically called the captain's, on account of its hanging from the starboard quarter. The figure that now stood by its bows was tall and swart, with one white tooth evilly protruding from its steel-like lips. A rumpled Chinese jacket of black cotton funereally invested him, with wide black trowsers of the same dark stuff. But strangely crowning his ebonness was a glistening white plaited turban, the living hair braided and coiled round and round upon his head. Less swart in aspect, the companions of this figure were of that vivid, tiger-yellow complexion peculiar to some of the aboriginal natives of the Manillas;—a race notorious for a certain diabolism of subtilty, and by some honest white mariners supposed to be the paid spies and secret confidential agents on the water of the devil, their lord, whose counting-room they suppose to be elsewhere.

While yet the wondering ship's company were gazing upon these strangers, Ahab cried out to the white-turbaned old man at their head, 'All ready there, Fedallah?'

'Ready,' was the half-hissed reply.

'Lower away then; d'ye hear?' shouting across the deck. 'Lower away there, I say.'

Such was the thunder of his voice, that spite of their amazement the men sprang over the rail; the sheaves whirled round in the blocks; with a wallow, the three boats dropped into the sea; while, with a dexterous, off-handed daring, unknown in any other vocation, the sailors, goat-like, leaped down the rolling ship's side into the tossed boats below.

Hardly had they pulled out from under the ship's lee, when a fourth keel, coming from the windward side, pulled round under the stern, and showed the five strangers rowing Ahab, who, standing erect in the stern, loudly hailed Starbuck, Stubb, and Flask, to spread themselves widely, so as to cover a large expanse of water, but with all their eyes again riveted upon the swart Fedallah and his crew, the inmates of the other boats obeyed not the command.

'Captain Ahab?—' said Starbuck.

'Spread yourselves,' cried Ahab; 'give way, all four boats. Thou, Flask, pull out more to leeward!'

'Aye, aye, sir,' cheerily cried little King-Post, sweeping round his great steering oar. 'Lay back!' addressing his crew. 'There!—there!—there again! There she blows right ahead, boys!—lay back!'

'Never heed yonder yellow boys, Archy.'

'Oh, I don't mind 'em, sir,' said Archy; 'I knew it all before now. Didn't I hear 'em in the hold? And didn't I tell Cabaco here of it? What say ye, Cabaco? They are stowaways, Mr. Flask.'

'Pull, pull, my fine hearts-alive; pull, my children; pull, my little ones,' drawingly and soothingly sighed Stubb to his crew, some of whom still showed signs of uneasiness. 'Why don't you break your back-bones, my boys? What is it you stare at? Those chaps in yonder boat? Tut! They are only five more hands come to help us—never mind from where—the more the merrier. Pull, then, do pull; never mind the brimstone—devils are good fellows enough. So, so; there you are now; that's the stroke for a thousand pounds; that's the stroke to sweep the stakes! Hurrah for the gold cup of sperm oil, my heroes! Three cheers, men—all hearts alive! Easy, easy; don't be in a hurry—don't be in a hurry. Why don't you snap your oars, you rascals? Bite something, you dogs! So, so, so, then;—softly, softly! That's it—that's it! long and strong. Give way there, give way! The devil fetch ye, ye ragamuffin rapscallions; ye are all asleep. Stop snoring, ye sleepers, and pull. Pull, will ye? pull, can't ye? pull, won't ye? Why in the name of gudgeons and ginger-cakes don't ye pull?—pull and break something! pull, and start your eyes out! Here!' whipping out the sharp knife from his girdle; 'every mother's son of ye draw his knife, and pull with the blade between his teeth. That's it—that's it. Now ye do something; that looks like it, my steel-bits. Start her—start her, my silver-spoons! Start her, marling-spikes!'

Stubb's exordium to his crew is given here at large, because he had rather a peculiar way of talking to them in general, and especially in inculcating the religion of rowing. But you must not suppose from this specimen of his sermonizings that he ever flew into downright passions with his congregation. Not at all; and therein consisted his chief peculiarity. He would say the most terrific things to his crew, in a tone so strangely compounded of fun and fury, and the fury seemed so calculated merely as a spice to the fun, that no oarsman could hear such queer invocations without pulling for dear life, and yet pulling for the mere joke of the thing. Besides he all the time looked so easy and indolent himself, so loungingly managed his steering-oar, and so broadly gaped—open-mouthed at times—that the mere sight of such a yawning commander, by sheer force of contrast, acted like a charm upon the crew. Then again, Stubb was one of

those odd sort of humorists, whose jollity is sometimes so curiously ambiguous, as to put all inferiors
on their guard in the matter of obeying them.

In obedience to a sign from Ahab, Starbuck was
now pulling obliquely across Stubb's bow; and when
for a minute or so the two boats were pretty near to
each other, Stubb hailed the mate.

'Mr. Starbuck! larboard boat there, ahoy! a word
with ye, sir, if ye please!'

'Halloa!' returned Starbuck, turning round not a
single inch as he spoke; still earnestly but whisper-
ingly urging his crew; his face set like a flint from
Stubb's.

'What think ye of those yellow boys, sir!'

'Smuggled on board, somehow, before the ship
sailed. (Strong, strong, boys!') in a whisper to his
crew, then speaking out loud again: 'A sad business,
Mr. Stubb! (seethe her, seethe her, my lads!) but
never mind, Mr. Stubb, all for the best. Let all your
crew pull strong, come what will. (Spring, my men,
spring!) There's hogsheads of sperm ahead, Mr.
Stubb, and that's what ye came for. (Pull, my boys!)
Sperm, sperm's the play! This at least is duty; duty
and profit hand in hand!'

'Aye, aye, I thought as much,' soliloquized Stubb,
when the boats diverged, 'as soon as I clapt on 'em, I
thought so. Aye, and that's what he went into the
after hold for, so often, as Dough-Boy long suspected. They were hidden down there. The White

Whale's at the bottom of it. Well, well, so be it! Can't be helped! All right! Give way, men! It ain't the White Whale to-day! Give way!'

Now the advent of these outlandish strangers at such a critical instant as the lowering of the boats from the deck, this had not unreasonably awakened a sort of superstitious amazement in some of the ship's company; but Archy's fancied discovery having some time previous got abroad among them, though indeed not credited then, this had in some small measure prepared them for the event. It took off the extreme edge of their wonder; and so what with all this and Stubb's confident way of accounting for their appearance, they were for the time freed from superstitious surmisings; though the affair still left abundant room for all manner of wild conjectures as to dark Ahab's precise agency in the matter from the beginning. For me, I silently recalled the mysterious shadows I had seen creeping on board the Pequod during the dim Nantucket dawn, as well as the enigmatical hintings of the unaccountable Elijah.

Meantime, Ahab, out of hearing of his officers, having sided the furthest to windward, was still ranging ahead of the other boats; a circumstance bespeaking how potent a crew was pulling him. Those tiger yellow creatures of his seemed all steel and whale-bone; like five trip-hammers they rose and fell with regular strokes of strength, which periodically started the boat along the water like a horizontal burst boiler out of a Mississippi steamer. As for Fedallah, who was seen pulling the harpooneer oar, he had thrown aside his black jacket, and displayed his naked chest with the whole part of his body above the gunwale, clearly cut against the alternating depressions of the watery horizon; while at the other end of the boat Ahab, with one arm, like a fencer's, thrown half backward into the air, as if to counterbalance any tendency to trip: Ahab was seen steadily managing his steering oar as in a thousand boat lowerings ere the White Whale had torn him. All at once the out-stretched arm gave a peculiar motion and then remained fixed, while the boat's five oars were seen simultaneously peaked. Boat and crew sat motionless on the sea. Instantly the three spread boats in the rear paused on their way. The whales had irregularly settled bodily down into the blue, thus giving no distantly discernible token of the movement, though from his closer vicinity Ahab had observed it.

'Every man look out along his oars!' cried Starbuck. 'Thou, Queequeg, stand up!'

Nimbly springing up on the triangular raised box in the bow, the savage stood erect there, and with intensely eager eyes gazed off towards the spot where the chase had last been described. Likewise upon the extreme stern of the boat where it was also triangularly platformed level with the gunwale, Starbuck himself was seen coolly and adroitly balancing

CLASSIC ADVENTURE STORIES

himself to the jerking tossings of his chip of a craft, and silently eyeing the vast blue eye of the sea.

Not very far distant Flask's boat was also lying breathlessly still; its commander recklessly standing upon the top of the loggerhead, a stout sort of post rooted in the keel, and rising some two feet above the level of the stern platform. It is used for catching turns with the whale line. Its top is not more spacious than the palm of a man's hand, and standing upon such a base as that, Flask seemed perched at the mast-head of some ship which had sunk to all but her trucks. But little King-Post was small and short, and at the same time little King-Post was full of a large and tall ambition, so that this loggerhead standpoint of his did by no means satisfy King-Post.

'I can't see three seas off; tip us up an oar there, and let me on to that.'

Upon this, Daggoo, with either hand upon the gunwale to steady his way, swiftly slid aft, and then erecting himself volunteered his lofty shoulders for a pedestal.

'Good a mast-head as any, sir. Will you mount?'

'That I will, and thank ye very much, my fine fellow; only I wish you fifty feet taller.'

Whereupon planting his feet firmly against two opposite planks of the boat, the gigantic negro, stooping a little, presented his flat palm to Flask's foot, and then putting Flask's hand on his hearse-plumed head and bidding him spring as he himself should toss, with one dexterous fling landed the little man high and dry on his shoulders. And here was Flask now standing, Daggoo with one lifted arm furnishing him with a breast-band to lean against and steady himself by.

At any time it is a strange sight to the tyro to see with what wondrous habitude of unconscious skill the whaleman will maintain an erect posture in his boat, even when pitched about by the most riotously perverse and cross-running seas. Still more strange to see him giddily perched upon the loggerhead itself, under such circumstances. But the sight of little Flask mounted upon gigantic Daggoo was yet more curious; for sustaining himself with a cool, indifferent, easy, unthought of, barbaric majesty, the noble negro to every roll of the sea harmoniously rolled his fine form. On his broad back, flaxen-haired Flask seemed a snow-flake. The bearer looked nobler than the rider. Though truly vivacious, tumultuous, ostentatious little Flask would now and then stamp with impatience; but not one added heave did he thereby give to the negro's lordly chest. So have I seen Passion and Vanity stamping the living magnanimous earth, but the earth did not alter her tides and her seasons for that.

Meanwhile Stubb, the third mate, betrayed no such far-gazing solicitudes. The whales might have made one of their regular soundings, not a temporary dive from mere fright; and if that were the case, Stubb, as his wont in such cases, it seems, was resolved to solace the languishing interval with his pipe. He withdrew it from his hatband, where he always wore it aslant like a feather. He loaded it, and rammed home the loading with his thumb-end; but hardly had he ignited his match across the rough sand-paper of his hand, when Tashtego, his harpooneer, whose eyes had been setting to windward like two fixed stars, suddenly dropped like light from his erect attitude to his seat, crying out in a quick phrensy of hurry, 'Down, down all, and give way!—there they are!'

To a landsman, no whale, nor any sign of a herring, would have been visible at that moment; nothing but a troubled bit of greenish white water, and thin scattered puffs of vapor hovering over it, and suffusingly blowing off to leeward, like the confused scud from white rolling billows. The air around suddenly vibrated and tingled, as it were, like the air over intensely heated plates of iron. Beneath this atmospheric waving and curling, and partially beneath a thin layer of water, also, the whales were swimming. Seen in advance of all the other indications, the puffs of vapor they spouted, seemed their forerunning couriers and detached flying outriders.

All four boats were now in keen pursuit of that one spot of troubled water and air. But it bade far to outstrip them; it flew on and on, as a mass of interblending bubbles borne down a rapid stream from the hills.

'Pull, pull, my good boys,' said Starbuck, in the lowest possible but intensest concentrated whisper to his men; while the sharp fixed glance from his eyes darted straight ahead of the bow, almost seemed as two visible needles in two unerring binnacle compasses. He did not say much to his crew, though, nor did his crew say anything to him. Only the silence of the boat was at intervals startlingly pierced by one of his peculiar whispers, now harsh with command, now soft with entreaty.

How different the loud little King-Post. 'Sing out and say something, my hearties. Roar and pull, my thunderbolts! Beach me, beach me on their black backs, boys; including wife and children, boys. Lay me on—lay me on! O Lord, Lord! but I shall go stark, staring mad: See! see that white water!' And so shouting, he pulled his hat from his head, and stamped up and down on it; then picking it up, flirted it far off upon the sea; and finally fell to rearing and plunging in the boat's stern like a crazed colt from the prairie.

'Look at that chap now,' philosophically drawled Stubb, who, with his unlighted short pipe, mechanically retained between his teeth, at a short distance, followed after—'He's got fits, that Flask has. Fits? yes, give him fits—that's the very word—pitch fits into 'em. Merrily, merrily, hearts-alive. Pudding for supper, you know;—merry's the word. Pull, babes— pull, sucklings—pull, all. But what the devil are you hurrying about? Softly, softly, and steadily, my men. Only pull, and keep pulling; nothing more. Crack all your backbones, and bite your knives in two—that's all. Take it easy—why don't ye take it easy, I say, and burst all your livers and lungs!'

But what it was that inscrutable Ahab said to that tiger-yellow crew of his—these were words best omitted here; for you live under the blessed light of the evangelical land.

Only the infidel sharks in the audacious seas may give ear to such words, when, with tornado brow, and eyes of red murder, and foam-glued lips, Ahab leaped after his prey.

Meanwhile, all the boats tore on. The repeated specific allusions of Flask to 'that whale', as he called the fictitious monster which he declared to be incessantly tantalizing his boat's bow with its tail—these allusions of his were at times so vivid and life-like, that they would cause some one or two of his men to snatch a fearful look over the shoulder. But this was against all rule; for the oarsmen must put out their eyes, and ram a skewer through their necks; usage pronouncing that they must have no organs but ears, and no limbs but arms, in these critical moments.

It was a sight full of quick wonder and awe! The vast swells of the omnipotent sea; the surging, hollow roar they made, as they rolled along the eight gunwales, like gigantic bowls in a boundless bowling-green; the brief suspended agony of the boat, as it would tip for an instant on the knife-like edge of the sharper waves, that almost seemed threatening to cut it in two; the sudden profound dip into the watery glens and hollows; the keen spurrings and goadings to gain the top of the opposite hill; the headlong, sled-like slide down its other side;—all these, with the cries of the headsmen and harpooneers, and the shuddering gasps of the oarsmen, with the wondrous sight of the ivory Pequod bearing down upon her boats with outstretched sails, like a wild hen after her screaming brood;—all this was thrilling. Not the raw recruit, marching from the bosom of his wife into the fever heat of his first battle; not the dead man's ghost encountering the first unknown phantom in the other world;—neither of these can feel stranger and stronger emotions than that man does, who for the first time finds himself pulling into the charmed, churned circle of the hunted Sperm Whale.

The dancing white water made by the chase was now becoming more and more visible, owing to the increasing darkness of the dun cloud-shadows flung upon the sea. The jets of vapor no longer blended, but tilted everywhere to right and left; the whales seemed separating their wakes. The boats were pulled more apart; Starbuck giving chase to three whales running dead to leeward. Our sail was now set, and, with the still rising wind, we rushed along; the boat going with such madness through the water, that the lee oars could scarcely be worked rapidly enough to escape being torn from the row-locks.

Soon we were running through a suffusing wide veil of mist; neither ship nor boat to be seen.

'Give way, men,' whispered Starbuck, drawing still further aft the sheet of his sail; 'there is time to kill a fish yet before the squall comes. There's white water again!—close to! Spring!'

Soon after, two cries in quick succession on each side of us denoted that the other boats had got fast; but hardly were they overheard, when with a lightning-like hurtling whisper Starbuck said: 'Stand up!' and Queequeg, harpoon in hand, sprang to his feet.

Though not one of the oarsmen was then facing the life and death peril so close to them ahead, yet with their eyes on the intense countenance of the mate in the stern of the boat, they knew that the imminent instant had come; they heard, too, an enormous wallowing sound as of fifty elephants stirring in their litter. Meanwhile the boat was still booming through the mist, the waves curling and hissing around us like the erected crests of enraged serpents.

'That's his hump. There, there, give it to him!' whispered Starbuck.

A short rushing sound leaped out of the boat; it was the darted iron of Queequeg. Then all in one welded commotion came an invisible push from astern, while forward the boat seemed striking on a ledge; the sail collapsed and exploded; a gush of scalding vapor shot up near by; something rolled and tumbled like an earthquake beneath us. The whole crew were half suffocated as they were tossed helter-skelter into the white curdling cream of the squall. Squall, whale, and harpoon had all blended together; and the whale, merely grazed by the iron, escaped.

Though completely swamped, the boat was nearly unharmed. Swimming round it we picked up the floating oars, and lashing them across the gunwale, tumbled back to our places. There we sat up to our knees in the sea, the water covering every rib and plank, so that to our downward gazing eyes the suspended craft seemed a coral boat grown up to us from the bottom of the ocean.

The wind increased to a howl; the waves dashed their bucklers together; the whole squall roared, forked, and crackled around us like a white fire upon the prairie, in which, unconsumed, we were burning; immortal in these jaws of death! In vain we hailed the other boats; as well roar to the live coals down the chimney of a flaming furnace as hail those boats in that storm. Meanwhile the driving scud, rack, and mist, grew darker with the shadows of night; no sign of the ship could be seen. The rising sea forbade all attempts to bale out the boat. The oars were useless as propellers, performing now the office of life-preservers. So, cutting the lashing of the water-proof match keg, after many failures Star-buck contrived to ignite the lamp in the lantern; then stretching it on a waif pole, handed it to Quee-queg as the standard-bearer of this forlorn hope. There, then, he sat, holding up that imbecile candle in the heart of that almighty forlornness. There, then, he sat, the sign and symbol of a man without faith, hopelessly holding up hope in the midst of despair.

Wet, drenched through, and shivering cold, despairing of ship or boat, we lifted up our eyes as the dawn came on. The mist still spread over the sea, the empty lantern lay crushed in the bottom of the boat. Suddenly Queequeg started to his feet, hollowing his hand to his ear. We all heard a faint creaking, as of ropes and yards hitherto muffled by the storm. The sound came nearer and nearer; the thick mists were dimly parted by a huge, vague form. Affrighted, we all sprang into the sea as the ship at last loomed into view, bearing right down upon us within a distance of not much more than its length.

Floating on the waves we saw the abandoned boat, as for one instant it tossed and gaped beneath the ship's bows like a chip at the base of a cataract; and then the vast hull rolled over it, and it was seen no more till it came up weltering astern. Again we swam for it, were dashed against it by the seas, and were at last taken up and safely landed on board. Ere the squall came close to, the other boats had cut loose from their fish and returned to the ship in good time. The ship had given us up, but was still cruising, if haply it might light upon some token of our perishing,—an oar or a lance pole.

The Pirate Crew Set Sail

[MARK TWAIN]

Tom's mind was made up now. He was gloomy and desperate. He was a forsaken, friendless boy, he said; nobody loved him; when they found out what they had driven him to, perhaps they would be sorry; he had tried to do right and get along, but they would not let him; since nothing would do them but to be rid of him, let it be so; and let them blame *him* for the consequences—why shouldn't they? What right had the friendless to complain? Yes, they had forced him to it at last: he would lead a life of crime. There was no choice.

By this time he was far down Meadow Lane, and the bell for school to "take up" tinkled faintly upon his ear. He sobbed, now, to think he should never, never hear that old familiar sound any more—it was very hard, but it was forced on him;

since he was driven out into the cold world, he must submit—but he forgave them. Then the sobs came thick and fast.

Just at this point he met his soul's sworn comrade, Joe Harper—hard-eyed, and with evidently a great and dismal purpose in his heart. Plainly here were "two souls with but a single thought." Tom, wiping his eyes with his sleeve, began to blubber out something about a resolution to escape from hard usage and lack of sympathy at home by roaming abroad into the great world never to return; and ended by hoping that Joe would not forget him.

But it transpired that this was a request which Joe had just been going to make to Tom, and had come to hunt him up for that purpose. His mother had whipped him for drinking some cream which he had never tasted and knew nothing about; it was plain that she was tired of him and wished him to go; if she felt that way, there was nothing for him to do but succumb; he hoped she would be happy, and never regret having driven her poor boy out into the unfeeling world to suffer and die.

As the two boys walked sorrowing along, they made a new compact to stand by each other and be brothers and never be separate till death relieved them of their troubles. Then they began to lay their plans. Joe was for being a hermit, and living on crusts in a remote cave, and dying, sometime, of cold and want and grief; but after listening to Tom, he conceded that there were some conspicuous advantages about a life of crime, and so he consented to be a pirate.

Three miles below St. Petersburg, at a point where the Mississippi River was a trifle over a mile wide, there was a long, narrow, wooded island, with a shallow bar at the head of it, and this offered well as a rendezvous. It was not inhabited; it lay far over toward the farther shore, abreast a dense and almost wholly unpeopled forest. So Jackson's Island was chosen. Who were to be the subjects of their piracies was a matter that did not occur to them. Then they hunted up Huckleberry Finn, and he joined them promptly, for all careers were one to him; he was indifferent. They presently separated to meet at a lonely spot on the riverbank two miles above the village at the favorite hour—which was midnight. There was a small log raft there which they meant to capture. Each would bring hooks and lines, and such provision as he could steal in the most dark and mysterious way—as became outlaws. And before the afternoon was done they had all managed to enjoy the sweet glory of spreading the fact that pretty soon the town would "hear something." All who got this vague hint were cautioned to "be mum and wait."

About midnight Tom arrived with a boiled ham and a few trifles, and stopped in a dense undergrowth on a small bluff overlooking the meeting place. It was starlight, and very still. The mighty river lay like an ocean at rest. Tom listened a moment, but no sound disturbed the quiet. Then he gave a low, distinct whistle. It was answered from under the bluff. Tom whistled twice more; these signals were answered in the same way. Then a guarded voice said:

"Who goes there?"

"Tom Sawyer, the Black Avenger of the Spanish Main. Name your names."

"Huck Finn the Red-Handed, and Joe Harper the Terror of the Seas." Tom had furnished these titles, from his favorite literature.

"'Tis well. Give the countersign."

Two hoarse whispers delivered the same awful word simultaneous to the brooding night:

"BLOOD!"

Then Tom tumbled his ham over the bluff and let himself down after it, tearing both skin and clothes to some extent in the effort. There was an easy, comfortable path along the shore under the bluff, but it lacked the advantages of difficulty and danger so valued by a pirate.

The Terror of the Seas had brought a side of bacon, and had about worn himself out with getting it there. Finn the Red-Handed had stolen a skillet and a quantity of half-cured leaf tobacco, and had also brought a few corncobs to make pipes with. But none of the pirates smoked or "chewed" but himself. The Black Avenger of the Spanish Main said it would

never do to start without some fire. That was a wise
thought; matches were hardly known there in that
day. They saw a fire smoldering upon a great raft a
hundred yards above, and they went stealthily thither
and helped themselves to a chunk. They made an
imposing adventure of it, saying, "Hist!" every now
and then, and suddenly halting with finger on lip;
moving with hands on imaginary dagger hilts; and
giving orders in dismal whispers that if "the foe"
stirred to "let him have it to the hilt," because "dead
men tell no tales." They knew well enough that the
raftsmen were all down at the village laying in stores
or having a spree, but still that was no excuse for their
conducting this thing in an unpiratical way.

They shoved off, presently, Tom in command,
Huck at the after oar and Joe at the forward. Tom
stood amidships, gloomy browed, and with folded
arms, and gave his orders in a low, stern whisper:

"Luff, and bring her to the wind!"

"Aye-aye, sir!"

"Steady, steady-y-y-y!"

"Steady it is, sir!"

"Let her go off a point!"

"Point it is, sir!"

As the boys steadily and monotonously drove the
raft toward midstream it was no doubt understood
that these orders were given only for "style," and
were not intended to mean anything in particular.

"What sail's she carrying?"

"Courses, tops'ls, and flying jib, sir."

"Send the r'yals up! Lay out aloft, there, half a dozen of ye—foretopmaststuns'l! Lively, now!"

"Aye-aye, sir!"

"Shake out that maintogalans'l! Sheets and braces! *Now*, my hearties!"

"Aye-aye, sir!"

"Hellum-a-lee—hard aport! Stand by to meet her when she comes! Port, port! *Now*, men! With a will! Steady-y-y-y!"

"Steady it is, sir!"

The raft drew beyond the middle of the river; the boys pointed her head right, and then lay on their oars. The river was not high, so there was not more than a two- or three-mile current. Hardly a word was said during the next three-quarters of an hour. Now the raft was passing before the distant town. Two or three glimmering lights showed where it lay, peacefully sleeping, unconscious of the tremendous event that was happening. The Black Avenger stood still with folded arms, "looking his last" upon the scene or his former joys and his later sufferings, and wishing "she" could see him now, abroad on the wild sea, facing peril and death with dauntless heart, going to his doom with a grim smile on his lips. It was but a small strain on his imagination to remove Jackson's Island beyond eyeshot of the village, and so he "looked his last" with a broken and satisfied heart. The other pirates were looking their last, too; and they all looked so long that they came near letting the current drift them out of the range of the island. But they discovered the danger in time, and made shift to avert it. About two o'clock in the morning the raft grounded on the bar two hundred yards above the head of the island, and they waded back and forth until they had landed their freight. Part of the little raft's belongings consisted of an old sail, and this they spread over a nook in the bushes for a tent to shelter their provisions; but they themselves would sleep in the open air in good weather, as became outlaws.

They built a fire against the side of a great log twenty or thirty steps within the somber depths of the forest, and then cooked some bacon in the frying pan for supper, and used up half of the corn "pone" stock they had brought. It seemed glorious sport to be feasting in that wild free way in the virgin forest of an unexplored and uninhabited island, far from the haunts of men, and they said they never would return to civilization. The climbing fire lit up their faces and threw its ruddy glare upon the pillared tree trunks of their forest temple, and upon the varnished foliage and festooning vines.

When the last crisp slice of bacon was gone and the last allowance of corn pone devoured, the boys stretched themselves out on the grass, filled with contentment. They could have found a cooler place, but they would not deny themselves such a romantic feature as the roasting campfire.

"*Ain't* it gay?" said Joe.

"It's *nuts!*" said Tom. "What would the boys say if they could see us?"

"Say? Well, they'd just die to be here—hey, Hucky!"

"I reckon so," said Huckleberry; "anyways, *I'm* suited. I don't want nothing better'n this. I don't ever get enough to eat, gen'ally—and here they can't come and pick at a feller and bullyrag him so."

"It's just the life for me," said Tom. "You don't have to get up, mornings, and you don't have to go to school, and wash, and all that blame foolishness. You see a pirate don't have to do *anything*, Joe, when he's ashore, but a hermit *he* has to be praying considerable, and then he don't have any fun, anyway, all by himself that way."

"Oh, yes, that's so," said Joe, "but I hadn't thought much about it, you know. I'd a good deal rather be a pirate, now that I've tried it."

"You see," said Tom, "people don't go much on hermits, nowadays, like they used to in old times, but a pirate's always respected. And a hermit's got to sleep on the hardest place he can find, and put sackcloth and ashes on his head, and stand out in the rain, and—"

"What does he put sackcloth and ashes on his head for?" inquired Huck.

"*I* dono. But they've *got* to do it. Hermits always do. You'd have to do that if you was a hermit."

"Derned if I would," said Huck.

"Well, what would you do?"

"I dunno. But I wouldn't do that."

"Why Huck, you'd *have* to. How'd you get around it?"

"Why, I just wouldn't stand it. I'd run away."

"Run away! Well, you *would* be a nice old slouch of a hermit. You'd be a disgrace."

The Red-Handed made no response, being better employed. He had finished gouging out a cob, and now he fitted a weed stem to it, loaded it with tobacco, and was pressing a coal to the charge and blowing a cloud of fragrant smoke—he was in the full bloom of luxurious contentment. The other pirates envied him this majestic vice, and secretly resolved to acquire it shortly. Presently Huck said:

"What does pirates have to do?"

Tom said:

"Oh, they have just a bully time—take ships and burn them, and get the money and bury it in awful places in their island where there's ghosts and things to watch it, and kill everybody in the ships—make 'em walk a plank."

"And they carry the women to the island," said Joe; "they don't kill the women."

"No," assented Tom, "they don't kill the women—they're too noble. And the women's always beautiful, too."

"And don't they wear the bulliest clothes! Oh, no! All gold and silver and di'monds," said Joe, with enthusiasm.

"Who?" said Huck.

"Why, the pirates."

Huck scanned his own clothing forlornly.

"I reckon I ain't dressed fitten for a pirate," said he, with a regretful pathos in his voice; "but I ain't got none but these."

But the other boys told him the fine clothes would come fast enough, after they should have begun their adventures. They made him understand that his poor rags would do to begin with, though it was customary for wealthy pirates to start with a proper wardrobe.

Gradually their talk died out and drowsiness began to steal upon the eyelids of the little waifs. The pipe dropped from the fingers of the Red-Handed, and he slept the sleep of the conscious-free and the weary. The Terror of the Seas and the Black Avenger of the Spanish Main had more difficulty in getting to sleep. They said their prayers inwardly, and lying down, since there was nobody there with authority to make them kneel and recite aloud; in truth, they had a mind not to say them at all, but they were afraid to proceed to such lengths as that, lest they might call down a sudden and special thunderbolt from heaven. Then at once they reached and hovered upon the imminent verge of sleep—but an intruder came, now, that would not "down." It was conscience. They began to feel a vague fear that they had been doing wrong to run away, and next they thought of the stolen meat, and then the real torture came. They tried to argue it away by reminding conscience that they had purloined sweetmeats and apples scores of times; but conscience was not to be appeased by such thin plausibilities; it seemed to them, in the end, that there was no getting around the stubborn fact that taking sweetmeats was only "hooking," while taking bacon and hams and such valuables was plain simple *stealing*—and there was a command against that in the Bible. So they inwardly resolved that so long as they remained in the business, their piracies should not again be sullied with the crime of stealing. Then conscience granted a truce, and these curiously inconsistent pirates fell peacefully to sleep.

In Which a Conversation Takes Place Which Seems Likely to Cost Phileas Fogg Dear

[JULES VERNE]

Phileas Fogg, having shut the door of his house at half-past eleven, and having put his right foot before his left five hundred and seventy-five times, and his left foot before his right five hundred and seventy-six times, reaches the Reform Club, an imposing edifice in Pall Mall, which could not have cost less than three millions. He repaired at once to the dining-room, the nine windows of which open upon a tasteful garden, where the trees were already gilded with an autumn colouring; and took his place at the habitual table, the cover of which had already been laid for him. His breakfast consisted of a side-dish, a broiled fish with Reading sauce, a scarlet slice of roast beef garnished with mushrooms, a rhubarb and gooseberry tart, and a morsel of Cheshire cheese, the whole being washed down with several cups of tea, for which the Reform is famous. He rose at thirteen minutes to one, and directed his steps towards the large hall, a sumptuous apartment adorned with lavishly-framed paintings. A flunkey handed him an uncut *Times,* which he proceeded to cut with a skill which betrayed familiarity with this delicate operation. The perusal of this paper absorbed Phileas Fogg until a quarter before four, whilst the *Standard,* his next task, occupied him till the dinner hour. Dinner passed as breakfast had done, and Mr. Fogg re-appeared in the reading-room and sat down to the Pall Mall at twenty minutes before six. Half an hour later several members of the Reform came in and drew up to the fireplace, where a coal fire was steadily burning. They were Mr. Fogg's usual partners at whist: Andrew Stuart, an engineer; John Sullivan and Samuel Fallentin, bankers; Thomas Flanagan, a brewer; and Gauthier Ralph, one of the Directors of the Bank of England—all rich and highly respectable personages, even in a club which comprises the princes of English trade and finance.

"Well, Ralph," said Thomas Flanagan, "what about that robbery?"

"Oh," replied Stuart, "the Bank will lose the money."

"On the contrary," broke in Ralph, "I hope we may put our hands on the robber. Skilful detectives have been sent to all the principal ports of America and the Continent, and he'll be a clever fellow if he slips through their fingers."

"But have you got the robber's description?" asked Stuart.

"In the first place, he is no robber at all," returned Ralph, positively.

"What! a fellow who makes off with fifty-five thousand pounds, no robber?"

"No."

"Perhaps he's a manufacturer, then."

"The Daily Telegraph says that he is a gentleman."

It was Phileas Fogg, whose head now emerged from behind his newspapers, who made this remark. He bowed to his friends, and entered into the conversation. The affair which formed its subject, and which was town talk, had occurred three days before at the Bank of England. A package of banknotes, to the value of fifty-five thousand pounds, had been taken from the principal cashier's table, that functionary being at the moment engaged in registering the receipt of three shillings and sixpence. Of course, he could not have his eyes everywhere. Let it be observed that the Bank of England reposes a touching confidence in the honesty of the public. There are neither guards nor gratings to protect its treasures; gold, silver, banknotes are freely exposed, at the mercy of the first comer. A keen observer of English customs relates that, being in one of the rooms of the Bank one day, he had the curiosity to examine a gold ingot weighing some seven or eight pounds. He took it up, scrutinised it, passed it to his neighbour, he to the next man, and so on until the ingot, going from hand to hand, was transferred to the end of a dark entry; nor did it return to its place for half an hour. Meanwhile, the cashier had not so much as raised his head. But in the present instance things had not gone so smoothly. The package of notes not being found when five o'clock sounded from the ponderous clock in the "drawing office," the amount was passed to the account of profit and loss. As soon as the robbery was discovered, picked detectives hastened off to Liverpool, Glasgow, Havre, Suez, Brindisi, New York, and other ports, inspired by the proffered reward of two thousand pounds, and five per cent on the sum that might be recovered. Detectives were also charged with narrowly watching those who arrived at or left London by rail, and a judicial examination was at once entered upon.

There were real grounds for supposing, as the Daily Telegraph said, that the thief did not belong to a professional band. On the day of the robbery a well-dressed gentleman of polished manners, and with a well-to-do air, had been observed going to and fro in the paying room where the crime was committed. A description of him was easily procured and sent to the detectives; and some hopeful spirits, of whom Ralph was one, did not despair of his apprehension. The papers and clubs were full of the affair, and everywhere people were discussing the probabilities of a successful pursuit; and the Reform Club was especially agitated, several of its members being Bank officials.

Ralph would not concede that the work of the detectives was likely to be in vain, for he thought that the prize offered would greatly stimulate their zeal and activity. But Stuart was far from sharing this confidence; and, as they placed themselves at the whist-table, they continued to argue the matter. Stuart and Flanagan played together, while Phileas Fogg had Fallentin for his partner. As the game proceeded the conversation ceased, excepting between the rubbers, when it revived again.

"I maintain," said Stuart, "that the chances are in favour of the thief, who must be a shrewd fellow."

"Well, but where can he fly to?" asked Ralph. "No country is safe for him."

"Pshaw!"

"Where could he go, then?"

"Oh, I don't know that. The world is big enough."

"It was once," said Phileas Fogg, in a low tone. "Cut, sir," he added, handing the cards to Thomas Flanagan.

The discussion fell during the rubber, after which Stuart took up its thread.

"What do you mean by 'once'? Has the world grown smaller?"

"Certainly," returned Ralph. "I agree with Mr. Fogg. The world has grown smaller, since a man can now go round it ten times more quickly than a hundred years ago. And that is why the search for this thief will be more likely to succeed."

"And also why the thief can get away more easily."

"Be so good as to play, Mr. Stuart," said Phileas Fogg.

But the incredulous Stuart was not convinced, and when the hand was finished, said eagerly: "You have a strange way, Ralph, of proving that the world has grown smaller. So, because you can go round it in three months—"

"In eighty days," interrupted Phileas Fogg.

"That is true, gentlemen," added John Sullivan. "Only eighty days, now that the section between Rothal and Allahabad, on the Great Indian Peninsula Railway, has been opened. Here is the estimate made by the Daily Telegraph.

From London to Suez via Mont Cenis and Brindisi, by rail and steamboats	7	days
From Suez to Bombay, by steamer	13	"
From Bombay to Calcutta, by rail	3	"

From Calcutta to Hong Kong, by steamer	13	"
From Hong Kong to Yokohama (Japan), by steamer	6	"
From Yokohama to San Francisco, by steamer	22	"
From San Francisco to New York, by rail	7	"
From New York to London, by steamer and rail	9	"
Total	**80**	**days**

"Yes, in eighty days!" exclaimed Stuart, who in his excitement made a false deal. "But that doesn't take into account bad weather, contrary winds, ship-wrecks, railway accidents, and so on."

"All included," returned Phileas Fogg, continuing to play despite the discussion.

"But suppose the Hindoos or Indians pull up the rails," replied Stuart; "suppose they stop the trains, pillage the luggage-vans, and scalp the passengers!"

"All included," calmly retorted Fogg; adding, as he threw down the cards, "Two trumps."

Stuart, whose turn it was to deal, gathered them up, and went on: "You are right, theoretically, Mr. Fogg, but practically—"

"Practically also, Mr. Stuart."

"I'd like to see you do it in eighty days."

"It depends on you. Shall we go?"

"Heaven preserve me! But I would wager four thousand pounds that such a journey, made under these conditions, is impossible."

"Quite possible, on the contrary," returned Mr. Fogg.

"Well, make it, then!"

"The journey round the world in eighty days?"

"Yes."

"I should like nothing better."

"When?"

"At once. Only I warn you that I shall do it at your expense."

"It's absurd!" cried Stuart, who was beginning to be annoyed at the persistency of his friend. "Come, let's go on with the game."

"Deal over again, then," said Phileas Fogg. "There's a false deal."

Stuart took up the pack with a feverish hand; then suddenly put them down again.

"Well, Mr. Fogg," said he, "it shall be so: I will wager the four thousand on it."

"Calm yourself, my dear Stuart," said Fallentin. "It's only a joke."

"When I say I'll wager," returned Stuart, "I mean it." "All right," said Mr. Fogg; and, turning to the others, he continued: "I have a deposit of twenty thousand at Baring's which I will willingly risk upon it."

"Twenty thousand pounds!" cried Sullivan. "Twenty

thousand pounds, which you would lose by a single accidental delay!"

"The unforeseen does not exist," quietly replied Phileas Fogg.

"But, Mr. Fogg, eighty days are only the estimate of the least possible time in which the journey can be made."

"A well-used minimum suffices for everything."

"But, in order not to exceed it, you must jump mathematically from the trains upon the steamers, and from the steamers upon the trains again."

"I will jump—mathematically."

"You are joking."

"A true Englishman doesn't joke when he is talking about so serious a thing as a wager," replied Phileas Fogg, solemnly. "I will bet twenty thousand pounds against anyone who wishes that I will make the tour of the world in eighty days or less; in nineteen hundred and twenty hours, or a hundred and fifteen thousand two hundred minutes. Do you accept?"

"We accept," replied Messrs. Stuart, Fallentin, Sullivan, Flanagan, and Ralph, after consulting each other.

"Good," said Mr. Fogg. "The train leaves for Dover at a quarter before nine. I will take it."

"This very evening?" asked Stuart.

"This very evening," returned Phileas Fogg. He took out and consulted a pocket almanac, and added,

"As today is Wednesday, the 2nd of October, I shall be due in London at this very room of the Reform Club, on Saturday, the 21st of December, at a quarter before nine p.m.; or else the twenty thousand pounds, now deposited in my name at Baring's, will belong to you, in fact and in right, gentlemen. Here is a cheque for the amount."

A memorandum of the wager was at once drawn up and signed by the six parties, during which Phileas Fogg preserved a stoical composure. He certainly did not bet to win, and had only staked the twenty thousand pounds, half of his fortune, because he foresaw that he might have to expend the other half to carry out this difficult, not to say unattainable, project. As for his antagonists, they seemed much agitated; not so much by the value of their stake, as because they had some scruples about betting under conditions so difficult to their friend.

The clock struck seven, and the party offered to suspend the game so that Mr. Fogg might make his preparations for departure.

"I am quite ready now," was his tranquil response. "Diamonds are trumps: be so good as to play, gentlemen."

Among the Crocodiles

[**H. HERVEY**]

" Take care! for goodness' sake! you'll be through the sleepers if you make a false step!"

Such was my greeting when next we met; but he didn't heed it. When did he ever heed me? He took not the slightest notice of my caution, and continued skipping along from sleeper to sleeper, although there were "way boards" on the other side of the metals purposely intended for pedestrians. *He* care? not he! and yet he had a heart of gold.

I, standing on a pier of the Dhodairoo railway-bridge, superintending the attachment of angle-iron telegraph brackets, had caught his eye as he passed on the engine of the mixed train. No sooner he "spotted" me than he ordered the driver to stop, and knowing that I would welcome him, he bawled to his servants to bundle out with his camp "kit," while he came titupping back across the open-work bridge with a recklessness that made my blood run cold.

"By Jove! I'm blown!" he exclaimed, bringing up above me. "If that's cold tea you've got in that bottle there, pass it along, and I'll take a pull. Phew! it was hot on that old rattle-trap," indicating the labouring loco-motive now getting into motion again with its load.

"Had a good time in Madras?" I asked, handing up the tea.

"Fairish; but hang old Maggs! he has played me something like a trick. I say, where are you stay-ing!—under an umbrella?"

I pointed to my tents beneath some trees on the river bank.

"You will remain the night, Sparkes?"

"Yes; but longer than for a night, I expect. Seen any crocodiles since you've been here?" he resumed, going off at one of his usual tangents.

"Yes, in the distance; the river swarms with them. Why?"

"How about elbow room?" nodding in the direc-tion of my camp.

"Plenty for you and me. I've a third tent also—unpitched."

"You have! How long will you be here?"

"Another week at least; this job will take quite that."

He deliberated for a while, I watching him from my lower level on the pier. I guessed he had something in contemplation, and I waited for him to unfold it.

"Bother! what's the odds?" he exclaimed at length. "I can always get them to slow down to drop me here, can't I? You don't mind putting up a couple of fellers besides me for a day or two, do you, Hervey? We'll share expenses as before."

"If you guarantee the 'fellers,' and they bring their camp cots, I've no objection."

"Well, this is how it is," said he, swinging down by my angle-iron bracket on to the pier-head, "directly I went to see old Maggs, he introduced me to a monied son-of-a-gun, some relative of one of our directors; he's a bit gone in the upper story, I think, and———

"Who's gone, Maggs, the director, or the son-of-a-gun?"

"The son-of-a-gun; he's out here on the mooch, the trot, and wants to see everything, try his hand at everything before the hot weather comes and drives him back to England. Tredethlin has shown him tiger and bison shooting; that is, the feller was present while the others did the work; and old Maggs has given him his *quantum suff.* of Anglo-Indian society at Madras. Now a hankering after crocodile shooting possesses the chap's soul, and he has been bothering Magg's life out of him about it. My turning up at Madras for that confounded ball gave the old boy his opportunity; he promptly shunted the son-of-a-gun and his toady on to me, and———"

"His toady?"

"Yes, a one-horse sort of an individual, who—figuratively—brushes the other feller's boots, and —————"

"What other fellow?"

"The son-of-a-gun; and as much as ordered me to arrange that he gets his stomach full of crocodile potting. Hang it all! I should like to ram one down his throat!"

"Well?"

"Well, I returned to Irodepett day before yesterday, and have been prospecting around for a likely place. Old Clarke mentioned the Yellavunka river. I've just come from it; but cholera has broken out there, so it won't do; then, spotting you, and Clarke having named the Dhodairoo also, I thought this would answer, provided other things fitted and you proved agreeable."

"I am agreeable. When will they be coming?"

"You're a brick! I'll send a man with a telegram to Cooloor, telling them to start at once. They ought to turn up by to-morrow's mixed train."

"All right; you go on to my camp, and tell them to pitch the third tent; ask for whatever you want, and make yourself comfortable; have a tub; tell them you're going to stay, and to see to the dinner accordingly; I'll be back by five or so."

Singing out to his people to tote along his *impedimenta*, he left me. I remained on the work till sundown, when I followed my chum to the tents. Poor chap! I was very glad to have him with me again, though only for a day or two; he always "shined me up" a bit, somehow.

The next morning, accompanied by the headmen of the village, we were shown a secluded reach of the river, about half a mile up, where it was fringed with thick jungle, and the stream itself broken by a small islet, and several sand-banks, on the latter of which, we were told, the crocodiles, or, more correctly speaking, the gavials, were wont to drag themselves high and dry to bask in the sun. Here, then, it was decided to conduct our expected guests on the morrow, and we instructed the villagers to bring along a coracle, for possible use in our operations. This settled, I went to the bridge to see after the work, and Sparkes returned to camp, where I joined him later on for breakfast.

In due course that afternoon the two men arrived, and Sparkes introduced me to them in the evening. That they were "verdants" with respect to their present surroundings, and the object of their visit was patent from the first; their speech, their manner, their very "kit" betrayed the fact. Mr. Brett—Sparkes' son-of-a-gun—was a florid, fair-faced, light-eyed, short, stout man of between twenty-five and thirty; while Mr. Walker—Sparkes' "toady"—was as direct an antithesis of his principal as you could imagine; having described the one, you can picture the other. In age they appeared about the same; but what lent comicality to the whole thing was the persistent manner in which Walker echoed Brett; this peculiarity will be made manifest further on.

"So you have set your heart on a shot at the crocodiles, Mr. Brett," said I, as soon as we were seated at dinner.

"Y—yes; being in the land of the great saurian, we thought it would not do to return to England and face our friends without having encountered the animal in his native haunts."

"In his native haunts," added Walker.

"Can't understand you waifs from home wanting to run your blessed necks into nooses like this," observed Sparkes. "However, to business. We'll have to start confoundedly early to get to the spot and take up our position before the brutes come out to bask, which they do at the first sun-blush. You and Mr. What's-his-name," nodding at Walker, "will have to take your stand on a bush-covered islet in the stream, which commands the sand-banks where the varmints lay themselves out to get warmed by the sun; it had better be the islet; for if you fire from the river-bank it would make the range about two hundred yards, and you might miss. All you have to do is wait till the first one gapes, when slap a bullet down its thorax, and you've got him; do you see?"

It was amusing to note their faces as Sparkes delivered himself of the above; they stared blankly at us, then at each other.

"But—but—er—er————" began Brett and stopped.

"But—but—er—er————" added Walker, and he stopped too.

"But what? Hang it all! out with it!" cried Sparkes.

"What—are—you two going to do? Mr. Tredethlin accompanied————"

"Oh, confound Mr. Tredethlin! You're here to shoot crocodiles; I am here to put you in the way. If Tredethlin chose to shoot the tiger for you, I'm not going to do ditto with the crocs. I and Mr. Hervey will *caché* on the bank,—to see fair play, *savez?*"

"But how are we to get to the islet? We can't swim!"

"Can't swim a stroke," added Walker.

"Who said you could? You can paddle, I suppose,—one or other of you?"

"Paddle what?"

"Paddle what?"

"Paddle your own canoe! There'll be a coracle, and the distance to be traversed a hundred yards or so; you can manage that surely! Living Mortlake way, as you say you do, you must have gone on the river occasionally and learnt how to propel a boat?"

"Oh, yes."

"Oh, frequently."

"That's all right. Your guns are somewhat antiquated affairs though. What are they sighted to?"

"Three hundred yards, I think."

"Yes, three hundred yards," said the echo.

"Pooh! then you are bound to go on to the islet. Shouldn't like to trust you with a Martini, especially as you told me you've never handled one. You can shoot straight enough to fire down a croc's open mouth at seventy or eighty yards?"

"No possible doubt of that," said Brett, gaining confidence.

"No possible doubt whatever," added Walker hilariously.

And so we conversed. They showed us their battery: old muzzle loaders—family heirlooms evidently; and we wondered that Brett, a man of means, should have come so poorly provided in respect to armament. They retired early, wishing—so they averred one after the other—to fortify themselves against the morrow.

We roused them before dawn, and after partaking of tea and toast, accompanied by two men carrying their guns, we sallied forth, and struck the river at the desired spot. Here we found the coracle moored to the steep bank, and a couple of villagers rolled up in their blankets, squatting by.

"There's your islet," said Sparkes, indicating it. "Lie down on the hither slope, and keep an eye through the bushes on the sand-bank lying beyond; wait till several of the animals lug themselves out and set to gape; select the one that gives you the squarer chance of sending your lead down into his insides, for you'll never be able to perforate his hide with those Brown Besses, and I don't suppose either of you could hit the eye. In you get; there's no time to lose," hustling them into the coracle.

"Do come with us!" pleaded Brett.

"Yes, do come with us!" tacked on Walker entreatingly.

"You be shot!" vociferated Sparkes. "What do you want me for? you fellers are bossing this show, not I."

They managed to paddle themselves across after a fashion. They landed, hitched the painter to a bush and took up their positions as instructed. I, Sparkes, and the natives concealed ourselves in the jungle that grew to the edge of the high bank, and waited in silence, our elevated vantage-ground enabling us to command a view of both islet and the sand-bank farther out.

Though as a rule timid of the human being, the Asiatic gavial is known to be a man-eater; its attack, under ordinary circumstances, is delivered insidiously. The usual *modus operandi* is to stalk the solitary bather, seize him below water, and carry him off to some secluded pool, where the huge lizards in numbers fall upon the perhaps still breathing victim and tear him in pieces. We knew that when assailed or otherwise roused to anger, the animal evinces courage and aggressiveness; but neither of us had actual experience of crocodiles, and we contented ourselves with the assurances of the villagers that so long as we kept clear of the water, there was nothing to fear, and that the gavials would vanish at the first report of a gun.

The sun rose,—up the river; and soon after his rays had burnished everything with a fiery effulgence we descried several ugly snouts protruding from the water. A little while, and more of the hideous bodies became visible; we heard their frequent harsh respirations, and then, from under the lea of the opposite bank which was marshy and much lower than ours, a general movement ensued towards deeper water: half a dozen of the reptiles drew their scaly lengths on to the sand-banks; others went up, some down stream, as if in quest of food—but our hearts ascended to our mouths when we saw the long shape of one brute emerge on to the islet occupied by Brett and his mate! And yet the natives had assured us that the lizards would confine themselves to the sand-banks! The crocodile drew clear of the water; it faced our friends; not five paces divided them! The men made no sign: perhaps they were waiting till the brute gaped. We looked on with a sickening sensation of horror! Then the saurian opened its fearful mouth, keeping it so for a few seconds, and closing it with a clash! What were those two fellows about? they must have heard that "snap"; the sound had penetrated to our ears. Why had they allowed so splendid an opportunity to slip by? Were they asleep? Sparkes could stand the suspense no longer.

"Shoot! can't you, you howling idiots? There he is under your very noses!"

Immediately on the sound of the human voice there was a simultaneous movement on the part of every gavial within our ken: one or two slid into the water, but the others only raised themselves on their squat limbs, closed their jaws, and seemed to eye the bank.

"Which one?" came in quavering accents from the islet: it was Brett who spoke.

"Confound you! the one within arm's length of you! Get up and look, you jackasses!" foamed Sparkes.

Brett and Walker erected themselves and peered over the bushes; no sooner did their eyes alight on the gruesome shape in such close proximity than Brett dropped his gun into the water, and set to wringing his hands, yelling at the top of his voice. Walker with better spirit, fired point blank at the gavial; the bullet glanced off the adamantine armouring into space, but the impact at so short a range was sufficient to sting the animal to madness, for it uttered a sort of bellow, and commenced— sluggishly, it is true—to approach Walker. The other saurians, attracted no doubt by their fellow's cry, tumbled helter-skelter into the water, and with their long, single-nostrilled snouts in the air, all swam converging on the islet. Before we could shout at him to desist, Brett, impelled by sheer panic, threw himself into the coracle, tore away the painter, and paddled frantically for the shore. Sparkes, with his brow black as thunder, rushed down the bank; I followed him; and as Brett, quaking with "funk," staggered out of the frail vessel, "You miserable son of a sea cook!" exclaimed my friend, "to leave the other feller in the lurch! Call yourself a man!" He had jumped into the boat as he spoke, and before I could join him was off to the rescue.

"Hold on!" I cried, wading after him; for he had used such despatch that he was off before I had well divined his intention. "Hold on! I'll come with you."

The lizards lay like dark logs of wood in the water, but the monster that Walker had fired at seemed determined to make a victim of him. The islet did not much exceed a few paces in length and breadth, rising to a bush-crested ridge about four feet high, the slopes on both sides were clear of vegetation: as a matter of fact there was not a sufficiency of level for a single saurian to spread himself out on in the sun; hence, I suppose, the natives saying that the spot was not frequented by the reptiles. Fortunately for Walker—and the human race in general—the gavial out of the water is neither nimble nor active, and had the space not been so confined, the man could have eluded his pursuer with ease. But as things stood the crocodile had drawn itself up to the bushes on the ridge, and was gradually pressing his enemy towards the water's edge. There was no room for Walker to dodge round the beast; he had clubbed his gun, and by showering blow after blow on the varmint's snout had hitherto arrested its final rush. I could see that the poor fellow's strength was fast failing him; in another second he must yield to the Scylla in front or the Charybdis in the water behind him and he would have eventually fallen into the clutches of one or the other if my plucky chum had not come up at this supreme moment. Yelling with all his voice, scaring thereby the gavials in the water, and managing his uncouth craft with consummate adroitness, he ran her shore just behind Walker, who by now was at his last gasp. "Jump back!" he shouted. "Jump for your life! I'll catch you!" standing up in the flimsy coracle as he uttered the words. Walker tumbled rather than jumped back; quick as thought Sparkes seized him, threw him into the bottom of the boat, and pushed off just as the gavial lunged ponderously forward to grasp his victim. Plying his paddle with all his might—for the whole swarm might take it into their heads to pursue the boat and "chaw" it up together with its occupants—he reached the bank, and we hauled them out in safety.

"Thank Heaven that's over," coolly remarked Sparkes, as we set our faces campwards.

Wild-Fowling Adventures

[**W. H. HUDSON**]

I have said I was not allowed to shoot before the age of ten, but the desire had come long before that; I was no more than seven when I used to wish to be a big, or at all events a bigger, boy, so that, like my brother, I too might carry a gun and shoot big wild birds. But he said "No" very emphatically, and there was an end of it.

He had virtually made himself the owner of all the guns and weapons generally in the house. These included three fowling-pieces, a rifle, an ancient Tower musket with a flint-lock—doubtless dropped from the dead hands of a slain British soldier in one of the fights in Buenos Ayres in 1807 or 1808; a pair of heavy horse pistols, and a ponderous, formidable-looking old blunderbuss, wide at the mouth as a tea-cup saucer. His, too, were the swords. To our native neighbours this appeared an astonishingly large collection of weapons, for in those days they possessed no fire-arm except, in some rare instances, a carbine, brought home by a runaway soldier and kept concealed lest the authorities should get wind of it.

As the next best thing to doing the shooting myself, I attended my brother in his expeditions, to hold his horse or to pick up and carry the birds, and was deeply grateful to him for allowing me to serve him in this humble capacity. We had some exciting adventures together. One summer day he came rushing home to get his gun, having just seen an immense flock of golden plover come down at a spot a mile or so from home. With his gun and a sack to put the birds in, he mounted his pony, I with him, as our ponies were accustomed to carry two and even three at a pinch. We found the flock where he had seen it alight—thousands of birds evenly scattered, running about busily feeding on the wet level ground.

The bird I speak of is the *Charadrius dominicana*, which breeds in Arctic America and migrates in August and September to the plains of La Plata and Patagonia, so that it travels about sixteen thousand miles every year. In appearance it is so like our golden plover, *Charadrius pluvialis*, as to be hardly distinguishable from it. The birds were quite tame: all our wild birds were if anything too tame, although not *shockingly* so as Alexander Selkirk found them on his island—the poet's, not the real

Selkirk. The birds being so scattered, all he could do
was to lie flat down and fire with the barrel of his
fowling-piece level with the flock, and the result was
that the shot cut through the loose flock to a distance
of thirty or forty yards, dropping thirty-nine birds,
which we put into the sack, and remounting our
pony set off home at a fast gallop. We were riding
barebacked, and as our pony's back had a forward
slope we slipped further and further forward until
we were almost on his neck, and I, sitting behind my
brother, shouted for him to stop. But he had his gun
in one hand and the sack in the other, and had lost
the reins; the pony, however, appeared to have understood, as he came to a dead stop of his own accord
on the edge of a rain-pool, into which we were
pitched headlong. When I raised my head I saw the
bag of birds at my side, and the gun lying under
water at a little distance; about three yards further on
my brother was just sitting up, with the water
streaming from his long hair, and a look of astonishment on his face. But the pool was quite clean, with
the soft grass for bottom, and we were not hurt.

However, we did sometimes get into serious
trouble. On one occasion he persuaded me and the
little brother to accompany him on a secret shooting expedition he had planned. We were to start on
horseback before daybreak, ride to one of the
marshes about two miles from home, shoot a lot of
duck, and get back about breakfast-time. The main

thing was to keep the plan secret, then it would be all right, since the sight of the number of wild duck we should have to show on our return would cause our escapade to be overlooked.

In the evening, instead of liberating our ponies as usual, we took and tethered them in the plantation, and next morning about three o'clock we crept cautiously out of the house and set off on our adventure. It was a winter morning, misty and cold when the light came, and the birds were excessively wild at that hour. In vain we followed the flocks, my brother stalking them through the sedges, above his knees in the water; not a bird could he get, and at last we were obliged to go back empty-handed to face the music. At half-past ten we rode to the door, wet and hungry and miserable, to find the whole house in a state of commotion at our disappearance. When we were first missed in the morning, one of the workmen reported that he had seen us taking our horses to conceal them in the plantation at a little after dark, and it was assumed that we had run away—that we had gone south where the country was more thinly settled and wild animals more abundant, in quest of new and more stirring adventures. They were greatly relieved to see us back, but as we had no ducks to placate them we could not be forgiven, and as a punishment we had to go breakfastless that day, and our leader was in addition sternly lectured and forbidden to use a gun for the future.

We thought this a very hard thing, and for the following days were inclinded to look at life as a rather
tame, insipid business; but soon, to our joy, the ban
was removed. In forbidding us the use of the guns
my father had punished himself as well as us, since he
never thoroughly enjoyed a meal—breakfast, dinner,
or supper—unless he had a bird on the table, wild
duck, plover, or snipe. A cold roast duck was his
favourite breakfast dish, and he was never quite
happy when he didn't get it.

Still, I was not happy, and could not be so long as
I was not allowed to shoot. It was a privilege to be
allowed to attend, but it seemed to me that at the
age of ten I was quite old enough to have a gun. I
had been a rider on horseback since the age of six,
and in some exercises I was not much behind my
brother, although when we practised with the foils
or with the gloves he punished me in rather a bar-
barous manner. He was my guide and philosopher,
and had also been a better friend ever since our fight
with knives and the cowbird episode; nevertheless
he still managed to dissemble his love, and when I
revolted against his tyranny I generally got well
punished for it.

About that time an old friend of the family, who
took an interest in me and wished to do something
to encourage me in my natural history tastes, made
me a present of a set of pen-and-ink drawings.
There was, however, nothing in these pictures to

help me in the line I had taken: they were mostly architectural drawings made by himself of buildings—houses, churches, castles, and so on, but my brother fell in love with them and began to try to get them from me. He could not rest without them, and was continually offering me something of his own in exchange for them; but though I soon grew tired of looking at them I refused to part with them, either because his anxiety to have them gave them a fictitious value in my sight, or because it was pleasing to be able to inflict a little pain on him in return for the many smarts I had suffered at his hands. At length one day, finding me still unmoved, he all at once offered to teach me to shoot and to allow me the use of one of the guns in exchange for the pictures. I could hardly believe my good fortune: it would have surprised me less if he had offered to give me his horse with "saddle and bridle also."

As soon as the drawings were in his hand he took me to our gun-room and gave me a quite unneeded lesson in the art of loading a gun—first so much powder, then a wad well rammed down with the old obsolete ramrod; then a percussion cap on the nipple. He then led the way to the plantation, and finding two wild pigeons sitting together in a tree, he ordered me to fire. I fired, and one fell, quite dead, and that completed my education, for now he declared he was not going to waste any more time on my instruction.

The gun he had told me to use was a single-barrel fowling-piece, an ancient converted flintlock, the stock made of an iron-hard black wood with silver mountings. When I stood it up and measured myself by it I found it was nearly two inches taller than I was, but it was light to carry and served me well: I became as much attached to it as to any living thing, and it was like a living being to me, and I had great faith in its intelligence.

My chief ambition was to shoot wild duck. My brother shot them in preference to anything else: they were so much esteemed and he was so much commended when he came in with a few in his bag that I looked on duck-shooting as the greatest thing I could go in for. Ducks were common enough with us and in great variety; I know not in what country more kinds are to be found. There were no fewer than five species of teal, the commonest a dark brown bird with black mottlings; another, very common, was pale grey, the plumage beautifully barred and pencilled with brown and black; then we had the blue-winged teal, a maroon-red duck which ranges from Patagonia to California; the ringed teal, with salmon-coloured breast and velvet-black collar; the Brazilian teal, a lovely olive-brown and velvet-black duck, with crimson beak and legs. There were two pintails, one of which was the most abundant species in the country; also a widgeon, a lake duck, a shoveller duck, with red plummage, grey head and neck, and blue wings; and two species of the long-legged whistling or tree duck. Another common species was the rosy-billed duck, now to be seen on ornamental waters in England; and occasionally we saw the wild Muscovy duck, called Royal duck by the natives, but it was a rare visitor so far south. We also had geese and swans: the upland geese from the Megellanic Straits that came to us in winter—that is to say, our winter from May to August. And there were two swans, the black-necked, which has black flesh and is unfit to eat, and the white or Coscoroba Swan, as good a table bird as there is in the world. And oddly enough this bird has been known to the natives as a "goose" since the discovery of America, and now after three centuries our scientific ornithologists have made the discovery that it is a link between the geese and swans, but is more goose than swan. It is a beautiful white bird, with bright red bill and legs, the wings tipped with black; and has a loud musical cry of three notes, the last prolonged note with a falling inflection.

These were the birds we sought after in winter; but we could shoot for the table all the year round, for no sooner was it the duck's pairing and breeding season than another bird-population from their breeding-grounds in the arctic and sub-arctic regions came on the scene—plover, sandpiper, godwit, curlew, whimbrel,—a host of northern species that made the summer-dried pampas their winter abode.

My first attempt at duck-shooting was made at a
pond not many minutes' walk from the house,
where I found a pair of shoveller ducks, feeding in
their usual way in the shallow water with head and
neck immersed. Anxious not to fail in this first trial,
I got down flat on the ground and crawled snake-
fashion for a distance of fifty or sixty yards, until I
was less then twenty yards from the birds, when I
fired and killed one.

That first duck was a great joy, and having succeeded so well with my careful tactics, I continued
in the same way, confining my attention to pairs or
small parties of three or four birds, when by
patiently creeping a long distance through the grass I
could get very close to them. In this way I shot teal,
widgeon, pintail, shovellers, and finally the noble
rosy-bill, which was esteemed for the table above all
the others.

My brother, ambitious of a big bag, invariably
went a distance from home in quest of the large
flocks, and despised my way of duck-shooting; but it
sometimes vexed him to find on his return from a
day's expedition that I had succeeded in getting as
many birds as himself without having gone much
more than a mile from home.

Some months after I had started shooting I began
to have trouble with my beloved gun, owing to a
weakness it had developed in its lock—one of the
infirmities incidental to age which the gunsmiths of

Buenos Ayres were never able to cure effectually. Whenever it got bad I was permitted to put it into the cart sent to town periodically, to have it repaired, and would then go gunless for a week or ten days. On one of these occasions I one day saw a party of shoveller duck dibbling in a small rain-pool at the side of the plantation, within a dozen yards of the old moat which surrounded it. Ducks always appeared to be exceptionally tame and bold when I was without a gun, but the boldness of those shovellers was more than I could stand, and running to the house I got out the old blunderbuss, which I had never been forbidden to use, since no one had ever thought it possible that I should want to use such a monster of a gun. But I was desperate, and loading it for the first (and last) time, I went after those shovellers.

I had once been told that it would be impossible to shoot wild duck or anything with the blunderbuss unless one could get within a dozen yards of them, on account of its tremendous scattering power. Well, by going along the bottom of the moat, which was luckily without water just then, I could get as near the birds as I liked and kill the whole flock. When I arrived abreast of the pool I crept up the grassy crumbling outside bank, and resting the ponderous barrel on the top of the bank, fired at the shovellers at a distance of about fifteen yards, and killed nothing, but received a kick which sent me flying to the bottom of the foss. It was several days before I got over that pain in my shoulder.

Later on there was a period of trouble and scarcity in the land. There was war, and the city from which we obtained our supplies was besieged by an army from the "upper provinces" which had come down to break the power and humble the pride of Buenos Ayres. Our elders missed their tea and coffee most, but our anxiety was that we should soon be without powder and shot. My brother constantly warned me not to be so wasteful, although he fired half a dozen shots to my one without getting more birds for the table. At length there came a day when there was little shot left—just about enough to fill one shot-pouch—and knowing it was his intention to have a day out, I sneaked into the gun-room and loaded my fowling-piece just to have one shot more. He was going to try for upland geese that day, and, as I had expected, carried off all the shot.

After he had gone I took my gun, and being determined to make the most of my one shot, refused to be tempted by any of the small parties of duck I found in the pools near home, even when they appeared quite tame. At length I encountered a good-sized flock of rosy-bills by the side of a marshy stream about two miles from home. It was a still, warm day in mid-winter, and the ducks were dozing on the green bank in a beautiful crowd, and as the land near them was covered with long grass, I saw it would be possible to get quite close to them. Leaving my pony at a good distance, I got down flat on the ground and began my long laborious crawl, and got within twenty-five yards of the flock. Never had I had such a chance before! As I peeped through the grass and herbage I imagined all sorts of delightful things—my brother far away vainly firing long shots at the wary geese, and his return and disgust at the sight of my heap of noble rosy-bills, all obtained near home at one shot!

Then I fired just as the birds, catching sight of my cap, raised their long necks in alarm. Bang! Up they rose with a noise of wings, leaving not one behind! Vainly I watched the flock, thinking that some of the birds I must have hit would soon be seen to waver in their course and then drop to earth. But none wavered or fell. I went home as much puzzled as disappointed. Late in the day my brother returned with one upland goose and three or four ducks and inquired if I had had any luck. I told him my sad story, whereupon he burst out laughing and informed me that he had taken care to draw the shot from my gun before going out. He was up to my little tricks, he said; he had seen what I had done, and was not going to allow me to waste the little shot we had left!

Our duck-shooting was carried on under difficulties during those days. We searched for ammunition at all the houses for some leagues around, and at one

house we found and purchased a quantity of exceedingly coarse gunpowder, with grain almost the size
of canary-seed. They told us it was cannon-powder
and to make it fit for use in our fowling-pieces we
ground it fine with glass and stone bottles for rollers
on a tin plate. Shot we could not find, so had to
make it for ourselves by cutting up plates of lead
into small square bits with a knife and hammer.

Eventually the civil war, which had dragged on for
a long time, brought an unexpected danger to our
house and caused us to turn our minds to more
important things than ducks. I have said that the city
was besieged by an army from the provinces, but
away on the southern frontier of the province of
Buenos Ayres the besieged party, or faction, had a
powerful friend in an estanciero in those parts who
was friendly with the Indians, and who collected an
army of Indians hungry for loot, and gauchos,
mostly criminals and deserters, who in those days
were accustomed to come from all parts of the
country to put themselves under the protection of
this good man.

This horde of robbers and enthusiasts was now
advancing upon the capital to raise the siege, and
each day brought us alarming reports—whether true
or false we could not know—of depredations they
were committing on their march. The good man,
their commander, was not a soldier, and there was no
pretence of discipline of any kind; the men, it was

said, did what they liked, swarming over the country on the line of march in bands, sacking and burning houses, killing or driving off the cattle and so on. Our house was unfortunately on the main road running south from the capital, and directly in the way of the coming rabble. That the danger was a real and very great one we could see in the anxious faces of our elders; besides, nothing was not talked of but the coming army and of all we had to fear.

At this juncture my brother took it upon himself to make preparations for the defence of the house. Our oldest brother was away, shut up in the besieged city, but the three of us at home determined to make a good fight, and we set to work cleaning and polishing up our firearms—the Tower musket, the awful blunderbuss, the three fowling-pieces, double and single-barrelled, and the two big horse-pistols and an old revolver. We collected all the old lead we could find about the place and made bullets in a couple of bullet-moulds we had found—one for ounce and one for small bullets, three to the ounce. The fire to melt the lead was in a shelter we had made behind an outhouse, and here one day, in spite of all our precautions, we were discovered at work, with rows and pyramids of shining bullets round us, and our secret was out. We were laughed at as a set of young fools for our pains. "Never mind," said my brother. "Let them mock now; by and by when it comes to choosing between having our throats cut and defending ourselves, they will probably be glad the bullets were made."

But though they laughed, our work was not interfered with, and some hundreds of bullets were turned out and made quite a pretty show.

Meanwhile the besiegers were not idle: they had in their army a cavalry officer who had had a long experience of frontier warfare and had always been successful in his fights with the pampas Indians; and this man, with a picked force composed of veteran fighters, was dispatched against the barbarians. They had already crossed the Salado river and were within two or three easy marches of us, when the small disciplined force met and gave them battle and utterly routed them. Indians and gauchos were sent flying south like thistle-down before the wind; but all being well-mounted, not many were killed.

So ended that danger, and I think we boys were all a little disappointed that no use had been made of our bright beautiful bullets. I am sure my brother was; but soon after that he left home for a distant country, and our shooting and other adventures together were ended for ever.

How the Brigadier
Slew the Fox

[ARTHUR CONAN DOYLE]

In all the great hosts of France there was only one officer toward whom the English of Wellington's Army retained a deep, steady, and unchangeable hatred.

There were plunderers among the French, and men of violence, gamblers, duellists, and roués. All these could be forgiven, for others of their kind were to be found among the ranks of the English. But one officer of Massena's force had committed a crime which was unspeakable, unheard of, abominable; only to be alluded to with curses late in the evening, when a second bottle had loosened the tongues of men. The news of it was carried back to England, and country gentlemen who knew little of the details of the war grew crimson with passion when they heard of it, and yeomen of the shires raised freckled fists to Heaven and swore. And yet who should be the doer of this dreadful deed but our friend the Brigadier, Etienne Gerard, of the Hussars of Conflans, gay-riding, plume-tossing, debonair, the darling of the ladies and of the six brigades of light cavalry.

But the strange part of it is that this gallant gentleman did this hateful thing, and made himself the most unpopular man in the Peninsula, without ever knowing that he had done a crime for which there is hardly a name amid all the resources of our language. He died of old age, and never once in that imperturbable self-confidence which adorned or disfigured his character knew that so many thousand Englishmen would gladly have hanged him with their own hands. On the contrary, he numbered this adventure among those other exploits which he has given to the world, and many a time he chuckled and hugged himself as he narrated it to the eager circle who gathered round him in that humble cafe where, between his dinner and his dominoes, he would tell, amid tears and laughter, of that inconceivable Napoleonic past when France, like an angel of wrath, rose up, splendid and terrible, before a cowering continent. Let us listen to him as he tells the story in his own way and from his own point of view.

You must know, my friends, said he, that it was toward the end of the year eighteen hundred and ten that I and Massena and the others pushed Wellington backward until we had hoped to drive him and his army into the Tagus. But when we were still twenty-five miles from Lisbon we found that we were betrayed, for what had this Englishman done but build an enormous line of works and forts at a place called Torres Vedras, so that even we were unable to get through them! They lay across the whole Peninsula, and our army was so far from home that we did not dare to risk a reverse, and we had already learned at Busaco that it was no child's play to fight against these people. What could we do, then, but sit down in front of these lines and blockade them to the best of our power? There we remained for six months, amid such anxieties that Massena said afterward that he had not one hair which was not white upon his body.

For my own part, I did not worry much about our situation, but I looked after our horses, who were in much need of rest and green fodder. For the rest, we drank the wine of the country and passed the time as best we might. There was a lady at Santarem—but my lips are sealed. It is the part of a gallant man to say nothing, though he may indicate that he could say a great deal.

One day Massena sent for me, and I found him in his tent with a great plan pinned upon the table. He looked at me in silence with that single piercing eye of his, and I felt by his expression that the matter was serious. He was nervous and ill at ease, but my bearing seemed to reassure him. It is good to be in contact with brave men.

"Colonel Etienne Gerard," said he, "I have always heard that you are a very gallant and enterprising officer."

It was not for me to confirm such a report, and yet it would be folly to deny it, so I clinked my spurs together and saluted.

"You are also an excellent rider."

I admitted it.

"And the best swordsman in the six brigades of light cavalry."

Massena was famous for the accuracy of his information.

"Now," said he, "if you will look at this plan you will have no difficulty in understanding what it is that I wish you to do. These are the lines of Torres Vedras. You will perceive that they cover a vast space, and you will realise that the English can only hold a position here and there. Once through the lines you have twenty-five miles of open country which lie between them and Lisbon. It is very important to me to learn how Wellington's troops are distributed throughout that space, and it is my wish that you should go and ascertain."

His words turned me cold.

"Sir," said I, "it is impossible that a colonel of light cavalry should condescend to act as a spy."

He laughed and clapped me on the shoulder.

"You would not be a Hussar if you were not a hot-head," said he. "If you will listen you will understand that I have not asked you to act as a spy. What do you think of that horse?"

He had conducted me to the opening of his tent, and there was a chasseur who led up and down a most admirable creature. He was a dapple grey, not very tall, a little over fifteen hands perhaps, but with the short head and splendid arch of the neck which comes with the Arab blood. His shoulders and haunches were so muscular, and yet his legs so fine, that it thrilled me with joy just to gaze upon him. A fine horse or a beautiful woman—I cannot look at them unmoved, even now when seventy winters have chilled my blood. You can think how it was in the year '10.

"This," said Massena, "is Voltigeur, the swiftest horse in our army. What I desire is that you should start tonight, ride round the lines upon the flank, make your way across the enemy's rear, and return upon the other flank, bringing me news of his disposition. You will wear a uniform, and will, therefore, if captured, be safe from the death of a spy. It is probable that you will get through the lines unchallenged, for the posts are very scattered. Once through, in daylight you can outride anything which you meet, and if you keep off the roads you may escape entirely unnoticed. If you have not reported yourself by to-morrow night, I will understand that you are taken, and I will offer them Colonel Petrie in exchange."

Ah, how my heart swelled with pride and joy as I sprang into the saddle and galloped this grand horse up and down to show the Marshal the mastery which I had of him! He was magnificent—we were both magnificent, for Massena clapped his hands and cried out in his delight.

It was not I, but he, who said that a gallant beast deserves a gallant rider. Then, when for the third time, with my panache flying and my dolman streaming behind me, I thundered past him, I saw upon his hard old face that he had no longer any doubt that he had chosen the man for his purpose. I drew my sabre, raised the hilt to my lips in salute, and galloped on to my own quarters.

Already the news had spread that I had been chosen for a mission, and my little rascals came swarming out of their tents to cheer me. Ah! It brings the tears to my old eyes when I think how proud they were of their Colonel.

And I was proud of them also. They deserved a dashing leader.

The night promised to be a stormy one, which was very much to my liking. It was my desire to keep my departure most secret, for it was evident that if the English heard that I had been detached from the army they would naturally conclude that something important was about to happen. My horse was taken, therefore, beyond the picket line, as if for watering, and I followed and mounted him there. I had a map, a compass, and a paper of instructions from the Marshal, and with these in the bosom of my tunic and my sabre at my side I set out upon my adventure.

A thin rain was falling and there was no moon, so you may imagine that it was not very cheerful. But my heart was light at the thought of the honour which had been done me and the glory which awaited me. This exploit should be one more in that brilliant series which was to change my sabre into a baton. Ah, how we dreamed, we foolish fellows, young, and drunk with success! Could I have foreseen that night as I rode, the chosen man of sixty thousand, that I should spend my life planting cabbages on a hundred francs a month! Oh, my youth, my hopes, my comrades! But the wheel turns and never stops. Forgive me, my friends, for an old man has his weakness.

My route, then, lay across the face of the high ground of Torres Vedras, then over a streamlet, past a farmhouse which had been burned down and was now only a landmark, then through a forest of young cork oaks, and so to the monastery of San Antonio, which marked the left of the English position. Here I turned south and rode quietly over the downs, for it was at this point that Massena thought that it would be most easy for me to find my way unobserved through the position. I went very slowly, for it was so dark that I could not see my hand in front of me. In such cases I leave my bridle loose and let my horse pick its own way. Voltigeur went confidently forward, and I was very content to sit upon his back and to peer about me, avoiding every light.

For three hours we advanced in this cautious way, until it seemed to me that I must have left all danger behind me. I then pushed on more briskly, for I wished to be in the rear of the whole army by day-break. There are many vineyards in these parts which in winter become open plains, and a horse-man finds few difficulties in his way.

But Massena had underrated the cunning of these English, for it appears that there was not one line of defence but three, and it was the third, which was the most formidable, through which I was at that instant passing. As I rode, elated at my own success, a lantern flashed suddenly before me, and I saw the glint of polished gun-barrels and the gleam of a red coat.

"Who goes there?" cried a voice—such a voice! I swerved to the right and rode like a madman, but a dozen squirts of fire came out of the darkness, and the bullets whizzed all round my ears. That was no new sound to me, my friends, though I will not talk like a foolish conscript and say that I have ever liked it. But at least it had never kept me from thinking clearly, and so I knew that there was nothing for it but to gallop hard and try my luck elsewhere. I rode round the English picket, and then, as I heard more of them, I concluded rightly that I had at last come through their defences.

For five miles I rode south, striking a tinder from time to time to look at my pocket compass. And then in an instant—I feel the pang once more as my memory brings back the moment—my horse, without a sob or staggers fell stone-dead beneath me!

I had never known it, but one of the bullets from that infernal picket had passed through his body. The gallant creature had never winced nor weakened, but had gone while life was in him. One instant I was secure on the swiftest, most graceful horse in Massena's army. The next he lay upon his side, worth only the price of his hide, and I stood there that most helpless, most ungainly of creatures, a dismounted Hussar. What could I do with my boots, my spurs, my trailing sabre? I was far inside the enemy's lines. How could I hope to get back again?

I am not ashamed to say that I, Etienne Gerard, sat upon my dead horse and sank my face in my hands in my despair.

Already the first streaks were whitening the east.

In half an hour it would be light. That I should have won my way past every obstacle and then at this last instant be left at the mercy of my enemies, my mission ruined, and myself a prisoner—was it not enough to break a soldier's heart?

But courage, my friends! We have these moments of weakness, the bravest of us; but I have a spirit like a slip of steel, for the more you bend it the higher it springs.

One spasm of despair, and then a brain of ice and a heart of fire. All was not yet lost. I who had come through so many hazards would come through this one also. I rose from my horse and considered what had best be done.

And first of all it was certain that I could not get back. Long before I could pass the lines it would be broad daylight. I must hide myself for the day, and then devote the next night to my escape. I took the saddle, holsters, and bridle from poor Voltigeur, and I concealed them among some bushes, so that no one finding him could know that he was a French horse. Then, leaving him lying there, I wandered on in search of some place where I might be safe for the day. In every direction I could see camp fires upon the sides of the hills, and already figures had begun to move around them. I must hide quickly, or I was lost.

But where was I to hide? It was a vineyard in which I found myself, the poles of the vines still standing, but the plants gone. There was no cover there. Besides, I should want some food and water before another night had come. I hurried wildly onward through the waning darkness, trusting that chance would be my friend.

And I was not disappointed. Chance is a woman, my friends, and she has her eye always upon a gallant Hussar.

Well, then, as I stumbled through the vineyard, something loomed in front of me, and I came upon a great square house with another long, low building upon one side of it. Three roads met there, and it was easy to see that this was the posada, or wine-shop.

There was no light in the windows, and everything was dark and silent, but, of course, I knew that such comfortable quarters were certainly occupied, and probably by someone of importance. I have learned, however, that the nearer the danger may really be the safer place, and so I was by no means inclined to trust myself away from this shelter. The low building was evidently the stable, and into this I crept, for the door was unlatched.

The place was full of bullocks and sheep, gathered there, no doubt, to be out of the clutches of marauders.

A ladder led to a loft, and up this I climbed and concealed myself very snugly among some bales of hay upon the top. This loft had a small open window, and I was able to look down upon the front of the inn and also upon the road. There I crouched and waited to see what would happen.

It was soon evident that I had not been mistaken when I had thought that this might be the quarters of some person of importance. Shortly after daybreak an English light dragoon arrived with a despatch, and from then onward the place was in a turmoil, officers continually riding up and away.

Always the same name was upon their lips: "Sir Stapleton—Sir Stapleton."

It was hard for me to lie there with a dry moustache and watch the great flagons which were brought out by the landlord to these English officers. But it amused me to look at their fresh-coloured, clean-shaven, careless faces, and to wonder what they would think if they knew that so celebrated a person was lying so near to them. And then, as I lay and watched, I saw a sight which filled me with surprise.

It is incredible the insolence of these English! What do you suppose Milord Wellington had done when he found that Massena had blockaded him and that he could not move his army? I might give you many guesses. You might say that he had raged, that he had despaired, that he had brought his troops together and spoken to them about glory and the fatherland before leading them to one last battle. No, Milord did none of these things. But he sent a fleet ship to England to bring him a number of fox-dogs; and he with his officers settled himself down to chase the fox. It is true what I tell you. Behind the lines of Torres Vedras these mad Englishmen made the fox chase three days in the week.

We had heard of it in the camp, and now I was myself to see that it was true.

For, along the road which I have described, there came these very dogs, thirty or forty of them, white

and brown, each with its tail at the same angle, like
the bayonets of the Old Guard. My faith, but it was
a pretty sight! And behind and amidst them there
rode three men with peaked caps and red coats,
whom I understood to be the hunters. After them
came many horsemen with uniforms of various
kinds, stringing along the roads in twos and threes,
talking together and laughing.

They did not seem to be going above a trot, and it
appeared to me that it must indeed be a slow fox
which they hoped to catch. However, it was their
affair, not mine, and soon they had all passed my
window and were out of sight. I waited and I
watched, ready for any chance which might offer.

Presently an officer, in a blue uniform not unlike
that of our flying artillery, came cantering down the
road—an elderly, stout man he was, with grey side-
whiskers. He stopped and began to talk with an
orderly officer of dragoons, who waited outside the
inn, and it was then that I learned the advantage of
the English which had been taught me. I could hear
and understand all that was said.

"Where is the meet?" said the officer, and I
thought that he was hungering for his *bifstek*. But
the other answered him that it was near Altara, so I
saw that it was a place of which he spoke.

"You are late, Sir George," said the orderly.

"Yes, I had a court-martial. Has Sir Stapleton Cotton gone?"

At this moment a window opened, and a handsome young man in a very splendid uniform looked out of it.

"Halloa, Murray!" said he. "These cursed papers keep me, but I will be at your heels."

"Very good, Cotton. I am late already, so I will ride on."

"You might order my groom to bring round my horse," said the young General at the window to the orderly below, while the other went on down the road.

The orderly rode away to some outlying stable, and then in a few minutes there came a smart English groom with a cockade in his hat, leading by the bridle a horse—and, oh, my friends, you have never known the perfection to which a horse can attain until you have seen a first-class English hunter. He was superb: tall, broad, strong, and yet as graceful and agile as a deer. Coal black he was in colour, and his neck, and his shoulder, and his quarters, and his fetlocks—how can I describe him all to you? The sun shone upon him as on polished ebony, and he raised his hoofs in a little playful dance so lightly and prettily, while he tossed his mane and whinnied with impatience. Never have I seen such a mixture of strength and beauty and grace. I had often wondered how the English Hussars had managed to ride over the chasseurs of the Guards in the affair at Astorga, but I wondered no longer when I saw the English horses.

There was a ring for fastening bridles at the door of the inn, and the groom tied the horse there while he entered the house. In an instant I had seen the chance which Fate had brought to me. Were I in that saddle I should be better off than when I started. Even Voltigeur could not compare with this magnificent creature. To think is to act with me. In one instant I was down the ladder and at the door of the stable. The next I was out and the bridle was in my hand. I bounded into the saddle.

Somebody, the master or the man, shouted wildly behind me. What cared I for his shouts! I touched the horse with my spurs and he bounded forward with such a spring that only a rider like myself could have sat him. I gave him his head and let him go—it did not matter to me where, so long as we left this inn far behind us. He thundered away across the vineyards, and in a very few minutes I had placed miles between myself and my pursuers. They could no longer tell in that wild country in which direction I had gone. I knew that I was safe, and so, riding to the top of a small hill, I drew my pencil and notebook from my pocket and proceeded to make plans of those camps which I could see and to draw the outline of the country.

He was a dear creature upon whom I sat, but it was not easy to draw upon his back, for every now and then his two ears would cock, and he would start and quiver with impatience. At first I could not understand this trick of his, but soon I observed that he only did it when a peculiar noise—"yoy, yoy, yoy"—came from somewhere among the oak woods beneath us. And then suddenly this strange cry changed into a most terrible screaming, with the frantic blowing of a horn. Instantly he went mad— this horse. His eyes blazed. His mane bristled. He bounded from the earth and bounded again, twisting and turning in a frenzy. My pencil flew one way and my note-book another. And then, as I looked down into the valley, an extraordinary sight met my eyes.

The hunt was streaming down it. The fox I could not see, but the dogs were in full cry, their noses down, their tails up, so close together that they might have been one great yellow and white moving carpet. And behind them rode the horsemen—my faith, what a sight! Consider every type which a great army could show. Some in hunting dress, but the most in uniforms: blue dragoons, red dragoons, red-trousered hussars, green riflemen, artillerymen, gold-slashed lancers, and most of all red, red, red, for the infantry officers ride as hard as the cavalry.

Such a crowd, some well mounted, some ill, but all flying along as best they might, the subaltern as good as the general, jostling and pushing, spurring and driving, with every thought thrown to the winds save that they should have the blood of this absurd fox! Truly, they are an extraordinary people, the English!

But I had little time to watch the hunt or to marvel at these islanders, for of all these mad creatures the very horse upon which I sat was the maddest. You understand that he was himself a hunter, and that the crying of these dogs was to him what the call of a cavalry trumpet in the street yonder would be to me. It thrilled him. It drove him wild. Again and again he bounded into the air, and then, seizing the bit between his teeth, he plunged down the slope and galloped after the dogs.

I swore, and tugged, and pulled, but I was powerless. This English General rode his horse with a snaffle only, and the beast had a mouth of iron. It was useless to pull him back. One might as well try to keep a grenadier from a wine-bottle. I gave it up in despair, and, settling down in the saddle, I prepared for the worst which could befall.

What a creature he was! Never have I felt such a horse between my knees. His great haunches gathered under him with every stride, and he shot forward ever faster and faster, stretched like a greyhound, while the wind beat in my face and whistled past my ears. I was wearing our undress jacket, a uniform simple and dark in itself—though some figures give distinction to any uniform—and I had taken the precaution to remove the long panache from my busby. The result was that, amidst the mixture of costumes in the hunt, there was no reason why mine should attract attention, or why these men, whose thoughts were all with the chase, should give any heed to me. The idea that a French officer might be riding with them was too absurd to enter their minds. I laughed as I rode, for, indeed, amid all the danger, there was something of comic in the situation.

I have said that the hunters were very unequally mounted, and so at the end of a few miles, instead of being one body of men, like a charging regiment, they were scattered over a considerable space, the better riders well up to the dogs and the others trailing away behind.

Now, I was as good a rider as any, and my horse was the best of them all, and so you can imagine that it was not long before he carried me to the front. And when I saw the dogs streaming over the open, and the red-coated huntsman behind them, and only seven or eight horsemen between us, then it was that the strangest thing of all happened, for I, too, went mad—I, Etienne Gerard!

In a moment it came upon me, this spirit of sport, this desire to excel, this hatred of the fox. Accursed animal, should he then defy us? Vile robber, his hour was come!

Ah, it is a great feeling, this feeling of sport, my friends, this desire to trample the fox under the hoofs of your horse. I have made the fox chase with the English. I have also, as I may tell you some day, fought the box-fight with the Bustler, of Bristol.

And I say to you that this sport is a wonderful thing—full of interest as well as madness.

The farther we went the faster galloped my horse, and soon there were but three men as near the dogs as I was.

All thought of fear of discovery had vanished. My brain throbbed, my blood ran hot—only one thing upon earth seemed worth living for, and that was to overtake this infernal fox. I passed one of the horsemen—a Hussar like myself. There were only two in front of me now: the one in a black coat, the other the blue artilleryman whom I had seen at the inn. His grey whiskers streamed in the wind, but he rode magnificently. For a mile or more we kept in this order, and then, as we galloped up a steep slope, my lighter weight brought me to the front.

I passed them both, and when I reached the crown I was riding level with the little, hard-faced English huntsman.

In front of us were the dogs, and then, a hundred paces beyond them, was a brown wisp of a thing, the fox itself, stretched to the uttermost. The sight of him fired my blood. "Aha, we have you then, assassin!" I cried, and shouted my encouragement to the huntsman. I waved my hand to show him that there was one upon whom he could rely.

And now there were only the dogs between me and my prey. These dogs, whose duty it is to point out the game, were now rather a hindrance than a

CLASSIC ADVENTURE STORIES

help to us, for it was hard to know how to pass them. The huntsman felt the difficulty as much as I, for he rode behind them, and could make no progress toward the fox. He was a swift rider, but wanting in enterprise. For my part, I felt that it would be unworthy of the Hussars of Conflans if I could not overcome such a difficulty as this.

Was Etienne Gerard to be stopped by a herd of fox-dogs?

It was absurd. I gave a shout and spurred my horse.

"Hold hard, sir! Hold hard!" cried the huntsman.

He was uneasy for me, this good old man, but I reassured him by a wave and a smile. The dogs opened in front of me. One or two may have been hurt, but what would you have? The egg must be broken for the omelette. I could hear the huntsman shouting his congratulations behind me. One more effort, and the dogs were all behind me. Only the fox was in front.

Ah, the joy and pride of that moment! To know that I had beaten the English at their own sport. Here were three hundred, all thirsting for the life of this animal, and yet it was I who was about to take it. I thought of my comrades of the light cavalry brigade, of my mother, of the Emperor, of France. I had brought honour to each and all. Every instant brought me nearer to the fox. The moment for action had arrived, so I unsheathed my sabre. I waved it in the air, and the brave English all shouted behind me.

Only then did I understand how difficult is this fox chase, for one may cut again and again at the creature and never strike him once. He is small, and turns quickly from a blow. At every cut I heard those shouts of encouragement from behind me, and they spurred me to yet another effort. And then at last the supreme moment of my triumph arrived. In the very act of turning I caught him fair with such another back-handed cut as that with which I killed the aide-de-camp of the Emperor of Russia. He flew into two pieces, his head one way and his tail another. I looked back and waved the blood-stained sabre in the air. For the moment I was exalted—superb!

Ah! how I should have loved to have waited to have received the congratulations of these generous enemies.

There were fifty of them in sight, and not one who was not waving his hand and shouting. They are not really such a phlegmatic race, the English. A gallant deed in war or sport will always warm their hearts. As to the old huntsman, he was the nearest to me, and I could see with my own eyes how over-come he was by what he had seen. He was like a man paralysed, his mouth open, his hand, with outspread fingers, raised in the air. For a moment my inclination was to return and to embrace him.

But already the call of duty was sounding in my ears, and these English, in spite of all the fraternity which exists among sportsmen, would certainly have made me prisoner. There was no hope for my mission now, and I had done all that I could do. I could see the lines of Massena's camp no very great distance off, for, by a lucky chance, the chase had taken us in that direction.

I turned from the dead fox, saluted with my sabre, and galloped away.

But they would not leave me so easily, these gallant huntsmen. I was the fox now, and the chase swept bravely over the plain. It was only at the moment when I started for the camp that they could have known that I was a Frenchman, and now the whole swarm of them were at my heels. We were within gunshot of our pickets before they would halt, and then they stood in knots and would not go away, but shouted and waved their hands at me. No, I will not think that it was in enmity. Rather would I fancy that a glow of admiration filled their breasts, and that their one desire was to embrace the stranger who had carried himself so gallantly and well.

Hunting Musk-Oxen
Near the Pole

[LIEUTENANT R. E. PERRY, USN]

On the fifteenth of May, 1895, the storm ceased which had held Lee, Hensen and myself prisoners for two days upon the Independence Bay moraine, the northern shore of the "Great Ice," more than four thousand feet above the level of the sea. Then, in a very short time, I completed all the preparations for a trip down over the land in search of the musk-oxen which would be our salvation. Matt and all the dogs were to accompany me.

I took the little "Chopsie" sledge, our rifles, four days' supply of tea, biscuits and oil—we had had no meat for several days—and the remainder of the dog-food, which was a lump of frozen walrus meat somewhat larger than a man's head. Lee was to remain at the tent during our absence.

The almost total lack of snow on this northern land was a surprise as well as an annoyance to me, since it threatened to damage my sledges seriously. But by keeping well ahead of the dogs, I was able to pick out a fairly good though circuitous path along the numerous snow drifts which lay on the leeward side of the hills and mountains.

After some twelve hours of steady marching, we were close to Musk-Ox Valley, where, three years before, Astrup and myself had first seen and killed some of these animals.

Leaving Matt with the sledge and dogs, I took my rifle and entered the valley, hoping to find them there again. So far we had not seen the slightest indication of musk-oxen though we had followed the same route, where, on my previous visit, their traces had been visible on almost every square rod of ground.

In the valley I found no trace of their presence, and I returned to the sledge in a gloomy mood. Could it be that the musk-oxen of this region were migratory? Did they retreat southward along the east coast in the autumn, and return in early summer, and were we too early for them? Or had the sight and smell of us and our dogs, and the sound of our guns and the sight of carcasses of the oxen we had slain three years before, terrified the others so that they had deserted this region completely?

These questions disturbed me deeply. We had now been marching for a long time; we were tired with the unaccustomed work of climbing up and down hills, and were weak and hungry from our long and scant diet of tea and biscuits.

Our hunger was partially appeased by the dog-food. True, this was a frozen mixture of walrus meat, blubber, hair, sand, and various other foreign substances, but we had to eat something, and the fact that the meat was "high" and the blubber more or less rancid did not deter us. Yet we dared not satisfy ourselves, even with dog-food, as we were dependent on the dogs, and they were more in need of food than we.

A few miles beyond Musk-Ox Valley I saw a fresh hare-track leading in the same direction in which we were going; and within five minutes I saw the hare itself squatting among the rocks a few paces distant. I called to Matt, who was some little distance back, to stop the dogs and come up with his rifle.

He was so affected by the prospect of a good dinner that his first and second bullets missed the mark, although usually he was a good marksman. But at the third shot the beautiful, spotless little animal collapsed into a shapeless mass, and on the instant gaunt hunger took from us the power of further endurance. We must stop at once and cook the hare.

Near us was a little pond surrounded by high banks. This offered the advantages of ice, from which to melt water for cooking purposes. So here we camped, lit our lamp, and cooked and ate the entire hare. It was the first full meal we had had for nearly six weeks—the first meal furnishing sufficient substance and nourishment for the doing of a heavy day's work.

Ease from hunger and pleasure in the process of digestion made us drowsy. Lying down as we were, upon the snow-covered shore of the little pond, without tent or sleeping-bag or anything except the clothes we wore, we slept the sleep of tired children in their cosy beds, though the snowflakes were falling thickly upon us.

The next morning we pushed on for a valley near Navy Cliff, where Astrup and myself had seen numerous musk-ox tracks. At the entrance of this valley I came upon a track, so indistinct that it might have been made the previous autumn. Following it a short distance, I saw the accompanying tracks of a calf, showing at once that the tracks were of this season; and a little farther on there were traces but a few days old.

Fastening our dogs securely to a rock and muzzling them so that they could neither gnaw themselves loose or make a noise to disturb the musk-oxen, we passed rapidly down the valley, Winchesters in hand, with our eyes fixed eagerly upon the tracks. Soon we reached the feeding-ground of the herd on the preceding day, and knew by their tracks and the places where they had dug away the snow in search of grass and moss that there was quite a herd of them.

We circled the feeding-ground as rapidly as we could, and at length found the tracks of the herd leading out of the labyrinth and up the slopes of the surrounding mountains. Following these, our eyes were soon gladdened by sight of a group of black spots on a little terrace just below the crest of the mountain.

Looking through the field-glass, we saw that some of the animals were lying down. Evidently the herd was beginning its midday snooze. We moved cautiously up to the edge of the terrace to leeward of the animals and sought shelter behind a big boulder. The musk-oxen were about two hundred yards distant and numbered twenty-two.

I wonder if one of my readers knows what hunger is. Hensen and I were worn to the bone with scant rations and hard work, which had left little on our bones except lean, tense muscles and wires of sinew. The supper from the hare—that meal of fresh, hot, luscious meat—the first adequate meal in nearly six hundred miles of snow-shoeing, had wakened every merciless hunger-fang that during the previous weeks had been gradually dulled into insensibility.

Gazing on the big black animals before us, we saw not game, but meat; and every nerve and fibre in my gaunt body was vibrating with a furious and savage hunger for that meat—meat that should be soft and warm; meat into which the teeth could sink and tear and rend; meat that would not blister the lips and tongue with its frost, nor ring like rock against the teeth.

Panting and quivering with excitement we lay for a few moments. We could not risk a shot at that distance.

"Do you think they will come for us?" said Matt.

"God knows I hope so, boy, for then we are sure of some of them. Are you ready?"

"Yes, sir."

"Come on, then."

Rising one of us one side of the boulder, the other on the other side, we dashed across the rocks and snow straight toward them.

There was a snort and stamp from the big bull guarding the herd, and the next instant every animal was on his feet, facing us, thank God! The next moment they were in close line, with lowered heads and horns. I could have yelled for joy if I had had the breath to spare.

Everyone one of us has read thrilling stories of deer chased by hungry wolves, and it is in the nature of man to sympathise with the creatures that are trying to escape. But did any of us ever stop to think how those other poor creatures, the wolves, were feeling? I know now just what *their* feelings are, and I cannot help sympathising with them. I was no better than a wolf myself at that moment.

We were within less than fifty yards of the herd when the big bull with a quick motion lowered his horns still more. Instinct, Providence—call it what you will—told me it was the signal for the herd to charge. Without slackening my pace, I pulled my Winchester to my shoulder and sent a bullet at the back of his neck over the white, impervious shield of the great horns.

Heart and soul and brain and eyes went with that singing bullet. I felt that I was strong enough, and hungry enough, and wild enough so that, had the bull been alone, I could have sprung upon him bare-handed and somehow made meat of him. But against the entire herd we should have been power-less; once the black avalanche had gained momen-tum, we should have been crushed by it like the crunching snow crystals under our feet.

As the bull fell upon his knees the herd wavered. A cow half turned and, as Matt's rifle cracked, fell with a bullet back of her fore-shoulder. Without raising my rifle above my hips another one dropped. Then another, for Matt; then the herd broke, and we hur-ried in pursuit.

A wounded cow wheeled and, with lowered head, was about to charge me; again Matt's rifle cracked, and she fell. As I rushed past her he shouted, "That was my last cartridge!"

A short distance beyond, the remainder of the herd faced about again and I put a bullet into the breast of another bull, but it did not stop him, and the herd broke again and disappeared over a sharp ridge. I had neither wind nor strength to follow.

Suddenly the back of one of the animals appeared above the ridge. I whirled and fired. I did not see the sights—I think I scarcely saw my rifle, but felt my aim as I would with harpoon or stone. I heard the thud of the bullet. I knew the beast was hit behind the fore-shoulder. As the animal disappeared I sank down on the snow, quite unable to go farther.

But after a little rest I was able to move. Matt came up. We instantly set about bleeding the last beast I had killed. How delicious that tender, raw, warm meat was—a mouthful here and a mouthful there, cut from the animal as we skinned it! It seems dreadful and loathsome to have made such a meal. But I wish those who stay at home at ease to realise what hunger drives men to. This was the barbarism out of which our race has risen. Matt and I were savages for the time. I ate till I dared eat no more, although still unsatisfied.

Then Matt went back to bring up the dogs and sledge, while I began removing the skins from our game. With Matt's return came the supremest luxury of all! That was to toss great lumps of meat to the gaunt shadows which we called dogs, till they, too, could eat no more, and lay gorged and quiet upon the rocks.

The removal of the great shaggy, black pelts of the musk-oxen was neither an easy nor a rapid job. By the time it was completed it was midnight; the sun was low over the mountains in the north, and a biting wind whistled about our airy location.

We were glad to drag the skins to a central place, construct a wind guard with the assistance of the sledge, a few stones and a couple of the skins, and make a bed of the others on the lee side of it.

We built up a little stone shelter for our cooking lamp, and then, stretched upon our luxurious, thick, soft, warm couch, we were, for the first time, able to spare the time to make ourselves some tea, and cook some of the delicious musk-ox meat.

Then, with the savage, sombre northern land lying like a map below us—the barren rocks, mottled here and there with eternal snowdrifts; with the summits of the distant mountains disappearing in a mist of driving snow; with the biting breath of the "Great Ice" following us even here and drifting the fine snow over and about our shelter, we slept again as tired children—nay as tired savages—sleep.

Youth

[JOSEPH CONRAD]

This could have occurred nowhere but in England, where men and sea interpenetrate, so to speak—the sea entering into the life of most men, and the men knowing something or everything about the sea, in the way of amusement, of travel, or of bread-winning.

We were sitting round a mahogany table that reflected the bottle, the claret-glasses, and our faces as we leaned on our elbows. There was a director of companies, an accountant, a lawyer, Marlow, and myself. The director had been a *Conway* boy, the accountant had served four years at sea, the lawyer—a fine crusted Tory, High Churchman, the best of old fellows, the soul of honour—had been chief officer in the P. & O. service in the good old days when mail-boats were square-rigged at least on two masts, and used to come down the China Sea before a fair monsoon with stun'-sails set alow and aloft. We all began life in the merchant service. Between the five of us there was the strong bond of the sea, and also the fellowship of the craft, which no amount of enthusiasm for yachting, cruising, and so on can give, since one is only the amusement of life and the other is life itself.

Marlow (at least I think that is how he spelt his name) told the story, or rather the chronicle, of a voyage:—

"Yes, I have seen a little of the Eastern seas; but what I remember best is my first voyage there. You fellows know there are those voyages that seem ordered for the illustration of life, that might stand for a symbol of existence. You fight, work, sweat, nearly kill yourself, sometimes do kill yourself, trying to accomplish something—and you can't. Not from any fault of yours. You simply can do nothing, neither great nor little—not a thing in the world—not even marry an old maid, or get a wretched 600-ton cargo of coal to its port of destination.

"It was altogether a memorable affair. It was my first voyage to the East, and my first voyage as second mate; it was also my skipper's first command. You'll admit it was time. He was sixty if a day; a little man, with a broad, not very straight back, with bowed shoulders and one leg more bandy than the other, he had that queer twisted-about appearance you see so often in men who work in the fields. He had a nut-cracker face—chin and nose trying to come together over a sunken mouth—and it was framed in iron-gray fluffy hair, that looked like a chin-strap of cotton-wool sprinkled with coal-dust. And he had blue eyes in that old face of his, which were amazingly like a boy's, with that candid expression some quite common men preserve to the end of their days by a rare internal gift of simplicity of heart and rectitude of soul. What induced him to accept me was a wonder. I had come out of a crack Australian clipper, where I had been a third officer, and he seemed to have a prejudice against crack clippers as aristocratic and high-toned. He said to me, 'You know, in this ship you will have to work,' I said I had to work in every ship I had ever been in. 'Ah, but this is different, and you gentlemen out of them big ships; . . . but there! I dare say you will do. Join to-morrow.'

"I joined to-morrow. It was twenty-two years ago; and I was just twenty. How time passes! It was one of the happiest days of my life. Fancy! Second mate for the first time—a really responsible officer! I wouldn't have thrown up my new billet for a fortune. The mate looked me over carefully. He was also an old chap, but of another stamp. He had a Roman nose, a snow-white, long beard, and his name was Mahon, but he insisted that it should be pronounced Mann. He was well connected; yet there was something wrong with his luck, and he had never got on.

"As to the captain, he had been for years in coasters, then in the Mediterranean, and last in the West Indian trade. He had never been round the Capes. He could just write a kind of sketchy hand, and didn't care for writing at all. Both were thorough good seamen of course, and between those two old chaps I felt like a small boy between two grandfathers.

"The ship also was old. Her name was the *Judea*. Queer name isn't it? She belonged to a man Wilmer, Wilcox—some name like that; but he has been bankrupt and dead these twenty years or more, and his name don't matter. She had been laid up in Shadwell basin for ever so long. You may imagine her state. She was all rust, dust, grime—soot aloft, dirt on deck. To me it was like coming out of a palace into a ruined cottage. She was about 400 tons, had a primitive windlass, wooden latches to the doors, not a bit of brass about her, and a big square stern. There was on it, below her name in big letters, a lot of scrollwork, with the gilt off, and some sort of a coat of arms, with the motto 'Do or Die' underneath. I remember it took my fancy immensely. There was a touch of romance in it, something that made me love the old thing—something that appealed to my youth!

"We left London in ballast—sand ballast—to load a cargo of coal in a northern port for Bankok. Bankok! I thrilled. I had been six years at sea, but had only seen Melbourne and Sydney, very good places, charming places in their way—but Bankok!

"We worked out of the Thames under canvas, with a North Sea pilot on board. His name was Jermyn, and he dodged all day long about the galley drying his handkerchief before the stove. Apparently he never slept. He was a dismal man, with a perpetual tear sparkling at the end of his nose, who either had been in trouble, or was in trouble, or expected to be in trouble—couldn't be happy unless something went wrong. He mistrusted my youth, my common-sense, and my seamanship, and made a point of showing it in a hundred little ways. I dare say he was right. It seems to me I knew very little then, and I know not much more now; but I cherish a hate for that Jermyn to this day.

"We were a week working up as far as Yarmouth Roads, and then we got into a gale—the famous October gale of twenty-two years ago. It was wind, lightning, sleet, snow, and a terrific sea. We were flying light, and you may imagine how bad it was when I tell you we had smashed bulwarks and a flooded deck. On the second night she shifted her ballast into the lee bow, and by that time we had been blown off somewhere on the Dogger Bank. There was nothing for it but go below with shovels and try to right her, and there we were in that vast hold, gloomy like a cavern, the tallow dips stuck and flickering on the beams, the gale howling above, the ship tossing about like mad on her side; there we all were, Jermyn, the captain, every one, hardly able to keep our feet, engaged on that gravedigger's work, and trying to toss shovelfuls of wet sand up to wind-ward. At every tumble of the ship you could see vaguely in the dim light men falling down with a great flourish of shovels. One of the ship's boys (we had two), impressed by the weirdness of the scene, wept as if his heart would break. We could hear him blubbering somewhere in the shadows.

"On the third day the gale died out, and by and by a north-country tug picked us up. We took sixteen days in all to get from London to the Tyne! When we got into dock we had lost our turn for loading, and they hauled us off to a tier where we remained for a month. Mrs. Beard (the captain's name was Beard) came from Colchester to see the old man. She lived on board. The crew of runners had left, and there remained only the officers, one boy and the steward, a mulatto who answered to the name of Abraham. Mrs. Beard was an old woman, with a face all wrinkled and ruddy like a winter apple, and the figure of a young girl. She caught sight of me once, sewing on a button, and insisted on having my shirts to repair. This was something different from the captains' wives I had known on board crack clippers. When I brought her the shirts, she said: 'And the socks? They want mending, I am sure, and John's— Captain Beard's—things are all in order now. I would be glad of something to do.' Bless the old woman. She overhauled my outfit for me, and meantime I read for the first time *Sartor Resartus* and Burnaby's *Ride to Khiva*. I didn't understand much of the first then; but I remember I preferred the soldier to the philosopher at the time; a preference which life has only confirmed. One was a man, and the other was either more—or less. However, they are both dead and Mrs. Beard is dead, and youth, strength, genius, thoughts, achievements, simple hearts—all die . . . No matter.

"They loaded us at last. We shipped a crew. Eight able seamen and two boys. We hauled off one evening to the buoys at the dock-gates, ready to go out, and with a fair prospect of beginning the voyage next day. Mrs. Beard was to start for home by a late train. When the ship was fast we went to tea. We sat rather silent through the meal—Mahon, the old couple, and I. I finished first, and slipped away for a smoke, my cabin being in a deck-house just against the poop. It was high water, blowing fresh with a drizzle; the double dock-gates were opened, and the steam-colliers were going in and out in the darkness with their lights burning bright, and a great plashing of propellers, rattling of winches, and a lot of hailing on the pier-heads. I watched the procession of head-lights gliding high and of green lights gliding low in the night, when suddenly a red gleam flashed at me, vanished, came into view again, and remained. The fore-end of a steamer loomed up close. I shouted down the cabin, 'Come up, quick!' and then heard a startled voice saying afar in the dark, 'Stop her, sir.' A bell jingled. Another voice cried warningly, 'We are going right into that barque, sir,' The answer to this was a gruff 'All right,' and the next thing was a heavy crash as the steamer struck a glancing blow with the bluff of her bow about our fore-rigging. There was a moment of confusion, yelling, and running about. Steam roared. Then somebody was heard saying, 'All clear, sir.' . . . 'Are you all right?" asked the gruff voice. I had jumped forward to see the damage, and hailed back, 'I think so.' 'Easy astern,' said the gruff voice. A bell jingled. 'What steamer is that?' screamed Mahon. By that time she was no more to us than a bulky shadow manoeuvring a little way off. They shouted at us some name—a woman's name, Miranda or Melissa—or some such thing. 'This means another month in this beastly hole,' said Mahon to me, as we peered with lamps about the splintered bulwarks and broken braces. 'But where's the captain?'

"We had not heard or seen anything of him all that time. We went aft to look. A doleful voice arose hailing somewhere in the middle of the dock, '*Judea* ahoy!' . . . How the devil did he get there? . . . 'Hallo!' we shouted. 'I am adrift in our boat without oars,' he cried. A belated water-man offered his services, and Mahon struck a bargain with him for half-a-crown to tow our skipper alongside; but it was Mrs. Beard that came up the ladder first. They had been floating about the dock in that mizzly cold rain for nearly an hour. I was never so surprised in my life.

"It appears that when he heard my shout 'Come up' he understood at once what was the matter, caught up his wife, ran on deck, and across, and down into our boat, which was fast to the ladder. Not bad for a sixty-year-old. Just imagine that old fellow saving heroically in his arms that old woman—the woman of his life. He set her down on a thwart, and was ready to climb back on board when the painter came adrift somehow, and away they went together. Of course in the confusion we did not hear him shouting. He looked abashed. She said cheerfully, 'I suppose it does not matter my losing the train now?' 'No, Jenny—you go below and get warm,' he growled. Then to us: 'A sailor has no business with a wife—I say. There I was, out of the ship. Well, no harm done this time. Let's go and look at what that fool of a steamer smashed.'

"It wasn't much, but it delayed us three weeks. At the end of that time, the captain being engaged with his agents, I carried Mrs. Beard's bag to the railway-station and put her all comfy into a third-class carriage. She lowered the window to say, 'You are a good young man. If you see John—Captain Beard—without his muffler at night, just remind him from me to keep his throat well wrapped up.' 'Certainly, Mrs. Beard,' I said. 'You are a good young man; I noticed how attentive you are to John—to Captain—' The train pulled out suddenly; I took my cap off to the old woman: I never saw her again. . . . Pass the bottle.

"We went to sea next day. When we made that start for Bankok we had been already three months out of London. We had expected to be a fortnight or so—at the outside.

"It was January, and the weather was beautiful— the beautiful sunny winter weather that has more charm than in the summer-time, because it is unexpected, and crisp, and you know it won't, it can't, last long. It's like a windfall, like a godsend, like an unexpected piece of luck.

"It lasted all down the North Sea, all down Channel; and it lasted till we were three hundred miles or so to the westward of the Lizards: then the wind went round to the sou'west and began to pipe up. In two days it blew a gale. The *Judea*, hove to, wallowed on the Atlantic like an old candle-box. It blew day after day: it blew with spite, without interval, without mercy, without rest. The world was nothing but an immensity of great foaming waves rushing at us, under a sky low enough to touch with the hand and dirty like a smoked ceiling. In the stormy space surrounding us there was as much flying spray as air. Day after day and night after night there was nothing round the ship but the howl of the wind, the tumult of the sea, the noise of water pouring over her deck. There was no rest for her and no rest for us. She tossed, she pitched, she stood on her head, she sat on her tail, she rolled, she groaned, and we had to hold on while on deck and cling to our bunks when below, in a constant effort of body and worry of mind.

"One night Mahon spoke through the small window of my berth. It opened right into my very bed, and I was lying there sleepless, in my boots, feeling as though I had not slept for years, and could not if I tried. He said excitedly—

"'You got the sounding-rod in here, Marlow? I can't get the pumps to suck. By God! it's no child's play.'

"I gave him the sounding-rod and lay down again, trying to think of various things—but I thought only of the pumps. When I came on deck they were still at it, and my watch relieved at the pumps. By the light of the lantern brought on deck to examine the sounding-rod I caught a glimpse of their weary, serious faces. We pumped all the four hours. We pumped all night, all day, all the week—watch and watch. She was working herself loose, and leaked badly—not enough to drown us at once, but enough to kill us with the work at the pumps. And while we pumped the ship was going from us piecemeal: the bulwarks went, the stanchions were torn out, the ventilators smashed, the cabin-door burst in. There was not a dry spot in the ship. She was being gutted bit by bit. The long-boat changed, as if by magic into matchwood where she stood in her gripes. I had lashed her myself, and was rather proud of my handiwork, which had withstood so long the malice of the sea. And we pumped. And there was no break in the weather. The sea was white like a sheet of foam, like a caldron of boiling milk; there was not a break in the clouds, no—not the size of a man's hand—no, not for so much as ten seconds. There was for us no sky, there were for us no stars, so sun, no universe— nothing but angry clouds and an infuriated sea. We pumped watch and watch, for dear life; and it seemed to last for months, for years, for all eternity, as though we had been dead and gone to a hell for sailors. We forgot the day of the week, the name of the month, what year it was, and whether we had ever been ashore. The sails blew away, she lay broadside on under a weather-cloth, the ocean poured over her, and we did not care. We turned those handles, and had the eyes of idiots. As soon as we had crawled on deck I used to take a round turn with a rope about the men, the pumps, and the mainmast, and we turned, we turned incessantly, with the water to our waists, to our necks, over our heads. It was all one. We had forgotten how it felt to be dry.

"And there was somewhere in me the thought: By Jove! this is the deuce of an adventure—something you read about; and it is my first voyage as second mate—and I am only twenty—and here I am lasting it out as well as any of these men, and keeping my chaps up to the mark. I was pleased. I would not have given up the experience for worlds. I had moments of exultation. Whenever the old dismantled craft pitched heavily with her counter high in the air, she seemed to me to throw up, like an appeal, like a defiance, like a cry to the clouds without mercy, the words written on her stern: '*Judea*, London. Do or Die.'

"O youth! The strength of it, the faith of it, the imagination of it! To me she was not an old rattle-trap carting about the world a lot of coal for a freight—to me she was the endeavour, the test, the trial of life. I think of her with pleasure, with affection, with regret—as you would think of someone dead you have loved. I shall never forget her. . . . Pass the bottle.

"One night when tied to the mast, as I explained, we were pumping on, deafened with the wind, and without spirit enough in us to wish ourselves dead, a heavy sea crashed aboard and swept clean over us. As soon as I got my breath I shouted, as in duty bound, 'Keep on boys!' when suddenly I felt something hard floating on deck strike the calf of my leg. I made a grab at it and missed. It was so dark we could not see each other's faces within a foot—you understand.

"After that thump the ship kept quiet for a while, and the thing, whatever it was, struck my leg again.

This time I caught it—and it was a saucepan. At first, being stupid with fatigue and thinking of nothing but the pumps, I did not understand what I had in my hand. Suddenly it dawned upon me, and I shouted, 'Boys, the house on deck is gone. Leave this, and let's look for the cook.'

"There was a deck-house forward, which contained the galley, the cook's berth, and the quarters of the crew. As we had expected for days to see it swept away, the hands had been ordered to sleep in the cabin—the only safe place in the ship. The steward, Abraham, however, persisted in clinging to his berth, stupidly, like a mule—from sheer fright I believe, like an animal that won't leave a stable falling in an earthquake. So we went to look for him. It was chancing death, since once out of our lashings we were as exposed as if on a raft. But we went. The house was shattered as if a shell had exploded inside. Most of it had gone overboard—stove, men's quarters, and their property, all was gone; but two posts, holding a portion of the bulkhead to which Abraham's bunk was attached, remained as if by a miracle. We groped in the ruins and came upon this, and there he was, sitting in his bunk, surrounded by foam and wreckage, jabbering cheerfully to himself. He was out of his mind; completely and for ever mad, with this sudden shock coming upon the fag-end of his endurance. We snatched him up, lugged him aft, and pitched him

head-first down the cabin companion. You understand there was no time to carry him down with
infinite precautions and wait to see how he got on.
Those below would pick him up at the bottom of
the stairs all right. We were in a hurry to go back to
the pumps. That business could not wait. A bad leak
is an inhuman thing.

"One would think that the sole purpose of that
fiendish gale had been to make a lunatic of that poor
devil of a mulatto. It eased before morning, and next
day the sky cleared, and as the sea went down the
leak took up. When it came to bending a fresh set of
sails the crew demanded to put back—and really
there was nothing else to do. Boats gone, decks
swept clean, cabin gutted, men without a stitch but
what they stood in, stores spoiled, ship strained. We
put her head for home, and—would you believe it?
The wind came east right in our teeth. It blew fresh,
it blew continuously. We had to beat up every inch
of the way, but she did not leak so badly, the water
keeping comparatively smooth. Two hours' pumping in every four is no joke—but it kept her afloat as
far as Falmouth.

"The good people there live on casualties of the
sea, and no doubt were glad to see us. A hungry
crowd of shipwrights sharpened their chisels at the
sight of that carcass of a ship. And, by Jove! they had
pretty pickings off us before they were done. I fancy
the owner was already in a tight place. There were

delays. Then it was decided to take part of the cargo out and caulk her topsides. This was done, the repairs finished, cargo reshipped; a new crew came on board, and we went out—for Bankok. At the end of a week we were back again. The crew said they weren't going to Bankok—a hundred and fifty days' passage—in a something hooker that wanted pumping eight hours out of the twenty-four; and the nautical papers inserted again the little paragraph: '*Judea.* Barque. Tyne to Bankok; coals; put back to Falmouth leaky and with crew refusing duty.'

"There were more delays—more tinkering. The owner came down for a day, and said she was as right as a little fiddle. Poor old Captain Beard looked like the ghost of a Geordie skipper—through the worry and humiliation of it. Remember he was sixty, and it was his first command. Mahon said it was a foolish business, and would end badly. I loved the ship more than ever, and wanted awfully to get to Bankok. To Bankok! Magic name, blessed name. Mesopotamia wasn't a patch on it. Remember I was twenty, and it was my first second-mate's billet, and the East was waiting for me.

"We went out and anchored in the outer roads with a fresh crew—the third. She leaked worse than ever. It was as if those confounded shipwrights had actually made a hole in her. This time we did not even go outside. The crew simply refused to man the windlass.

"They towed us back to the inner harbour, and we became a fixture, a feature, an institution of the place. People pointed us out to visitors as "That 'ere barque that's going to Bankok—has been here six months—put back three times.' On holidays the small boys pulling about in boats would hail '*Judea*, ahoy!' and if a head showed above the rail shouted, 'Where you bound to?—Bankok?' and jeered. We were only three on board. The poor old skipper mooned in the cabin. Mahon undertook the cooking, and unexpectedly developed all a Frenchman's genius for preparing nice little messes. I looked languidly at the rigging. We became citizens of Falmouth. Every shopkeeper knew us. At the barber's or tobacconist's they asked familiarly, 'Do you think you will ever get to Bankok?' Meantime the owner, the underwriters, and the charterers squabbled amongst themselves in London, and our pay went on. . . . Pass the bottle.

"It was horrid. Morally it was worse than pumping for life. It seemed as though we had been forgotten by the world, belonged to nobody, and would get nowhere; it seemed that, as if bewitched, we would have to live for ever and ever in that inner harbour, a derision and a byword to generations of long-shore loafers and dishonest boatmen. I obtained three months' pay and a five days leave, and made a rush for London. It took me a day to get there and pretty well another to come back—but three months' pay went all the same. I don't know what I did with it. I went to a music-hall, I believe, lunched, dined, and supped in a swell place in Regent Street, and was back to time, with nothing but a complete set of Byron's works and a new railway rug to show for three months' work. The boat-man who pulled me off to the ship said: 'Hallo! I thought you had left the old thing. *She* will never get to Bankok.' 'That's all *you* know about it,' I said scornfully—but I didn't like that prophecy at all.

"Suddenly a man, some kind of agent to somebody, appeared with full powers. He had grog-blossoms all over his face, an indomitable energy, and was a jolly soul. We leaped into life again. A hulk came alongside, took our cargo, and then we went into dry dock to get our copper stripped. No wonder she leaked. The poor thing, strained beyond endurance by the gale, had, as if in disgust, spat out all the oakum of her lower seams. She was recaulked, new coppered, and made as tight as a bottle. We went back to the hulk and re-shipped our cargo.

"Then, on a fine moonlight night, all the rats left the ship.

"We had been infested with them. They had destroyed our sails, consumed more stores than the crew, affably shared our beds and our dangers, and now, when the ship was made seaworthy, concluded to clear out. I called Mahon to enjoy the spectacle. Rat after rat appeared on our rail, took a last look over his shoulder, and leaped with a hollow thud into the empty hulk. We tried to count them, but soon lost the tale. Mahon said: 'Well, well! don't talk to me about the intelligence of rats. They ought to have left before, when we had that narrow squeak from foundering. There you have proof how silly is the superstition about them. They leave a good ship for an old rotten hulk, where there is nothing to eat, too, the fools! . . . I don't believe they know what is safe or what is good for them, any more than you or I.'

"And after some more talk we agreed that the wisdom of rats had been grossly overrated, being in fact no greater than that of men.

"The story of the ship was known, by this, all up the Channel from Land's End to the Forelands, and we could get no crew on the south coast. They sent us one all complete from Liverpool, and we left once more—for Bankok.

"We had fair breezes, smooth water right into the tropics and the old *Judea* lumbered along in the sunshine. When she went eight knots everything cracked aloft, and we tied our caps to our heads; but mostly she strolled on at the rate of three miles an hour. What could you expect? She was tired—that old ship. Her youth was where mine is—where yours is—you fellows who listen to this yarn; and what friend would throw your years and your weariness in your face? We didn't grumble at her. To us aft, at least, it seemed as though we had been born in her, reared in her, had lived in her for ages, had never known any other ship. I would just as soon have abused the old village church at home for not being a cathedral.

"And for me there was also my youth to make me patient. There was all the East before me, and all life, and the thought that I had been tried in that ship and had come out pretty well. And I thought of men of old, who centuries ago, went that road in ships that sailed no better, to the land of palms, and spices, and yellow sands, and of brown nations ruled by kings more cruel than Nero the Roman, and more splendid than Solomon the Jew. The old bark lumbered on, heavy with her age and the burden of her cargo, while I lived the life of youth in ignorance and hope. She lumbered on through an interminable procession of days; and the fresh gilding flashed back at the setting sun, seemed to cry out over the darkening sea the words painted on her stern, '*Judea*, London. Do or Die.'

"Then we entered the Indian Ocean and steered northerly for Java Head. The winds were light. Weeks slipped by. She crawled on, do or die, and people at home began to think of posting us as overdue.

"One Saturday evening, I being off duty, the men asked me to give them an extra bucket of water or so—for washing clothes. As I did not wish to screw on the fresh-water pump so late, I went forward whistling, and with a key in my hand to unlock the forepeak scuttle, intending to serve the water out of a spare tank we kept there.

"The smell down below was as unexpected as it was frightful. One would have thought hundreds of paraffin-lamps had been flaring and smoking in that hole for days. I was glad to get out. The man with me coughed and said, 'Funny smell, sir.' I answered negligently, 'It's good for the health they say,' and walked aft.

"The first thing I did was to put my head down the square of the midship ventilator. As I lifted the lid a visible breath, something like a thin fog, a puff of faint haze, rose from the opening. The ascending air was hot, and had a heavy, sooty, paraffiny smell. I gave one sniff, and put down the lid gently. It was no use choking myself. The cargo was on fire.

"Next day she began to smoke in earnest. You see it was to be expected, for though the coal was of a safe kind, that cargo had been so handled, so broken up with handling, that it looked more like smithy coal than anything else. Then it had been wetted—more than once. It rained all the time we were taking it back from the hulk, and now with this long passage it got heated, and there was another case of spontaneous combustion.

"The captain called us into the cabin. He had a chart spread on the table, and looked unhappy. He said, 'The coast of West Australia is near, but I mean to proceed to our destination. It is the hurricane month, too; but we will just keep her head for Bankok, and fight the fire. No more putting back anywhere, if we all get roasted. We will try first to stifle this 'ere damned combustion by want of air.'

"We tried. We battened down everything, and still she smoked. The smoke kept coming out through imperceptible crevices; it forced itself through bulkheads and covers; it oozed here and there and everywhere in slender threads, in an invisible film, in an incomprehensible manner. It made its way into the cabin, into the forecastle; it poisoned the sheltered places on the deck, it could be sniffed as high as the mainyard. It was clear that if the smoke came out the air came in. This was disheartening. This combustion refused to be stifled.

"We resolved to try water, and took the hatches off. Enormous volumes of smoke, whitish, yellowish, thick, greasy, misty, choking, ascended as high as the trucks. All hands cleared out aft. Then the poisonous cloud blew away, and we went back to work in a smoke that was no thicker now than that of an ordinary factory chimney.

"We rigged the force-pump, got the hose along, and by and by it burst. Well, it was as old as the ship—a prehistoric hose, and past repair. Then we pumped with the feeble head-pump, drew water with buckets, and in this way managed in time to pour lots of Indian Ocean into the main hatch. The bright stream flashed in sunshine, fell into a layer of white crawling smoke, and vanished on the black surface of coal. Steam ascended mingling with the smoke. We poured salt water as into a barrel without a bottom. It was our fate to pump in that ship, to pump out of her, to pump into her; and after keeping water out of her to save ourselves from being drowned, we frantically poured water into her to save ourselves from being burnt.

"And she crawled on, do or die, in the serene weather. The sky was a miracle of purity, a miracle of azure. The sea was polished, was blue, was pellucid, was sparkling like a precious stone, extending on all sides, all round to the horizon—as if the whole terrestrial globe had been one jewel, one colossal sapphire, a single gem fashioned into a planet. And on the lustre of the great calm waters the *Judea* glided imperceptibly, enveloped in languid and unclean vapours, in a lazy cloud that drifted to leeward, light and slow; a pestiferous cloud defiling the splendour of sea and sky.

"All this time of course we saw no fire. The cargo smouldered at the bottom somewhere. Once Mahon, as we were working side by side, said to me with a queer smile: 'Now, if she only would spring a tidy leak—like that time when we first left the Channel—it would put a stopper on this fire. Wouldn't it?' I remarked irrelevantly, 'Do you remember the rats?'

"We fought the fire and sailed the ship too as carefully as though nothing had been the matter. The steward cooked and attended on us. Of the other twelve men, eight worked while four rested. Everyone took his turn, captain included. There was equality, and if not exactly fraternity, then a deal of good feeling. Sometimes a man, as he dashed a bucketful of water down the hatchway, would yell out, 'Hurrah for Bankok!' and the rest laughed. But generally we were taciturn and serious—and thirsty. Oh! how thirsty! And we had to be careful with the water. Strict allowance. The ship smoked, the sun blazed. . . . Pass the bottle.

"We tried everything. We even made an attempt to dig down to the fire. No good, of course. No man could remain more than a minute below. Mahon, who went first, fainted there, and the man who went to fetch him out did likewise. We lugged them out on deck. Then I leaped down to show how easily it could be done. They had learned wisdom by that time, and contented themselves by fishing for me with a chain-hook tied to a broom-handle, I believe. I did not offer to go and fetch up my shovel, which was left down below.

"Things began to look bad. We put the long-boat into the water. The second boat was ready to swing out. We had also another, a 14-foot thing, on davits aft, were it was quite safe.

"Then, behold, the smoke suddenly decreased. We redoubled our efforts to flood the bottom of the ship. In two days there was no smoke at all. Everybody was on the broad grin. This was on a Friday. On Saturday no work, but sailing the ship of course was done. The men washed their clothes and their faces for the first time in a fortnight, and had a special dinner given them. They spoke of spontaneous combustion with contempt, and implied *they* were the boys to put out combustions. Somehow we all felt as though we each had inherited a large fortune. But a beastly smell of burning hung about the ship. Captain Beard had hollow eyes and sunken cheeks. I had never noticed so much before how twisted and bowed he was. He and Mahon prowled soberly about hatches and ventilators, sniffing. It struck me suddenly poor Mahon was a very, very old chap. As to me, I was as pleased and proud as though I had helped to win a great naval battle. O! Youth!

"The night was fine. In the morning a homeward-bound ship passed us hull down—the first we had seen for months; but we were nearing the land at last, Java Head being about 190 miles off, and nearly due north.

"Next day it was my watch on deck from eight to twelve. At breakfast the captain observed, 'It's wonderful how that smell hangs about the cabin.' About ten, the mate being on the poop, I stepped down on the main-deck for a moment. The carpenter's bench stood abaft the mainmast: I leaned against it sucking at my pipe, and the carpenter, a young chap, came to talk to me. He remarked, 'I think we have done very well, haven't we?' and then I perceived with annoyance the fool was trying to tilt the bench. I said curtly, 'Don't Chips,' and immediately became aware of a queer sensation, of an absurd delusion,—I seemed somehow to be in the air. I heard all round me like a pent-up breath released—as if a thousand giants simultaneously had said Phoo!—and felt a dull concussion which made my ribs ache suddenly. No doubt about it—I was in the air, and my body was describing a short parabola. But short as it was, I had the time to think several thoughts in, as far as I can remember, the following order: 'This can't be the carpenter—What is it?—Some accident—Submarine volcano?—Coals, gas!—By Jove! we are being blown up—Everybody's dead—I am falling into the after-hatch—I see fire in it.'

"The coal-dust suspended in the air of the hold had glowed dull-red at the moment of the explosion. In the twinkling of an eye, in an infinitesimal fraction of a second since the first tilt of the bench, I was sprawling full length on the cargo. I picked myself up and scrambled out. It was quick like a rebound. The deck was a wilderness of smashed timber, lying crosswise like trees in a wood after a hurricane; an immense curtain of soiled rags waved gently before me—it was the mainsail blown to strips. I thought, The masts will be toppling over directly; and to get out of the way bolted on all-fours towards the poop-ladder. The first person I saw was Mahon, with eyes like saucers, his mouth open, and the long white hair standing straight on end round his head like a silver halo. He was just about to go down when the sight of the main-deck stirring, heaving up, and changing into splinters before his eyes, petrified him on the top stop. I stared at him in unbelief, and he stared at me with a queer kind of shocked curiosity. I did not know that I had no hair, no eyebrows, no eyelashes, that my young moustache was burnt off, that my face was black, one cheek laid open, my nose cut, and my chin bleeding. I had lost my cap, one of my slippers, and my shirt was torn to rags. Of all this I was not aware. I was amazed to see the ship still afloat, the poop-deck whole—and, most of all, to see anybody alive. Also the peace of the sky and the serenity of the sea were distinctly surprising. I suppose I expected to see them convulsed with horror. . . . Pass the bottle.

"There was a voice hailing the ship from some-where—in the air, in the sky—I couldn't tell. Presently I saw the captain—and he was mad. He asked me eagerly, 'Where's the cabin-table?' and to hear such a question was a frightful shock. I had just been blown up, you understand, and vibrated with that experience—I wasn't quite sure whether I was alive. Mahon began to stamp with both feet and yelled at him, "Good God! don't you see the decks blown out of her?' I found my voice, and stammered out as if conscious of some gross neglect of duty, 'I don't know where the cabin-table is.' It was like an absurd dream.

"Do you know what he wanted next? Well, he wanted to trim the yards. Very placidly, and as if lost in thought, he insisted on having the foreyard squared. 'I don't know if there's anybody alive,' said Mahon, almost tearfully. 'Surely,' he said, gently, 'there will be enough left to square the foreyard.'

"The old chap, it seems, was in his own berth winding up the chronometers, when the shock sent him spinning. Immediately it occurred to him—as he said afterwards—that the ship had struck something, and he ran out into the cabin. There, he saw, the cabin-table had vanished somewhere. The deck being blown up, it had fallen down into the lazarette of course. Where we had our breakfast that morning he saw only a great hole in the floor. This appeared to him so awfully mysterious, and impressed him so immensely, that what he saw and heard after he got on deck were mere trifles in comparison. And, mark, he noticed directly the wheel deserted and his barque off her course—and his only thought was to get that miserable, stripped, undecked, smouldering shell of a ship back again with her head pointing at her port of destination. Bankok! That's what he was after. I tell you this quiet, bowed, bandy-legged, almost deformed little man was immense in the singleness of his idea and in his placid ignorance of our agitation. He motioned us forward with a commanding gesture, and went to take the wheel himself.

"Yes; that was the first thing we did—trim the yards of that wreck! No one was killed, or even disabled, but everyone was more or less hurt. You should have seen them! Some were in rags, with black faces, like coal-heavers, like sweeps, and had bullet heads that seemed closely cropped, but were in fact singed to the skin. Others, of the watch below, awakened by being shot out from their collapsing bunks, shivered incessantly, and kept on groaning even as we went about our work. But they all worked. That crew of Liverpool hard cases had in them the right stuff. It's my experience they always have. It is the sea that gives it—the vastness, the loneliness surrounding their dark stolid souls. Ah! Well! we stumbled, we crept, we fell, we barked our shins on the wreckage, we hauled. The masts stood, but we did not know how much they might be charred down below. It was nearly calm, but a long swell ran from the west and made her roll. They might go at any moment. We looked at them with apprehension. One could not foresee which way they would fall.

"Then we retreated aft and looked about us. The deck was a tangle of planks on edge, of planks on end, of splinters, of ruined woodwork. The masts rose from that chaos like big trees above a matted undergrowth. The interstices of that mass of wreckage were full of something whitish, sluggish, stirring—of something that was like a greasy fog. The smoke of the invisible fire was coming up again, was trailing, like a poisonous thick mist in some valley choked with dead wood. Already lazy wisps were beginning to curl upwards amongst the mass of splinters. Here and there a piece of timber, stuck upright, resembled a post. Half of a fife-rail had been shot through the foresail, and the sky made a patch of glorious blue in the ignobly soiled canvas. A portion of several boards holding together had fallen across the rail, and one end protruded overboard, like a gangway leading upon nothing, like a gangway leading over the deep sea, leading to death—as if inviting us to walk the plank at once and be done with our ridiculous troubles. And still the air, the sky—a ghost, something invisible was hailing the ship.

"Someone had the sense to look over, and there was the helmsman, who had impulsively jumped overboard, anxious to come back. He yelled and swam lustily like a merman, keeping up with the ship. We threw him a rope, and presently he stood amongst us streaming with water and very crestfallen. The captain had surrendered the wheel, and apart, elbow on rail and chin in hand, gazed at the sea wistfully. We asked ourselves, What next? I thought, Now, this is something like. This is great. I wonder what will happen. O youth!

"Suddenly Mahon sighted a steamer far astern, Captain Beard said, 'We may do something with her yet.' We hoisted two flags, which said in the international language of the sea, 'On fire. Want immediate assistance.' The steamer grew bigger rapidly, and by and by spoke with two flags on her foremast, 'I am coming to your assistance.'

"In half an hour she was abreast, to windward, within hail, and rolling slightly, with her engines stopped. We lost our composure, and yelled all together with excitement, 'We've been blown up'. A man in a white helmet, on the bridge, cried, 'Yes! All right! all right!' and he nodded his head, and smiled, and made soothing motions with his hand as though at a lot of frightened children. One of the boats dropped in the water, and walked towards us upon the sea with her long oars. Four Calashes pulled a swinging stroke. This was my first sight of Malay seamen. I've known them since, but what struck me then was their unconcern: they came alongside, and even the bowman standing up and holding to our main-chains with the boat-hook did not deign to lift his head for a glance. I thought people who had been blown up deserved more attention.

"A little man, dry like a chip and agile like a monkey, clambered up. It was the mate of the steamer. He gave one look, and cried, 'O boys—you had better quit.'

"We were silent. He talked apart with the captain for a time,—seemed to argue with him. Then they went away together to the steamer.

"When our skipper came back we learned that the steamer was the *Somerville*, Captain Nash, from West Australia to Singapore *via* Batavia with mails, and that the agreement was she should tow us to Anjer or Batavia, if possible, where we could extinguish the fire by scuttling, and then proceed on our voyage— to Bankok! The old man seemed excited. 'We will do it yet,' he said to Mahon, fiercely. He shook his fist at the sky. Nobody else said a word.

"At noon the steamer began to tow. She went ahead slim and high, and what was left of the *Judea* followed at the end of seventy fathom of tow-rope,—followed her swiftly like a cloud of smoke with mast-heads protruding above. We went aloft to furl the sails. We coughed on the yards, and were careful about the bunts. Do you see the lot of us there, putting a neat furl on the sails of that ship doomed to arrive nowhere? There was not a man who didn't think that any moment the masts would topple over. From aloft we could not see the ship for smoke, and they worked carefully, passing the gaskets with even turns. 'Harbour furl—aloft there!' cried Mahon from below.

"You understand this? I don't think one of those chaps expected to get down in the usual way. When we did I heard them saying to each other, 'Well, I thought we would come down overboard, in a lump—blame me if I didn't.' 'That's what I was thinking to myself,' would answer wearily another battered and bandaged scarecrow. And, mind, these were men without the drilled-in habit of obedience. To an onlooker they would be a lot of profane scallywags without a redeeming point. What made them do it—what made them obey me when I, thinking consciously how fine it was, made them drop the bunt of the foresail twice to try and do it better? What? They had no professional reputation—no examples, no praise. It wasn't a sense of duty; they all knew well enough how to shirk, and laze, and dodge—when they had a mind to it—and mostly they had. Was it the two pounds ten a-month that sent them there? They didn't think their pay half good enough. No; it was something in them, something inborn and subtle and everlasting. I don't say positively that the crew of a French or German merchantman wouldn't have done it, but I doubt whether it would have been done in the same way. There was a completeness in it, something solid like a principle, and masterful like an instinct—a disclosure of something secret—of that hidden something, that gift of good or evil that makes racial difference, that shapes the fate of nations.

"It was that night at ten that, for the first time since we had been fighting it, we saw the fire. The speed of the towing had fanned the smouldering destruction. A blue gleam appeared forward, shining below the wreck of the deck. It wavered in patches, it seemed to stir and creep like the light of a glowworm. I saw it first, and told Mahon. 'Then the game's up,' he said. 'We had better stop this towing, or she will burst out suddenly fore and aft before we can clear out.' We set up a yell; rang bells to attract their attention; they towed on. At last Mahon and I had to crawl forward and cut the rope with an axe. There was no time to cast off the lashings. Red tongues could be seen licking the wilderness of splinters under our feet as we made our way back to the poop.

"Of course they very soon found out in the steamer that the rope was gone. She gave a loud blast of her whistle, her lights were seen sweeping in a wide circle, she came up ranging close along-side, and stopped. We were all in a tight group on the poop looking at her. Every man had saved a little bundle or a bag. Suddenly a conical flame with a twisted top shot up forward and threw upon the black sea a circle of light, with the two vessels side by side and heaving gently in its centre. Captain Beard had been sitting on the gratings still and mute for hours, but now he rose slowly and advanced in front of us, to the mizzen-shrouds. Captain Nash hailed: 'Come along! Look sharp. I have mail-bags on board. I will take you and your boats to Singapore.'

"'Thank you! No!' said our skipper. 'We must see the last of the ship.'

"'I can't stand by any longer,' shouted the other. 'Mails—you know.'

"'Ay! ay! We are all right.'

"Very well! I'll report you in Singapore. . . . Good-bye!'

"He waved his hand. Our men dropped their bundles quietly. The steamer moved ahead, and passing out of the circle of light, vanished at once from our sight, dazzled by the fire which burned fiercely. And then I knew that I would see the East first as commander of a small boat. I thought it fine; and the fidelity to the old ship was fine. We should see the last of her. Oh, the glamour of youth! Oh, the fire of it, more dazzling than the flames of the burning ship, throwing a magic light on the wide earth, leaping audaciously to the sky, presently to be quenched by time, more cruel, and more pitiless, more bitter than the sea—and like the flames of the burning ship surrounded by an impenetrable night.

"The old man warned us in his gentle and inflexible way that it was part of our duty to save for the underwriters as much as we could of the ship's gear. Accordingly we went to work aft, while she blazed forward to give us plenty of light. We lugged out a lot of rubbish. What didn't we save? An old barometer fixed with an absurd quantity of screws nearly cost me my life: a sudden rush of smoke came upon me, and I just got away in time. There were various stores, bolts of canvas, coils of rope; the poop looked like a marine bazaar, and the boats were lumbered to the gunwales. One would have thought the old man wanted to take as much as he could of his first command with him. He was very, very quiet, but off his balance evidently. Would you believe it? He wanted to take a length of old stream-cable and a kedge-anchor with him in the long-boat. We said, 'Ay, ay, sir,' deferentially, and on the quiet let the things slip overboard. The heavy medicine-chest went that way, two bags of green coffee, tins of paint—fancy, paint!—a whole lot of things. Then I was ordered with two hands into the boats to make a storage and get them ready against the time it would be proper for us to leave the ship.

"We put everything straight, stepped the long-boat's mast for our skipper, who was to take charge of her, and I was not sorry to sit down for a moment. My face felt raw, every limb ached as if broken, I was aware of all my ribs, and would have sworn to a twist in the backbone. The boats, fast astern, lay in a deep shadow, and all around I could the circle of the sea lighted by the fire. A gigantic flame arose forward straight and clear. It flared fierce, with noises like the whirr of wings, with rumbles as of thunder. There were cracks, detonations, and from the cone of flame the sparks flew upwards, as man is born to trouble, to leaky ships, and to ships that burn.

"What bothered me was that the ship, lying broadside to the swell and to such wind as there was—a mere breath—the boats would not keep astern where they were safe, but persisted, in a pig-headed way boats have, in getting under the counter and then swinging alongside. They were knocking about dangerously and coming near the flame, while the ship rolled on them, and, of course, there was always the danger of the masts going over the side at any moment. I and my two boat-keepers kept them off as best we could, with oars and boat-hooks; but to be constantly at it became exasperating, since there was no reason why we should not leave at once. We could not see those on board, nor could we imagine what caused the delay. The boat-keepers were swearing feebly, and I had not only my share of the work but also had to keep at it two men who showed a constant inclination to lay themselves down and let things slide.

"At last I hailed, 'On deck there,' and someone looked over. 'We're ready here,' I said. The head disappeared, and very soon popped up again. 'The captain says, All right, sir, and to keep the boats well clear of the ship.'

"Half an hour passed. Suddenly there was a frightful racket, rattle, clanking of chain, hiss of water, and millions of sparks flew up into the shivering column of smoke that stood leaning slightly above the ship. The cat-heads had burned away, and the two red-hot anchors had gone to the bottom, tearing out after them two hundred fathom of red-hot chain. The ship trembled, the mass of flame swayed as if ready to collapse, and the fore top-gallant-mast fell. It darted down like an arrow of fire, shot under, and instantly leaping up within an oar's-length of the boats, floated quietly, very black on the luminous sea. I hailed the deck again. After some time a man in an unexpectedly cheerful but also muffled tone, as though he had been trying to speak with his mouth shut, informed me, 'Coming directly, sir,' and vanished. For a long time I heard nothing but the whirr and roar of the fire. There were also whistling sounds. The boats jumped, tugged at the painter, ran at each other playfully, knocked their sides together, or, do what we would, swung in a bunch against the ship's side. I couldn't stand it any longer, and swarming up a rope, clambered aboard over the stern.

"It was as bright as day. Coming up like this, the sheet of fire facing me was a terrifying sight, and the heat seemed hardly bearable at first. On a settee cushion dragged out of the cabin Captain Beard, his legs drawn up and one arm under his head, slept with the light playing on him. Do you know what the rest were busy about? They were sitting on deck right aft, round an open case, eating bread and cheese and drinking bottled stout.

"On the background of flames twisting in fierce tongues above their heads they seemed at home like salamanders, and looked like a band of desperate pirates. The fire sparkled in the whites of their eyes, gleamed on patches of white skin seen through the torn shirts. Each had the marks as of a battle about him—bandaged heads, tied-up arms, a strip of dirty rag round a knee—and each man had a bottle between his legs and a chunk of cheese in his hand. Mahon got up. With his handsome and disreputable head, his hooked profile, his long white beard, and with an uncorked bottle in his hand, he resembled one of those reckless sea-robbers of old making merry amidst violence and disaster. 'The last meal on board,' he explained solemnly. 'We had nothing to eat all day, and it was no use leaving all this.' He flourished the bottle and indicated the sleeping skipper. 'He said he couldn't swallow anything, so I got him to lie down,' he went on; and as I stared, 'I don't know whether you are aware, young fellow, the man had no sleep to speak of for days—and there will be dam' little sleep in the boats.' 'There will be no boats by-and-by if you fool about much longer,' I said, indignantly. I walked up to the skipper and shook him by the shoulder. At last he opened his eyes, but did not move. 'Time to leave her, sir,' I said quietly.

"He got up painfully, looked at the flames, at the sea sparkling round the ship, and black, black as ink farther away; he looked at the stars shining dim through a thin veil of smoke in a sky black, black as Erebus.

"'Youngest first,' he said.

"And the ordinary seaman, wiping his mouth with the back of his hand, got up, clambered over the taffrail, and vanished. Others followed. One, on the point of going over, stopped short to drain his bottle, and with a great swing of his arm flung it at the fire. 'Take this!' he cried.

"The skipper lingered disconsolately, and we left him to commune alone for a awhile with his first command. Then I went up again and brought him away at last. It was time. The ironwork on the poop was hot to the touch.

"Then the painter of the long-boat was cut, and the three boats, tied together, drifted clear of the ship. It was just sixteen hours after the explosion when we abandoned her. Mahon had charge of the second boat, and I had the smallest—the 14-foot thing. The long-boat would have taken the lot of us; but the skipper said we must save as much property as we could—for the under-writers—and so I got my first command. I had two men with me, a bag of biscuits, a few tins of meat, and a breaker of water. I was ordered to keep close to the long-boat, that in case of bad weather we might be taken into her.

"And do you know what I thought? I thought I would part company as soon as I could. I wanted to have my first command all to myself. I wasn't going to sail in a squadron if there were a chance for independent cruising. I would make land by myself. I would beat the other boats. Youth! All youth! The silly, charming, beautiful youth.

"But we did not make a start at once. We must see the last of the ship. And so the boats drifted about that night, heaving and setting on the swell. The men dozed, waked, sighed, groaned. I looked at the burning ship.

"Between the darkness of earth and heaven she was burning fiercely upon a disc of purple sea shot by the blood-red play of gleams; upon a disc of water glittering and sinister. A high, clear flame, an immense and lonely flame, ascended from the ocean, and from its summit the black smoke poured continuously at the sky. She burned furiously; mournful and imposing like a funeral pile kindled in the night, surrounded by the sea, watched over by the stars. A magnificent death had come like a grace, like a gift, like a reward to that old ship at the end of her laborious days. The surrender of her weary ghost to the keeping of stars and sea was stirring like the sight of a glorious triumph. The masts fell just before daybreak, and for a moment there was a burst and turmoil of sparks that seemed to fill with flying fire the night patient and watchful, the vast night lying silent upon the sea. At daylight she was only a charred shell, floating still under a cloud of smoke and bearing a glowing mass of coal within.

"Then the oars were got out, and the boats forming in a line moved round her remains as if in procession—the long-boat leading. As we pulled across her stern a slim dart of fire shot out viciously at us, and suddenly she went down, head first, in a great hiss of steam. The unconsumed stern was the last to sink; but the paint had gone, had cracked, had peeled off, and there were no letters, there was no word, no stubborn device that was like her soul, to flash at the rising run her creed and her name.

"We made our way north. A breeze sprang up, and about noon all the boats came together for the last time. I had no mast or sail in mine, but I made a mast out of a spare oar and hoisted a boat-awning for a sail, with a boat-hook for a yard. She was certainly over-masted, but I had the satisfaction of know that with the wind aft I could beat the other two. I had to wait for them. Then we all had a look at the captain's chart, and, after a sociable meal of hard bread and water, got our last instructions. These were simple: steer north, and keep together as much as possible. 'Be careful with that jury-rig, Marlow,' said the captain; and Mahon, as I sailed proudly past his boat, wrinkled his curved nose and hailed, 'You will sail that ship of yours under water, if you don't look out, young fellow.' He was a malicious old man—and may the deep sea where he sleeps now rock him gently, rock him tenderly to the end of time!

"Before sunset a thick rain-squall passed over the two boats, which were far astern, and that was the last I saw of them for a time. Next day I sat steering my cockle-shell—my first command—with nothing but water and sky around me. I did sight in the afternoon the upper sails of a ship far away, but said nothing, and my men did not notice her. You see I was afraid she might be homeward bound, and I had no mind to turn back from the portals of the East. I was steering for Java—another blessed name—like Bankok, you know. I steered many days.

"I need not tell you what it is to be knocking about in an open boat. I remember nights and days of calm, when we pulled, we pulled, and the boat seemed to stand still, as if bewitched within the circle of the sea horizon. I remember the heat, the deluge of rain-squalls that kept us baling for dear life (but filled our water-cask), and I remember sixteen hours on end with a mouth dry as a cinder and a steering-oar over the stern to keep my first command head on to a breaking sea. I did not know how good a man I was till then. I remember the drawn faces, the dejected figures of my two men, and I remember my youth and the feeling that will never come back any more—the feeling that I could last for ever, outlast the sea, the earth, and all men; the deceitful feeling that lures us on to joys, to perils, to love, to vain effort—to death; the triumphant conviction of strength, the heat of life in the handful of dust, the glow in the heart that with every year grows dim, grows cold, grows small, and expires—and expires, too soon, too soon—before life itself.

"And this is how I see the East. I have seen its secret places and have looked into its very soul; but now I see it always from a small boat, a high outline of mountains, blue and afar in the morning; like faint mist at noon; a jagged wall of purple at sunset. I have the feel of the oar in my hand, the vision of a scorching blue sea in my eyes. And I see a bay, a wide bay, smooth as glass and polished like ice, shimmering in the dark. A red light burns far off upon the gloom of the land, and the night is soft and warm. We drag at the oars with aching arms, and suddenly a puff of wind, a puff faint and tepid and laden with strange odours of blossoms, of aromatic wood, comes out of the still night—the first sigh of the East on my face. That I can never forget. It was impalpable and enslaving, like a charm, like a whispered promise of mysterious delight.

"We had been pulling this finishing spell for eleven hours. Two pulled, and he whose turn it was to rest sat at the tiller. We had made out the red light in that bay and steered for it, guessing it must mark some small coasting port. We passed two vessels, outlandish and high-sterned, sleeping at anchor, and, approaching the light, now very dim, ran the boat's nose against the end of a jutting wharf. We were blind with fatigue. My men dropped the oars and fell off the thwarts as if dead. I made fast to a pile. A current rippled softly. The scented obscurity of the shore was grouped into vast masses, a density of colossal clumps of vegetation, probably—mute and fantastic shapes. And at their foot the semicircle of a beach gleamed faintly, like an illusion. There was not a light, not a stir, not a sound. The mysterious East faced me, perfumed like a flower, silent like death, dark like a grave.

"And I sat weary beyond expression, exulting like a conqueror, sleepless and entranced as if before a profound, a fateful enigma.

"A splashing of oars, a measured dip reverberating on the level of water, intensified by the silence of the shore into loud claps, made me jump up. A boat, a European boat, was coming in. I invoked the name of the dead; I hailed; *Judea* ahoy! A thin shout answered.

"It was the captain. I had beaten the flagship by three hours, and I was glad to hear the old man's voice again, tremulous and tired. 'Is it you, Marlow?' 'Mind the end of that jetty sir,' I cried.

"He approached cautiously, and brought up with the deep-sea lead-line which we had saved—for the underwriters. I eased my painter and fell alongside. He sat, a broken figure at the stern, wet with dew, his hands clasped in his lap. His men were asleep already. 'I had a terrible time of it,' he murmured. 'Mahon is behind—not very far.' We conversed in whispers, in low whispers, as if afraid to wake up the land. Guns, thunder, earthquakes would not have awakened the men just then.

"Looking round as we talked, I saw away at sea a bright light travelling in the night. 'There's a steamer passing the bay,' I said. She was not passing, she was entering, and she even came close and anchored. 'I wish,' said the old man, 'you would find out whether she is English. Perhaps they could give us a passage somewhere.' He seemed nervously anxious. So by dint of punching and kicking I started one of my men into a state of somnambulism, and giving him an oar, took another and pulled towards the lights of the steamer.

"There was a murmur of voices in her, metallic hollow clang of the engine-room, footsteps on the deck. Her ports shown, round like dilated eyes. Shapes moved about, and there was a shadowy man high up on the bridge. He heard my oars.

"And then, before I could open my lips, the East spoke to me, but it was in a Western voice. A torrent of words was poured into the enigmatical, the fateful silence; outlandish, angry words, mixed with words and even whole sentences of good English, less strange but even more surprising. The voice swore and cursed violently; it riddled the solemn peace of the bay by a volley of abuse. It began by calling me Pig, and from that went crescendo into unmentionable adjectives—in English. The man up there raged aloud in two languages, and with a sincerity in his fury that almost convinced me I had, in some way, sinned against the harmony of the universe. I could hardly see him, but began to think he would work himself into a fit.

"Suddenly he ceased, and I could hear him snorting and blowing like a porpoise. I said—

"'What steamer is this, pray?'

"'Eh? What's this? And who are you?'

"'Castaway crew of an English barque burnt at sea. We came here to-night. I am the second mate. The captain is in the long-boat, and wishes to know if you would give us a passage somewhere.'

"'Oh, my goodness! I say. . . . This is the *Celestial* from Singapore on her return trip. I'll arrange with your captain in the morning, . . . and, . . . I say, . . . did you hear me just now?'

"'I should think the whole bay heard you.'

"'I thought you were a shore-boat. Now, look here—this infernal lazy scoundrel of a caretaker has gone to sleep again—curse him. The light is out, and I nearly ran foul of the end of this damned jetty. This is the third time he plays me this trick. Now, I ask you, can anybody stand this kind of thing? It's enough to drive a man out of his mind. I'll report him. . . . I'll get the Assistant Resident to give him the sack, by . . . ! See—there's no light. It's out, isn't it? I take you to witness the light's out. There should be a light, you know. A red light on the—'

"'There was a light,' I said, mildly.

"'But it's out, man! What the use of talking like this? You can see for yourself it's out—don't you? If you had to take a valuable steamer along this God-forsaken coast you would want a light, too. I'll kick him from end to end of his miserable wharf. You'll see if I don't. I will—'

"'So may I tell my captain you'll take us?' I broke in.

"'Yes, I'll take you. Good-night,' he said brusquely.

"I pulled back, made fast again to the jetty, and then went to sleep at last. I had faced the silence of the East. I had heard some of its language. But when I opened my eyes again the silence was as complete as though it had never been broken. I was lying in a flood of light, and the sky had never looked so far, so high, before. I opened my eyes and lay without moving.

"And then I saw the men of the East—they were looking at me. The whole length of the jetty was full of people. I saw brown, bronze, yellow faces, the black eyes, the glitter, the colour of an Eastern crowd. And all these beings stared without a murmur, without a sigh, without a movement. They stared down at the boats, at the sleeping men who at night had come to them from the sea. Nothing moved. The fronds of the palms stood still against the sky. Not a branch stirred along the shore, and the brown roofs of hidden houses peeped through the green foliage, through the big leaves that hung shining and still like leaves forged of heavy metal. This was the East of the ancient navigators, so old, so mysterious, resplendent and sombre, living and unchanged, full of danger and promise. And these were the men. I sat up suddenly. A wave of movement passed through the crowd from end to end, passed along the heads, swayed the bodies, ran along the jetty like a ripple on the water, like a breath of wind on a field—and all was still again. I see it now—the wide sweep of the bay, the glittering sands, the wealth of green infinite and varied, the sea blue like the sea of a dream, the crowd of attentive faces, the blaze of vivid colour—the water reflecting it all, the curve of the shore, the jetty, the high-sterned outlandish craft floating still, and the three boats with the tired men from the West sleeping, unconscious of the land and the people and of the violence of sunshine. They slept thrown across the thwarts, curled on bottom-boards, in the careless attitudes of death. The head of the old skipper, leaning back in the stern of the long-boat, had fallen on his breast, and he looked as though he would never wake. Farther out old Mahon's face was upturned to the sky, with the long white beard spread out on his breast, as though he had been shot where he sat at the tiller; and a man, all in a heap in the bows of the boat, slept with both arms embracing the stem-head and with his cheek laid on the gunwale. The East looked at them without a sound.

"I have known its fascination since; I have seen the mysterious shores, the still water, the lands of brown nations, where a stealthy Nemesis lies in wait, pursues, overtakes so many of the conquering race, who are proud of their wisdom, of their knowledge, of their strength. But for me all the East is contained in that vision of my youth. It is all in that moment when I opened my young eyes on it. I came upon it from a tussle with the sea—and I was young—and I saw it looking at me. And this is all that is left of it! Only a moment; a moment of strength, of romance, of glamour—of youth! . . . A flick of sunshine upon a strange shore, the time to remember, the time for a sigh, and—good-bye!—Night—Good-bye . . . !"

He drank.

"Ah! The good old time—the good old time. Youth and the sea. Glamour and the sea! The good, strong sea, the salt, bitter sea, that could whisper to you and roar at you and knock your breath out of you."

He drank again.

"By all that's wonderful it is the sea, I believe, the sea itself—or is it youth alone? Who can tell? But you here—you all had something out of life: money, love—whatever one gets on shore—and, tell me, wasn't that the best time, that time when we were young at sea; young and had nothing, on the sea that gives nothing, except hard knocks—and sometimes a chance to feel your strength—that only—what you all regret?"

And we all nodded at him: the man of finance, the man of accounts, the man of law, we all nodded at him over the polished table that like a still sheet of brown water reflected our faces, lined, wrinkled; our face marked by toil, by deceptions, by success, by love; our weary eyes looking still, looking always, looking anxiously for something out of life, that while it is expected is already gone—has passed unseen, in a sigh, in a flash—together with the youth, with the strength, with the romance of illusions.

The Strange Days That Came to Jimmie Friday

[FREDERIC REMINGTON]

The "Abwee-chemun" Club was organized with six charter members at a heavy lunch in the Savarin restaurant—one of those lunches which make through connections to dinner without change. One member basely deserted, while two more lost all their enthusiasm on the following morning, but three of us stuck. We vaguely knew that somewhere north of the Canadian Pacific and south of Hudson Bay were big lakes and rapid rivers—lakes whose names we did not know; lakes bigger than Champlain, with unnamed rivers between them. We did not propose to be boated around in a big birch-bark by two voyagers among blankets and crackers and ham, but each provided himself a little thirteen-foot cedar canoe, twenty-nine inches in the beam, and weighing less than forty pounds. I cannot tell you precisely how our party was sorted, but one was a lawyer with eyeglasses and settled habits, loving nature, though detesting canoes; the other was nominally a merchant, but in reality an atavic Norseman of the wolf and raven kind; while I am not new. Together we started.

Presently the Abwees sat about the board of a lumbermen's hotel, filled with house-flies and slatternly waiter-girls, who talked familiarly while they served greasy food. The Abwees were yet sore in their minds at the thoughts of the smelly beds upstairs, and discouragement sat deeply on their souls. But their time was not yet.

After breakfast they marched to the Hudson Bay Company's store, knowing as they did that in Canada there are only two places for a traveller to go who wants anything—the great company or the parish priest; and then, having explained to the factor their dream, they were told "that beyond, beyond some days' journey"—oh! that awful beyond, which for centuries has stood across the path of the pioneer, and in these latter days confronts the sportsman and wilderness-lover—"that beyond some days' journey to the north was a country such as they had dreamed up Temiscamingue and beyond."

The subject of a guide was considered.

Jimmie Friday always brought a big toboggan-load of furs into Fort Tiemogamie every spring, and was accounted good in his business. He and his big brother trapped together, and in turn followed the ten days' swing through the snow-laden forest which they had covered with their dead-falls and steel-jawed traps; but when the ice went out in the rivers, and the great pines dripped with the melting snows, they had nothing more to do but cut a few cords of wood for their widowed mother's cabin near the post. Then the brother and he paddled down to Bais des Pierres, where the brother engaged as a deck hand on a steamboat, and Jimmie hired himself as a guide for some bush-rangers, as the men are called who explore for pine lands for the great lumber firms. Having worked all summer and got through with that business, Jimmie bethought him to dissipate for a few days in the bustling lumber town down on the Ottawa River. He had been there before to feel the exhilaration of civilization, but beyond that clearing he had never known anything more inspiring than a Hudson Bay post, which is generally a log store, a house where the agent lives, and a few tiny Indian cabins set higgledy-piggledy in a suburnt gash of stumps and bowlders, lost in the middle of the solemn, unresponsive forest. On this morning in question he had stepped from his friend's cabin up in the Indian village, and after lighting a perfectly round and rather yellow cigar, he had instinctively wandered down to the Hudson Bay store, there to find himself amused by a strange sight.

The Abwees had hired two French-Indian voyagers of sinister mien, and a Scotch-Canadian boy
bred to the bush. They were out on the grass,
engaged in taking burlaps off three highly polished
canoes, while the clerk ran out and asked questions
about "how much bacon," and, "will fifty pounds of
pork be enough, sir?"

The round yellow cigar was getting stubby, while
Jimmie's modest eyes sought out the points of interest in the new-comers when he was suddenly and
sharply addressed:

"Can you cook?"

Jimmie couldn't do anything in a hurry, except
chop a log in two, paddle very fast, and shoot
quickly, so he said, as was his wont:

"I think—I dun'no'—"

"Well, how much?" came the query.

"Two daul—ars—" said Jimmie.

The transaction was complete. The yellow butt
went over the fence, and Jimmie shed his coat. He
was directed to lend a hand by the bustling sportsmen, and requested to run and find things of which
he had never before in his life heard the name.

After two days' travel the Abwees were put
ashore—boxes, bags, rolls of blankets, canoes, Indians, and plunder of many sorts—on a pebbly beach,
and the steamer backed off and steamed away. They
had reached the "beyond" at last, and the odoriferous
little bedrooms, the bustle of the preparation, the

cares of their lives, were behind. Then there was a girding up of the loins, a getting out of tump-lines and canvas packs, and the long portage was begun.

The voyagers carried each two hundred pounds as they stalked away into the wilderness, while the attorney-at-law "hefted" his pack, wiped his eye-glasses with his pocket-handkerchief, and tried cheerfully to assume the responsibilities of a "dead game sport."

"I cannot lift the thing, and how I am going to carry it is more than I know; but I'm a dead game sport, and I am going to try. I do not want to be dead game, but it looks as though I couldn't help it. Will some gentleman help me to adjust this cargo?"

The night overtook the outfit in an old beaver meadow half-way through the trail. Like all first camps, it was tough. The lean-to tents went up awk-wardly. No one could find anything. Late at night the Abwees lay on their backs under the blankets, while the fog settled over the meadow and blotted out the stars.

On the following day the stuff was all gotten through, and by this time the lawyer had become a voyager, willing to carry anything he could stagger under. It is strange how one can accustom himself to "pack." He may never use the tump-line, since it goes across the head, and will unseat his intellect if he does, but with shoulder-straps and a tump-line a man who thinks he is not strong will simply amaze himself inside of a week by what he can do. As for our little canoes, we could trot with them. Each Abwee carried his own belongings and his boat, which entitled him to the distinction of "a dead game sport," whatever that may mean, while the Indians portaged their larger canoes and our mass of supplies, making many trips backward and forward in the process.

At the river everything was parcelled out and arranged. The birch-barks were re-pitched, and every man found out what he was expected to portage and do about camp. After breaking and making camp three times, the outfit could pack up, load the canoes, and move inside of fifteen minutes. At the first camp the lawyer essayed his canoe, and was cautioned that the delicate thing might flirt with him. He stepped in and sat gracefully down in about two feet of water, while the "delicate thing" shook herself saucily at his side. After he had crawled dripping ashore and wiped his eyeglasses, he engaged to sell the "delicate thing" to an Indian for one dollar and a half on a promissory note. The trade was suppressed, and he was urged to try again. A man who has held down a canebottom chair conscientiously for fifteen years looks askance at so fickle a thing as a canoe twenty-nine inches in the beam. They are nearly as hard to sit on in the water as a cork; but once one is in the bottom they are stable enough, though they do not submit to liberties or palsied movements. The staid lawyer was filled with horror at the prospect of another go at his polished beauty; but remembering his resolve to be dead game, he abandoned his life to the chances, and got in this time safely.

So the Abwees went down the river on a golden morning, their double-blade paddles flashing the sun and sending the drip in a shower on the glassy water. The smoke from the lawyer's pipe hung behind him in the quiet air, while the note of the reveille clangored from the little buglette of the Norseman. Jimmie and the big Scotch backwoodsman swayed their bodies in one boat, while the two sinister voyagers dipped their paddles in the big canoe.

The Norseman's gorge came up, and he yelled back: "Say! this suits me. I am never going back to New York."

Jimmie grinned at the noise; it made him happy. Such a morning, such a water, such a lack of anything to disturb one's peace! Let man's better nature revel in the beauties of existence; they inflate his soul. The colors play upon the senses—the reddish-yellow of the birch-barks, the blue of the water, and the silver sheen as it parts at the bows of the canoes; the dark evergreens, the steely rocks with their lichens, the white trunks of the birches, their fluffy tops so greeny green, and over all the gold of a sunny day. It is my religion, this thing, and I do not know how to tell all I feel concerning it.

The rods were taken out, a gang of flies put on and trolled behind—but we have all seen a man fight a five-pound bass for twenty minutes. The waters fairly swarmed with them, and we could always get enough for the "pot" in a half-hour's fishing at any time during the trip. The Abwees were canoeing, not hunting or fishing; though in truth, they did not need to hunt spruce-partridge or fish for bass in any sporting sense they simply went out after them, and never stayed over half an hour. On a point we stopped for lunch: the Scotchman always struck the beach a-cooking. He had a "kit," which was a big camp-pail, and inside of it were more dishes than are to be found in some hotels. He broiled the bacon, instead of frying it, and thus we were saved the terrors of indigestion. He had many luxuries in his commissary, among them dried apples, with which he filled a camp-pail one day and put them on to boil. They subsequently got to be about a foot deep all over the camp, while Furguson stood around and regarded the black-magic of the thing with overpowering emotions and Homeric tongue. Furguson was a good genius, big and gentle, and a woodsman root and branch. The Abwees had intended their days in the wilderness to be happy singing flights of time, but with grease and paste in one's stomach what may not befall the mind when it is bent on nature's doings?

And thus it was that the gloomy Indian Jimmie Friday, despite his tuberculosis begotten of insufficient nourishment, was happy in these strange days—even to the extent of looking with wondrous eyes on the nooks which we loved—nooks which previously for him had only sheltered possible "dead-falls" or not, as the discerning eye of the trapper decided the prospects for pelf.

Going ashore on a sandy beach, Jimmie wandered down its length, his hunter mind seeking out the footprints of his prey. He stooped down, and then beckoned me to come, which I did.

Pointing at the sand, he said, "You know him?"

"Wolves," I answered.

"Yes—first time I see 'em up here—they be fol-lerin' the deers—bad—bad. No can trap 'em—ver-rie smart."

A half-dozen wolves had chased a deer into the water; but wolves do not take to the water, so they had stopped and drank, and then gone rollicking together up the beach. There were cubs, and one great track as big as a mastiff might make.

"See that—moose track—he go by yesterday;" and Jimmie pointed to enormous footprints in the muck of a marshy place. "Verrie big moose—we make call at next camp—think it is early for call."

At the next camp Jimmie made the usual birchbark moose-call, and at evening blew it, as he also did on the following morning. This camp was a divine spot on a rise back of a long sandy beach, and we con-cluded to stop for a day. The Norseman and I each took a man in our canoes and started out to explore. I wanted to observe some musk-rat hotels down in a big marsh, and the Norseman was fishing. The attorney was content to sit on a log by the shores of the lake, smoke lazily, and watch the sun shimmer through the lifting fog. He saw a canoe approaching from across the lake. He gazed vacantly at it, when it grew strange and more unlike a canoe. The paddles did not move, but the phantom craft drew quickly on.

"Say, Furguson—come here—look at that canoe."

The Scotchman came down, with a pail in one hand, and looked. "Canoe—hell—it's a moose—and there ain't a pocket-pistol in this camp," and he fairly jumped up and down.

"You don't say—you really don't say!" gasped the lawyer, who now began to exhibit signs of insanity.

"Yes—he's going to be d——d sociable with us—he's coming right bang into this camp."

The Indian too came down, but he was long past talking English, and the gutturals came up in lumps, as though he was trying to keep them down.

The moose finally struck a long point of sand and rushes about two hundred yards away, and drew majestically out of the water, his hide dripping, and the sun glistening on his antlers and back.

The three men gazed in spellbound admiration at the picture until the moose was gone. When they had recovered their senses they slowly went up to the camp on the ridge—disgusted and dumfounded.

"I could almost put a cartridge in that old guncase and kill him," sighed the backwoodsman.

"I have never hunted in my life," mused the attorney, "but few men have seen such a sight," and he filled his pipe.

"Hark—listen!" said the Indian. There was a faint cracking, which presently became louder. "He's coming into camp;" and the Indian nearly died from excitement as he grabbed a hatchet. The three unfortunate men stepped to the back of the tents, and as big a bull moose as walks the lonely woods came up to within one hundred fifty feet of the camp, and stopped, returning their gaze.

Thus they stood for what they say was a minute, but which seemed like hours. The attorney composedly admired the unusual sight. The Indian and Furguson swore softly but most viciously until the moose moved away. The Indian hurled the hatchet at the retreating figure, with a final curse, and the thing was over.

"Those fellow who are out in their canoes will be sick abed when we tell them what's been going on in the camp this morning," sighed Mr. Furguson, as he scoured a cooking-pot.

I fear we would have had that moose on our consciences if we had been there: the game law was not up at the time, but I should have asked for strength from a higher source than my respect for law.

The golden days passed and the lake grew great. The wind blew at our backs. The waves rolled in restless surges, piling the little canoes on their crests and swallowing them in the troughs. The canoes thrashed the water as they flew along, half in, half out, but they rode like ducks. The Abwees took off their hats, gripped their double blades, made the water swirl behind them, howled in glee to each other through the rushing storm. To be five miles from shore in a seaway in kayaks like ours was a sensation. We found they stood it well, and grew contented. It was the complement to the golden lazy days when the water was glass, and the canoes rode upsidedown over its mirror surface. The Norseman grinned and shook his head in token of his pleasure, much as an epicure might after a sip of superior Burgundy.

"How do you fancy this?" we asked the attorney-at-law.

"I am not going to deliver an opinion until I get ashore. I would never have believed that I would be here at my time of life, but one never knows what a —— fool one can make of one's self. My glasses are covered with water, and I can hardly see, but I can't let go of this paddle, to wipe them," shrieked the man of the office chair, in the howl of the weather.

But we made a long journey by the aid of the wind, and grew a contempt for it. How could one imagine the stability of those little boats until one had tried it?

That night we put into a natural harbor and camped on a gravel beach. The tents were up and the supper cooking, when the wind hauled and blew furiously into our haven. The fires were scattered and the rain came in blinding sheets. The tent-pegs pulled from the sand. We sprang to our feet and held on to the poles, wet to the skin. It was useless; the rain blew right under the canvas. We laid the tents on the "grub" and stepped out into the dark. We could not be any wetter, and we did not care. To stand in the dark in the wilderness, with nothing to eat, and a fire-engine playing a hose on you for a couple of hours—if you have imagination enough, you can fill in the situation. But the gods were propitious. The wind died down. The stars came out by myriads. The fires were relighted, and the ordinary life begun. It was late in the night before our clothes, blankets, and tents were dry, but, like boys, we forgot it all.

Then came a river—blue and flat like the sky above—running through rushy banks, backed by the masses of the forest; anon the waters rushed upon us over the rocks, and we fought, plunk-plunk-plunk, with the paddles, until our strength gave out. We stepped out into the water, and getting our lines, and using our long double blades as fenders, "tracked" the canoes up through the boil. The Indians in their heavier boats used "setting-poles" with marvellous dexterity, and by furious exertion were able to draw steadily up the grade—though at times they too "tracked," and even portaged. Our largest canoe weighed two hundred pounds, but a little voyager

managed to lug it, though how I couldn't compre-
hend, since his pipe-stem legs fairly bent and wobbled
under the enormous ark. None of us by this time
were able to lift the loads which we carried, but, like
a Western pack-mule, we stood about and had things
piled on to us, until nothing more would stick.
Some of the backwoodsmen carry incredible masses
of stuff, and their lore is full of tales which no one
could be expected to believe. Our men did not hes-
itate to take two hundred and fifty pounds over short
portages, which were very rough and stony, though
they all said if they slipped they expected to break a
leg. This is largely due to the tump-line, which is
laid over the head, while persons unused to it must
have shoulder-straps in addition, which are not as
good, because the "breastbone," so called, is not
strong enough.

We were getting day by day farther into "the
beyond." There were no traces here of the hand of
man. Only Jimmie knew the way—it was his trapping-
ground. Only once did we encounter people. We
were blown into a little board dock, on a gray day,
with the waves piling up behind us, and made a difficult landing. Here were a few tiny log houses—an
outpost of the Hudson Bay Company. We renewed
our stock of provisions, after laborious trading with
the stagnated people who live in the lonely place.
There was nothing to sell us but a few of the most
common necessities; however, we needed only pota-

toes and sugar. This was Jimmie's home. Here we saw his poor old mother, who was being tossed about in the smallest of canoes as she drew her nets. Jimmie's father had gone on a hunting expedition and had never come back. Some day Jimmie's old mother will go out on the wild lake to tend her nets, and she will not come back. Some time Jimmie too will not return—for this Indian struggle with nature is appalling in its fierceness.

There was a dance at the post, which the boys attended, going by canoe at night, and they came back early in the morning, with much giggling at their gallantries.

The loneliness of this forest life is positively discouraging to think about. What the long winters must be in the little cabins I cannot imagine, and I fear the traders must be all avarice, or have none at all; for there can certainly be absolutely no intellectual life. There is undoubtedly work, but no one single problem concerning it. The Indian hunters do fairly well in a financial way, though their lives are beset with weakening hardships and constant danger. Their meagre diet wears out their constitutions, and they are subject to disease. The simplicity of their minds makes it very difficult to see into their life as they try to narrate it to one who may be interested.

From here on was through beautiful little lakes, and the voyagers rigged blanket sails on the big canoes, while we towed behind. Then came the river and the rapids, which we ran, darting between rocks, bumping on sunken stones—shooting fairly out into the air, all but turning over hundred of times. One day the Abwees glided out in the big lake Tesmiaque-mang, and saw the steamer going to Bais des Pierres. We hailed her, and she stopped, while the little canoes danced about in the swell as we were loaded one by one. On the deck above us the passengers admired a kind of boat the like of which had not appeared in these parts.

At Bais des Pierres we handed over the residue of the commissaries of the Abwee-Chemun to Jimmie Friday, including personally many pairs of well-worn golf-breeches, sweaters, rubber coats, knives which would be proscribed by law in New York. If Jimmie ever parades his solemn wilderness in these garbs, the owls will laugh from the trees. Our simple forest friend laid in his winter stock—traps, flour, salt, tobacco, and pork, a new axe—and accompanied us back down the lake again on the steamer. She stopped in mid-stream, while Jimmie got his bundles into his "bark" and shoved off, amid a hail of "good-byes."

The engine palpitated, the big wheel churned the water astern, and we drew away. Jimmie bent on his paddle with the quick body-swing habitual to the Indian, and after a time grew a speck on the reflection of the red sunset in Temiscamingue.

The Abwees sat sadly leaning on the after-rail, and agreed that Jimmie was "a lovely Injun." Jimmie had gone into the shade of the overhang of the cliffs, when the Norseman started violently up, put his hands in his pockets, stamped his foot, said, "By George, fellows, any D.F. would call this a sporting trip!"

Lion-Hunting

[ALFRED H. MILES]

All hunted animals are wild. The popular belief is that they are hunted because they are wild, the truth is, they are wild because they are hunted.

Men and women would become wild under similar circumstances.

The same causes which stir up strife among men make animals fight, and these are, hunger, jealousy and danger, the struggle for existence, and the care of the dependent.

The lion does not appear to have any particular antipathy to man, and at close quarters often shows him a generosity but rarely reciprocated. Why men should take pleasure in killing such an animal for the mere sake of killing him, it is difficult to understand. It is popularly put down to a love of "sport," surely it is more often the result of vanity or the love of self.

Sir William Jardine tells a story of a Dutchman named Diederik Muller who encountered a lion at close quarters. The man fired and missed. The lion faced him, and on his proceeding to reload, approached him. The man then lowered his gun, and the lion turned to make off. On looking round the lion saw that the man was again proceeding to reload, whereupon he again turned and made towards him. The man again dropped his gun, and the lion once more made off. This occurred several times, until the lion finally made good his escape. From this it would seem that the lion had some idea of the use of the gun, but had no desire to injure the man, and though not in any way afraid of his enemy, was too wise to face a union of forces which he knew he could not withstand.

This was not weak cowardice, but generous prudence.

That lions are capable of great affection for those who show them kindness is well known, and there is nothing more beautiful in living phenomena than the union of love and strength.

Notwithstanding what is alleged by some lion-tamers as to the necessity of governing their charges by fear, it cannot be admitted that fear is capable of accomplishing half so much as kindness in establishing safe relations between man and beast. The lion-tamer has to compel his animals to go through certain performances night after night, performances quite foreign to their nature, and often when the animal is more or less out of sorts. He can only do this by conquering the will of the animal. This involves him in constant danger, especially when unusual causes make the animals very irritable.

If the public were content to see the lion as he might be, in affectionate frolic with his keeper in the same kind of play that is so entertaining in a kitten—which is only a small member of his family—it might be delighted and edified by the spectacle of what love can do to tame the savage instinct born of long ages of the struggle for existence, but which need not survive the necessity for that struggle. But the public will pay a penny more if the lion roars, so the lion must be prodded until he does, in order that he may earn the extra penny.

Men and women would show the same resentment if they were continually stimulated by pin pricks to dance for the delight of animals.

The *Youth's Companion* of America gives an interesting account of an interview with the late Rosa Bonheur and her pet lion, which shows the way in which the lion will repay kindness with affection.

"After the 'Horse Fair' (says that journal) there is perhaps no picture of Rosa Bonheur's more often reproduced and more popular with the public than that called 'An Old Monarch'—the head of a superb lion, which gazes from the canvas with a look of dignity, tranquillity, and power, that impresses alike the critic and the child. No one can look at it without believing that the artist understood the nature, no less than the form and colour, of her noble model.

"Indeed, Mlle. Bonheur was fond of lions. She owned many at different times which she kept in easy captivity at her beautiful country estate of By, consoled for imprisonment by her own affection and the society—at a respectful distance—of enough other animals, wild and tame, to people a fair-sized forest.

"Cats, dogs, sheep, deer, goats, bulls, ponies, horses, monkeys, leopards and panthers have been at different times, and sometimes simultaneously, dwellers in the chateau and park of By, subjects of the quiet little lady with bright eyes and odd masculine dress—half-cavalier, half-peasant, which she has found most convenient for her work—who ruled over them gently and fearlessly.

"A journalist who once visited By found her the proud possessor of a new lion from Africa, which had already become so attached to her that she petted the great creature as if it were an ordinary cat, while it writhed its tawny body and stretched itself luxuriously under her hand, purring a tremendous purr as she rubbed and fondled its enormous head; but even while caressing her new pet, Mlle. Bonheur regretfully related the career of the first lion she ever owned.

"He was named Nero, and had the reputation of being untamably ferocious when she bought him; but after being comfortably established in a suitable residence in her garden, he soon learned to know and love his mistress. She kept him there several years. Then, because she was about to travel, she sold him to the Jardin des Plantes (the Paris 'Zoo'), supposing he would be better cared for there than anywhere else. Unfortunately, she was mistaken. Returning two years later from her wanderings, she went to see him, and found that through accident or carelessness in his treatment his eyes had become inflamed, then entirely sightless.

"He was lying in his cage when she arrived, heedless of the staring and chatting crowd about it, quite blind and ailing. She looked at him a moment, then called: "Nero!" Instantly he rose to his feet, uttered the peculiar note of welcome which he reserved only for her (as household cats often do for their friends), and sprang towards the remembered voice so impetuously that he dashed himself against the bars of his cage and rolled over backward, half-stunned, upon its floor.

"She went to the authorities of the Jardin des Plantes at once and bought her old pet back from them, took him home with her to By, and kept and tended him until his death. He died in the chateau itself, at the foot of the great staircase, clinging piteously to her with his huge paws at the last, as if entreating not to be forsaken. And she was so sure of his devotion that she dared hold and caress him, even in his death struggle. She was not mistaken in her confidence, for Nero's last movement was a faint and feeble attempt to lick her hands."

"You see," said Rosa Bonheur to her visitor as she ended the story, thoughtfully ruffling the mane of her new lion as she spoke, "to be really beloved by wild beasts, you must really love them."

An old lion story, which in the light of Rosa Bonheur's experience need not be doubted, is told in the history of the Crusades, when it is related that Geoffrey de la Tour, one of the knights who went upon the first Crusade to the Holy Land, as he rode through a forest suddenly heard a cry of distress. Hoping to rescue some unfortunate sufferer, he rode boldly into the thicket; but what was his astonishment when he beheld a lion with a large serpent coiled round his body? To relieve the distressed was the duty of every true knight. With a single stroke of his sword he killed the serpent, and extricated the lion from his perilous situation.

From that hour the thankful animals constantly accompanied his deliverer, whom he followed like a dog, and never displayed his natural ferocity but at his command. At length the Crusade terminated, and the knight prepared to sail for Europe. He had wished to take his faithful lion with him; but the master of the vessel in which he sailed would not admit him on board, and he was obliged to leave him on shore.

The lion, when separated from his beloved master, first began to roar hideously; and, seeing the ship diverging from him, plunged into the waves and endeavoured to swim after it. But all his efforts were in vain. At length, his strength exhausted, he sank; and the ocean engulfed a generous animal whose fidelity had well deserved a better fate.

More adventurous, but surely not so interesting, are the stories of lion-hunting told by Mr. Selous, Captain Melliss, and others, who, veritable Nimrods, seem to love hunting for the sake of hunting, and who appear to calculate "sport" arithmetically.

Among the many African adventures described by Mr. Selous is one which may be quoted from *Animal Life* of a night passed in a temporary hut built by his Kaffirs as a shelter from which to shoot lions, which were baited by the carcass of an ox placed ten paces away. Soon after dark, footsteps were heard outside on the dry leaves, and then some dark object loomed upon beyond the carcass of the ox. It might be a hyena, especially as it held its head up. But it passed the ox and came near the hut. From its boldness it ought to be a lion. At that instant two more vague forms appeared, and the one first seen came still nearer, and presently was within three yards of Mr. Selous's rifle.

Mr. Selous fired, and the report, loud as it was in the silence of the night, was at once "dwarfed and drowned by the terrific roaring grunts of the wounded lion." A few moments more, and a gurgling noise assured the hunter that the beast was at the point of death.

Even while this was passing, and almost before Mr. Selous had got another cartridge into his rifle, a second lion came up and he fired again. The roar that followed could have been heard a mile away. It was followed by moans, and then by stillness. The second lion was dead.

Mr. Selous whispered to his companion that the sport was probably over for that night, but the words were hardly out of his mouth before they heard some animal breathing within a few feet of them. The next instant the hut was shaken, and one of the loose branches of its outer covering was torn off.

Another lion was there, and was trying to get in! It tore off one bough after another, and soon came to the place at which the men had entered. That was now blocked with poles. There the lion stopped, and from the noises—it was too dark to see anything—it was plain that he was trying to get his paw through.

Finding it impossible to see the beast, and fearing that he would topple the whole structure over upon their heads, Mr. Selous pushed his rifle between the poles in the direction of the sounds, and fired at a venture. This report, like the others, was answered by the most terrific "grunting roars," followed by moans.

"Three lions in about five minutes," one of the men said to the other. That was pretty good luck.

There were two more of the beasts, but it was not likely that they would venture near the hut, so the men lay down. Before midnight they several times heard some animal sniffing round the back of the hut; but it never came in front of the shooting holes, nor did it touch the poles, thought sometimes the sniffings were very loud and came right up to the hut.

Before very long it was plain that the remaining two lions were still present—"less than ten yards from the muzzles of the rifles"—though absolutely nothing could be seen. For hours they lay devouring the carcass of the ox, crunching the bones, and now and then snarling at each other.

One curious feature of the case is mentioned by Mr. Selous.

"It would be supposed," he says, "that to lie thus in the wilds of Africa within ten yards of a couple of lions feeding noisily, and sometimes snarling loudly, would be enough to keep one awake; yet to show how 'familiarity breeds contempt' I may mention that twice I had to wake my young companion, and tell him not to snore, as the noise might disturb the lions."

The upshot of the matter was that the two lions went away before the first ray of light, and at daybreak the two men found two lions lying dead not far from the hut. The third one they could not find, although they had no doubt it lay dead in the thick bush and grass within a few hundred yards.

"Three lions in about five minutes," as the man said, and yet it took as many *ages* to produce them.

Lion-hunting was a very different thing before the introduction of firearms gave the human side of the argument the greater weight. It may be a very courageous thing for the modern traveller armed with the best appliances and accompanied by servants carrying an unlimited supply to face an animal having no means of defence but those which nature gave him; but what must it have been to our ancestors, who were not only without such advantageous aids, but who had to fight an animal of even larger size and powers.

Some years ago there were discovered in a cave on the French side of the Pyrenees—the cave of Herm—some remains of prehistoric man, such as arrowheads and other implements made of flint, mingled with the bones of animals which, like the men of those ancient days, have disappeared. Among these remains is the jaw of the celebrated cave-lion, an animal which must have been a most formidable enemy to his human contemporaries.

The study of this jaw has thrown some new light upon the characteristics of the cave-lion, indicating that it was intermediate in its bodily structure between the lion and the tiger. The imagination is strangely moved by the suggestion as to the kind of life that was led by the early representatives of our race upon the earth, forced to battle, even for the possession of the caves in which they dwelt, with fierce and powerful beasts, and that, too, at a time when only the rudest weapons had been invented, and when bodily strength and agility must have been their main dependence in such contests.

Lion-hunting is, however, still dangerous enough, even when the hunter's health and strength are of the best. But an inveterate sportsman does not count cost, and the author of "Sport in East Central Africa" gives an account of a foolhardy adventure which he seems to have enjoyed. He was ill with fever in a little settlement of blacks, but since lions were in the neighbourhood he must needs insist upon having the carcass of a boar placed as bait not far from his hut; and although his legs were too weak to allow him to walk a dozen steps, he had himself propped against the door-jamb, and laid his double-barrelled rifle across his knees.

It was nearly one o'clock, he says, when the lions gave notice of their whereabouts. I heard the heavy grunting sighs of three or four of them as they moved about in the scrub two hundred yards away. Then followed a series of rushes, as they leaped down the bank of the creek and lapped noisily at the water. Next came a terrified voice from a neighbouring hut.

"White man, we are going," it said, and the "boys" rushed pell-mell from their shelter, some passing in front of me, others behind me, making for a grove of trees.

Scarcely had the first of them got well outside the huts, before it seemed as if a lion were right amongst them, as, with deep, savage grunts, it dashed past my hut, bounding through the scrub in close pursuit.

Suddenly a yell rang out from the darkness, and I was convinced that one of my blacks was being devoured; but I was too weak to stand, and was powerless to act.

After some further noise and confusion, I heard a lion treading over the dead leaves near by. Then came a prolonged muffled sound, half-roar, half-moan, uttered in a deep voice, which even under the circumstances I recognised as profoundly musical. Then there was a heavy but silent footfall as the beast walked to the back of my hut, and thrusting his nose amongst the thatched grass, sniffed loudly till I could see the lighter stalks stirring with his breath and hear the rustling when he endeavoured to insert a paw between the interstices of the wattles.

Each instant I expected the whole structure to collapse, but luckily the beast forbore to take a mean advantage, which would have secured my destruction. I should have fired, had I not been afraid of setting fire to the hut.

At length the brutes cleared out, uttering deep growls. They had destroyed one hut and pretty much ruined two more, not to speak of smashing the hut next mine, which contained all my stores. I could hear them there, making a terrific noise, snuffing, grunting and snarling, breaking sticks and clanking metal, while every now and then one would leap down the bank into the water and then come tearing back, breathing heavily and growling low. Yet not a whisker hair did one of them show in the firelight in front of me.

The excitement did me good. The next morning I was up and about in pyjamas and an ulster. Not one of the boys had been injured, although one had had a marvellous escape. The lions were close upon him as he reached a tree. He sprang at a branch, and in his terror seized the leg of another black who had clambered up before him. Fearing lest he, too, should fall into the lion's maw, the other fellow kicked his leg clear, so that the unfortunate fugitive fell to the ground, uttering the yell I had heard.

Why the nearest lion did not seize him, I cannot say. The boy explained that it merely growled as he scrambled to his feet and climbed up another tree as fast as his black legs could shin.

Captain Melliss, who met with great success as a lion-hunter, had gone on "a shooting trip" into the interior of Somaliland, in East Africa. At Berbera he procured ten camels, two donkeys, and twelve Somalis, and with this caravan set forth in pursuit of lions. After a march of some days, news reached him one afternoon that two lions had been seen that morning out on the plain. His pony was saddled, and with three Somalis he set out at a brisk pace. Away and away they rode, till the speed and the heat began to tell on the pony. At last the wild-eyed Somali who had brought word to the camp pointed to a clump of bushes defined against the horizon some miles in advance. Onward the party rode, the bushes grew more and more distinct, and at last the Somali cried, "There are the lions," just as Captain Melliss caught sight of two yellow animals lying outside the bushes.

"Here," says the captain, "I had two lions, actually waiting for me, all to myself, a vast plain on all sides, clear of jungle as a lawn, not another bush in sight. I was going to get them or they to get me. Could the situation have been more perfect?"

The afternoon was wearing away, and he was in a hurry to begin, though he regretted afterwards that he had not sat down awhile and tasted the full rapture of the moment. He rode within a hundred yards of the bush, pulled up, gave orders to his men how to proceed, and then dismounted, with Jama, one of his assistants, who was to walk behind him carrying a second gun.

The lions let the two men come within a hundred yards. Then they rose—"huge, yellow brutes"—and retired through the bush to the other side. The men circled the bush, and presently the captain came upon one of them—"a magnificent lion"—lying down not fifty yards away, and facing the hunter.

"I sat down promptly, and fired at his shoulder," the captain says. "As the bullet struck him he leaped into the air, and then stood uttering savage coughing roars. The majesty of the grand brute I shall never forget, as he stood there with his great jaws open, breathing out his wrath. There was a grand, furious indignant air about him that made one feel rather small, as being an unprovoked aggressor. His roars were nothing very tremendous, but his open hanging jaws were most impressive."

The lion was disabled, it was plain. Captain Melliss fired again, but missed, and the beast attempted to charge, but fell forward, and was killed by two shots from the second gun.

Then the hunter ran to his pony, and galloped off after the other lion, which two of his men had been instructed to watch. Yes, there he was, facing the two horsemen. Captain Melliss rode up, dismounted, though the lion "looked in an exceedingly nasty temper" and welcomed the intruder with a show of teeth and much snarling.

At a distance of fifty yards the hunter sat down, fired between the lion's eyes, and then jumped to his feet.

"I was not a bit too soon," he says. "At the shot the lion sprang up with a furious roar. I had a lightning glimpse of him rearing on his hind legs pawing the air. Then he came for me. It was a fierce rush across the ground, no springing that I could see.

"How close he got before I fired I cannot say; but it was very near. I let him come on, aiming the muzzles of the rifle at his chest. Jama says he was about to spring when I pulled the trigger and ran back a pace or two to one side, but as I did so I saw through the smoke that the lion was stopped within a few paces of me.

"The second gun and Jama were not as near as they might have been. The lion struggled up on his hind quarters, uttering roars. I rammed two cartridges into my rifle, and fired again, and the grand brute fell over dying."

The Englishman was in a great state of jubilee as he rode back to the camp, and the Somalis were very merry. One of them broke into an impromptu song, full of compliments for the mighty hunter. The next day people poured into camp from all directions, all anxious to see the lions' heads. One of the beasts was reported to have killed several persons.

"It was a great day for Captain Melliss when he shot five lions in one afternoon, or rather in one half-hour. This was in Somaliland. He had been out for the forenoon, and both he and his pony were pretty well fatigued; but when some one brought word of several lions out on the plain, about eight miles away, there was no resisting the temptation. Off he went with two Somalis, and at last, when his pony had "no more canter in him," they came in sight of some horsemen who had

been keeping watch of the game until the Englishman should arrive.

Captain Melliss jumped to the ground, handed his
pony to one of his men, crammed his pockets with
cartridges, and ran toward a pair of lionesses which
were walking calming through the grass. Meanwhile
he was in a fever of excitement, for the nearer Somalis were shouting, "Five lions! Five lions!" In the
hunter's own words, it was a "dream of bliss."

Not to make too long a story, he shot both the
lionesses, and then another, though his arm was very
unsteady from his exhausting ride, and in a minute
more galloped after the fourth—a "yellow beauty."
She was making for a distant line of jungle, but he
cut her off.

"Suddenly," he says, "she stopped, swung round,
and looked at me. I pulled up too, and the next
moment she was charging straight for me. I thought
I was caught, for my pony was dead beat; but he, too,
saw the danger, and with equal suddenness he turned
tail, and we made a flying retreat."

The lioness did not long pursue, but lay down in
the grass. The Englishman waiting till one of the
Somalis came up; then he dismounted and proceeded to load, while the lioness "made it unpleasant" for him by a continuous angry growling, as if
she were coming on at every moment.

"At last I was loaded, and having walked forward a
little way, sat down and fired at her chest. At the shot,

a very shaky one, which only wounded her inside the forearm, she sprang up and charged.

"I jumped to my feet and aimed at her chest, but, good heavens, how my arm shook! To and fro swayed the muzzle of the rifle, now on her, now very much off her, and for the life of me I could not steady myself. My second gun was nowhere, and my right barrel empty. It looked bad for me, I thought, and I must hang on to my only shot until she was almost on me.

"How long that wait of a second or two seemed, while the lioness charged over the forty paces of level ground between us I very well remember. More than once my finger pressed more heavily on the trigger, but I held on, fortunately, as I believe.

"On and on she comes, and still my aim wavers. Now she is within eight or ten paces, and in another instant I must fire, when, to my great surprise and relief, she stops short right before me, and glances to her left.

"I look at her in astonishment, see her right shoulder exposed, change my aim instantly and fire. The thinning smoke reveals her stretched on her side."

The New York *Sun* prints an amusing tale which is not impossible, but the reader may receive it with as many ounces of allowance as he thinks necessary. It is connected with the wreck of a circus train in a rather wild Southern country. Many of the cages of the menagerie were broken, it appears, and their occupants had full opportunity to escape to the woods and fields. While all hands were waiting the arrival of a wrecking-train, an old coloured man, with a business look about him, approached the circus manager.

"Boss," he said, "do I get antying' if I cotch de giraffee what got away last night?"

"No giraffee got away," was the reply.

"Wal, I cotched something' over on my place dat must ha' got away from somebody. My ole woman done say it's a giraffee, but mebbe it's a elephant."

"Our elephants are all here, but one of the camels is gone."

"Maybe it's a camel. I nebber seed no camel. He ain't got no wings nor nuffin'."

"Does it look like a horse or a cow?"

"No, sah. My boy Henry says it's a 'nosceros, but I'se a little suspicious dat it hain't."

"We have no rhinoceros, but it may be our sacred bull from India."

"Does yo' sacred bull growl like a dawg an' show his teef?"

"No."

"Does he walk roun' a nigger's cabin, an' take a dawg by de neck and shake de life outen him, an' roar an' roar?"

"No. It must be one of our lions! You don't mean to say you have captured a lion?"

"Can't say, boss. It's somethin' dat growls an' roars an' switches his tail. Him didn't wanter come along, but I just tied a rope roun' his neck an' made him. He's tied up to dat tree ober dere, an' I reckon yo' oughter gimme 'bout two bits for my trouble."

The circus hands went up the road with the old man, and about a quarter of a mile away, tied to a persimmon-tree and looking much disgusted, was the biggest lion of the menagerie.

"Dunno if it's an elephant or a 'nosceros or a giraffee," said the coloured man, as he went up and began loosening the rope, "but yere he am, an' sein' as he killed my dawg, an' sein' as I had ter drag him all de way ober, mebbe you'll make it fo' bits."

"Man alive!" gasped the manager, as he handed the negro a silver coin. "Didn't you know this was a lion?"

"No. Nebber done knowed what he was. Jest got a rope an' made him come along; an' when he growled an' roared I hammered him wid dis stick. Much obleeged, sah."

The Forcing of the Trap

[ANTHONY HOPE]

The night came fine and clear. I had prayed for dirty weather, such as had favoured my previous voyage in the moat, but Fortune was this time against me. Still I reckoned that by keeping close under the wall and in the shadow I could escape detection from the windows of the chateau that looked out on the scene of my efforts. If they searched the moat, indeed, my scheme must fail; but I did not think they would. They had made "Jacob's Ladder" secure against attack. Johann had himself helped to fix it closely to the masonry on the under side, so that it could not now be moved from below any more than from above. An assault with explosives or a long battering with picks alone could displace it, and the noise involved in either of these operations put them out of the question. What harm, then, could a man do in the moat? I trusted that Black Michael, putting this query to himself, would answer confidently, "None;" while, even if Johann meant treachery, he did not know my scheme, and would doubtless expect to see me, at the head of my friends, before the front entrance to the chateau. "There," I said to Sapt, was the real danger. "And there," I added, "you shall be. Doesn't that content you?"

But it did not. Dearly would he have liked to come with me, had I not utterly refused to take him. One man might escape notice, to double the party more than doubled the risk; and when he ventured to hint once again that my life was too valuable, I, knowing the secret thought he clung to, sternly bade him be silent, assuring him that unless the King lived through the night, I would not live through it either.

At twelve o'clock, Sapt's command left the chateau of Tarlenheim and struck off to the right, riding by unfrequented roads, and avoiding the town of Zenda. If all went well, they would be in front of the Castle by about a quarter to two. Leaving their horses half a mile off, they were to steal up to the entrance and hold themselves in readiness for the opening of the door. If the door were not opened by two, they were to send Fritz von Tarlenheim round to the other side of the Castle. I would meet him there if I were alive, and we would consult whether to storm the Castle or not. If I were not there, they were to return with all speed to Tarlenheim, rouse the Marshal, and march in force to Zenda. For if not there, I should be dead; and

I knew that the King would not be alive five minutes after I ceased to breathe. I must now leave Sapt and his friends, and relate how I myself proceeded on this eventful night. I went out on the good horse which had carried me, on the night of the coronation, back from the hunting lodge to Strelsau. I carried a revolver in the saddle and my sword. I was covered with a large cloak, and under this I wore a warm, tight-fitting woollen jersey, a pair of knickerbockers, thick stockings, and light canvas shoes. I had rubbed myself thoroughly with oil, and I carried a large flask of whisky. The night was warm, but I might probably be immersed a long while, and it was necessary to take every precaution against cold: for cold not only saps a man's courage if he has to die, but impairs his energy if others have to die, and, finally, gives him rheumatics, if it be God's will that he lives. Also I tied round my body a length of thin but stout cord, and I did not forget my ladder. I, starting after Sapt, took a shorter route, skirting the town to the left, and found myself in the outskirts of the forest at about half-past twelve. I tied my horse up in a thick clump of trees, leaving the revolver in its pocket in the saddle—it would be no use to me—and, ladder in hand, made my way to the edge of the moat. Here I unwound my rope from about my waist, bound it securely round the trunk of a tree on the bank, and let myself down. The Castle clock struck a quarter to one as I felt the water under me and began to swim round the keep, pushing the ladder before me, and hugging the Castle wall. Thus voyaging, I came to my old friend, "Jacob's Ladder," and felt the ledge of the masonry under me. I crouched down in the shadow of the great pipe—I tried to stir it, but it was quite immovable—and waited. I remember that my predominant feeling was neither anxiety for the king nor longing for Flavia, but an intense desire to smoke; and this craving, of course, I could not gratify.

The drawbridge was still in its place. I saw its airy, slight framework above me, some ten yards to my right, as I crouched with my back against the wall of the King's cell. I made out a window two yards my side of it and nearly on the same level. That, if Johann spoke true, must belong to the duke's apartments; and on the other side, in about the same relative position, must be Madame de Mauban's window. Women are careless, forgetful creatures. I prayed that she might not forget that she was to be the victim of a brutal attempt at two o'clock precisely. I was rather amused at the part I had assigned to my young friend Rupert Hentzau; but I owed him a stroke—for, even as I sat, my shoulder ached where he had, with an audacity that seemed half to hide his treachery, struck at me, in the sight of all my friends, on the terrace at Tarlenheim.

Suddenly the duke's window grew bright. The shutters were not closed, and the interior became partially visible to me as I cautiously raised myself till I stood on tiptoe. Thus placed, my range of sight embraced a yard or more inside the window, while the radius of light did not reach me. The window was flung open and someone looked out. I marked Antoinette de Mauban's graceful figure, and, though her face was in shadow, the fine outline of her head was revealed against the light behind. I longed to cry softly, "Remember!" but I dared not—and happily, for a moment later a man came up and stood by her. He tried to put his arm round her waist, but with a swift motion she sprang away and leant against the shutter, her profile towards me. I made out who the newcomer was: it was young Rupert. A low laugh from him made me sure, as he leant forward, stretching out his hand towards her.

"Gently, gently!" I murmured. "You're too soon, my boy!"

His head was close to hers. I suppose he whispered to her, for I saw her point to the moat, and I heard her say, in slow and distinct tones:

"I had rather throw myself out of this window!"

He came close up to the window and looked out.

"It looks cold," said he. "Come, Antoinette, are you serious?"

She made no answer so far as I heard; and he smiting his hand petulantly on the window-sill, went on, in the voice of some spoilt child:

"Hang Black Michael! Isn't the princess enough for him? Is he to have everything? What the devil do you see in Black Michael?"

"If I told him what you say—" she began.

"Well, tell him," said Rupert, carelessly; and, catching her off her guard, he sprang forward and kissed her, laughing, and crying, "There's something to tell him!"

If I had kept my revolver with me, I should have been very sorely tempted. Being spared the temptation, I merely added this new score to his account.

"Though, faith," said Rupert, "it's little he cares. He's mad about the princess, you know. He talks of nothing but cutting the play-actor's throat."

Didn't he, indeed?

"And if I do it for him, what do you think he's promised me?"

The unhappy woman raised her hands above her head, in prayer or in despair.

"But I detest waiting," said Rupert; and I saw that he was about to lay his hand on her again, when there was a noise of a door in the room opening, and a harsh voice cried:

"What are you doing here, sir?"

Rupert turned his back to the window, bowed low, and said, in his loud, merry tones: "Apologizing for your absence, sir. Could I leave the lady alone?"

The newcomer must be Black Michael. I saw him directly, as he advanced towards the window. He caught young Rupert by the arm.

"The moat would hold more than the King!" said he, with a significant gesture.

"Does your Highness threaten me?" asked Rupert.

"A threat is more warning than most men get from me."

"Yet," observed Rupert, "Rudolf Rassendyll has been much threatened, and yet lives!"

"Am I in fault because my servants bungle?" asked Michael scornfully.

"Your Highness has run no risk of bungling!" sneered Rupert.

It was telling the duke that he shirked danger as plain as ever I have heard a man told. Black Michael had self-control. I dare say he scowled—it was a great regret to me that I could not see their faces better— but his voice was even and calm, as he answered:

"Enough, enough! We mustn't quarrel, Rupert. Are Detchard and Bersonin at their posts?"

"They are, sir."

"I need you no more."

"Nay, I'm not oppressed with fatigue," said Rupert.

"Pray, sir, leave us," said Michael, more impatiently. "In ten minutes the drawbridge will be drawn back, and I presume you have no wish to swim to your bed."

Rupert's figure disappeared. I heard the door open and shut again. Michael and Antoinette de Mauban were left together. To my chagrin, the duke laid his hand on the window and closed it. He stood talking to Antoinette for a moment or two.

She shook her head, and he turned impatiently away. She left the window. The door sounded again, and Black Michael closed the shutters.

"De Gautet, De Gautet, man!" sounded from the drawbridge. "Unless you want a bath before your bed, come along!"

It was Rupert's voice, coming from the end of the drawbridge. A moment later he and De Gautet stepped out on the bridge. Rupert's arm was through De Gautet's, and in the middle of the bridge he detained his companion and leant over. I dropped behind the shelter of "Jacob's Ladder."

Then Master Rupert had a little sport. He took from De Gautet a bottle which he carried, and put it to his lips.

"Hardly a drop!" he cried discontentedly, and flung it in the moat.

It fell, as I judged from the sound and the circles on the water, within a yard of the pipe. And Rupert, taking out his revolver, began to shoot at it. The first two shots missed the bottle, but hit the pipe. The third shattered the bottle. I hoped that the young ruffian would be content; but he emptied the other barrels at the pipe, and one, skimming over the pipe, whistled through my hair as I crouched on the other side.

"Ware bridge!" a voice cried, to my relief.

Rupert and De Gautet cried, "A moment!" and ran across. The bridge was drawn back, and all became still. The clock struck a quarter-past one. I rose and stretched myself and yawned.

I think some ten minutes had passed when I heard a slight noise to my right. I peered over the pipe, and saw a dark figure standing in the gateway that led to the bridge. It was a man. By the careless, graceful poise, I guessed it to be Rupert again. He held a sword in his hand, and he stood motionless for a minute or two. Wild thoughts ran through me. On what mischief was the young fiend bent now? Then he laughed low to himself; then he turned his face to the wall, took a step in my direction, and, to my surprise, began to climb down the wall. In an instant I saw that there must be steps in the wall; it was plain. They were cut into or affixed to the wall, at intervals of about eighteen inches. Rupert set his foot on the lower one. Then he placed his sword between his teeth, turned round, and noiselessly let himself into the water. Had it been a matter of my life only, I would have swum to meet him. Dearly would I have loved to fight it out with him then and there—with steel, on a fine night, and none to come between us. But there was the King! I restrained myself, but I could not bridle my swift breathing, and I watched him with the intensest eagerness.

He swam leisurely and quietly across. There were more steps up on the other side, and he climbed them. When he set foot in the gateway, standing on the drawn-back bridge, he felt in his pocket and took something out. I heard him unlock the door. I could hear no noise of its closing behind him. He vanished from my sight.

Abandoning my ladder—I saw I did not need it now—I swam to the side of the bridge and climbed half way up the steps. There I hung with my sword in my hand, listening eagerly. The duke's room was shuttered and dark. There was a light in the window on the opposite side of the bridge. Not a sound broke the silence, till half-past one chimed from the great clock in the tower of the chateau.

There were other plots than mine afoot in the Castle that night.

The position wherein I stood does not appear very favourable to thought; yet for the next moment or two I thought profoundly. I had, I told myself, scored one point. Be Rupert Hentzau's errand what it might, and the villainy he was engaged on what it would, I had scored one point. He was on the other side of the moat from the King, and it would be by no fault of mine if ever he set foot on the same side again. I had three left to deal with: two on guard and De Gautet in his bed. Ah, if I had the keys! I would have risked everything and attacked Detchard and Bersonin before their friends could join them. But I was powerless. I must wait till the coming of my friends enticed someone to cross the bridge— someone with the keys. And I waited, as it seemed, for half an hour, really for about five minutes, before the next act in the rapid drama began.

All was still on the other side. The duke's room remained inscrutable behind its shutters. The light burnt steadily in Madame de Mauban's window. Then I heard the faintest, faintest sound: it came from behind the door which led to the drawbridge on the other side of the moat. It but just reached my ear, yet I could not be mistaken as to what it was. It was made by a key being turned very carefully and slowly. Who was turning it? And of what room was it the key? There leapt before my eyes the picture of young Rupert, with the key in one hand, his sword in the other, and an evil smile on his face. But I did not know what door it was, nor on which of his favourite pursuits young Rupert was spending the hours of that night.

I was soon to be enlightened, for the next moment—before my friends could be near the chateau door—before Johann the keeper would have thought to nerve himself for his task—there was a sudden crash from the room with the lighted window. It sounded as though someone had flung down a lamp; and the window went dark and black. At the same instant a cry rang out, shrill in the night: "Help, help! Michael, help!" and was followed by a shriek of utter terror.

I was tingling in every nerve. I stood on the topmost step, clinging to the threshold of the gate with my right hand and holding my sword in my left. Suddenly I perceived that the gateway was broader than the bridge; there was a dark corner on the opposite side where a man could stand. I darted across and stood there. Thus placed, I commanded the path, and no man could pass between the chateau and the old Castle till he had tried conclusions with me.

There was another shriek. Then a door was flung open and clanged against the wall, and I heard the handle of a door savagely twisted.

"Open the door! In God's name, what's the matter?" cried a voice—the voice of Black Michael himself.

He was answered by the very words I had written in my letter.

"Help, Michael—Hentzau!"

A fierce oath rang out from the duke, and with a loud thud he threw himself against the door. At the same moment I heard a window above my head open, and a voice cried: "What's the matter?" and I heard a man's hasty footsteps. I grasped my sword. If De Gautet came my way, the Six would be less by one more.

Then I heard the clash of crossed swords and a tramp of feet and—I cannot tell the thing so quickly as it happened, for all seemed to come at once. There was an angry cry from madame's room, the cry of a wounded man; the window was flung open; young

Rupert stood there sword in hand. He turned his back, and I saw his body go forward to the lunge.

"Ah, Johann, there's one for you! Come on, Michael!"

Johann was there, then—come to the rescue of the duke! How would he open the door for me? For I feared that Rupert had slain him.

"Help!" cried the duke's voice, faint and husky.

I heard a step on the stairs above me; and I heard a stir down to my left, in the direction of the King's cell. But, before anything happened on my side of the moat, I saw five or six men round young Rupert in the embrasure of madame's window. Three or four times he lunged with incomparable dash and dexterity. For an instant they fell back, leaving a ring round him. He leapt on the parapet of the window, laughing as he leapt, and waving his sword in his hand. He was drunk with blood, and he laughed again wildly as he flung himself headlong into the moat.

What became of him then? I did not see: for as he leapt, De Gautet's lean face looked out through the door by me, and, without a second's hesitation, I struck at him with all the strength God had given me, and he fell dead in the doorway without a word or a groan. I dropped on my knees by him. Where were the keys? I found myself muttering: "The keys, man, the keys?" as though he had been yet alive and could listen; and when I could not find them, I—God forgive me!—I believe I struck a dead man's face.

At last I had them. There were but three. Seizing the largest, I felt the lock of the door that led to the cell. I fitted in the key. It was right. The lock turned. I drew the door close behind me and locked it as noiselessly as I could, putting the key in my pocket.

I found myself at the top of a flight of steep stone stairs. An oil lamp burnt dimly in the bracket. I took it down and held it in my hand; and I stood and listened.

"What in the devil can it be?" I heard a voice say.

It came from behind a door that faced me at the bottom of the stairs.

And another answered:

"Shall we kill him?"

I strained to hear the answer, and could have sobbed with relief when Detchard's voice came grating and cold:

"Wait a bit. There'll be trouble if we strike too soon."

There was a moment's silence. Then I heard the bolt of the door cautiously drawn back. Instantly I put out the light I held, replacing the lamp in the bracket.

"It's dark—the lamp's out. Have you a light?" said the other voice—Bersonin's.

No doubt they had a light, but they should not use it. It was come to the crisis now, and I rushed down the steps and flung myself against the door. Bersonin had unbolted it and it gave way before me. The Belgian stood there sword in hand, and Detchard was

sitting on a couch at the side of the room. In astonishment at seeing me, Bersonin recoiled; Detchard
jumped to his sword. I rushed madly at the Belgian:
he gave way before me, and I drove him up against
the wall. He was no swordsman, though he fought
bravely, and in a moment he lay on the floor before
me. I turned—Detchard was not there. Faithful to
his orders, he had not risked a fight with me, but had
rushed straight to the door of the King's room,
opened it and slammed it behind him. Even now he
was at his work inside.

And surely he would have killed the King, and
perhaps me also, had it not been for one devoted
man who gave his life for the King. For when I
forced the door, the sight I saw was this: the King
stood in the corner of the room: broken by his sickness, he could do nothing; his fettered hands moved
uselessly up and down, and he was laughing horribly
in half-mad delirium. Detchard and the doctor were
together in the middle of the room; and the doctor
had flung himself on the murderer, pinning his
hands to his sides for an instant. Then Detchard
wrenched himself free from the feeble grip, and, as I
entered, drove his sword through the hapless man.
Then he turned on me, crying:

"At last!"

We were sword to sword. By blessed chance, neither he nor Bersonin had been wearing their
revolvers. I found them afterwards, ready loaded, on

the mantelpiece of the outer room: it was hard by the door, ready to their hands, but my sudden rush in had cut off access to them. Yes, we were man to man: and we began to fight, silently, sternly, and hard. Yet I remember little of it, save that the man was my match with the sword—nay, and more, for he knew more tricks than I; and that he forced me back against the bars that guarded the entrance to "Jacob's Ladder." And I saw a smile on his face, and he wounded me in the left arm.

No glory do I take for that contest. I believe that the man would have mastered me and slain me, and then done his butcher's work, for he was the most skilful swordsman I have ever met; but even as he pressed me hard, the half-mad, wasted, wan creature in the corner leapt high in lunatic mirth, shrieking:

"It's cousin Rudolf! Cousin Rudolf! I'll help you, cousin Rudolf!" and catching up a chair in his hands (he could but just lift it from the ground and hold it uselessly before him) he came towards us. Hope came to me. "Come on!" I cried. "Come on! Drive it against his legs."

Detchard replied with a savage thrust. He all but had me.

"Come on! Come on, man!" I cried. "Come and share the fun!"

And the King laughed gleefully, and came on, pushing his chair before him. With an oath Detchard skipped back, and, before I knew what he was doing, had turned his sword against the King. He made one fierce cut at the King, and the King, with a piteous cry, dropped where he stood. The stout ruffian turned to face me again. But his own hand had prepared his destruction: for in turning he trod in the pool of blood that flowed from the dead physician. He slipped; he fell. Like a dart I was upon him. I caught him by the throat, and before he could recover himself I drove my point through his neck, and with a stifled curse he fell across the body of his victim.

Was the King dead? It was my first thought. I rushed to where he lay. Ay, it seemed as if he were dead, for he had a great gash across his forehead, and he lay still in a huddled heap on the floor. I dropped on my knees beside him, and leant my ear down to hear if he breathed. But before I could there was a loud rattle from the outside. I knew the sound: the drawbridge was being pushed out. A moment later it rang home against the wall on my side of the moat. I should be caught in a trap and the King with me, if he yet lived. He must take his chance, to live or die. I took my sword, and passed into the outer room. Who were pushing the drawbridge out—my men? If so, all was well. My eye fell on the revolvers, and I seized one; and paused to listen in the doorway of the outer room. To listen, say I? Yes, and to get my breath: and I tore my shirt and twisted a strip of it round my bleeding arm; and stood listening again. I would have given the world to hear Sapt's voice. For

I was faint, spent, and weary. And that wild-cat Rupert Hentzau was yet at large in the Castle. Yet, because I could better defend the narrow door at the top of the stairs than the wider entrance to the room, I dragged myself up the steps, and stood behind it listening.

What was the sound? Again a strange one for the place and time. An easy, scornful, merry laugh—the laugh of young Rupert Hentzau! I could scarcely believe that a sane man would laugh. Yet the laugh told me that my men had not come; for they must have shot Rupert ere now, if they had come. And the clock struck half-past two! My God! The door had not been opened! They had gone to the bank! They had not found me! They had gone by now back to Tarlenheim, with the news of the King's death—and mine. Well, it would be true before they got there. Was not Rupert laughing in triumph?

For a moment, I sank, unnerved, against the door. Then I started up alert again, for Rupert cried scornfully:

"Well, the bridge is there! Come over it! And in God's name, let's see Black Michael. Keep back, you curs! Michael, come and fight for her!"

If it were a three-cornered fight, I might yet bear my part. I turned the key in the door and looked out.

For a moment I could see nothing, for the glare of lanterns and torches caught me full in the eyes from the other side of the bridge. But soon the scene grew clear: and it was a strange scene. The bridge was in its place. At the far end of it stood a group of the duke's servants; two or three carried the lights which had dazzled me, three or four held pikes in rest. They were huddled together; their weapons were protruded before them; their faces were pale and agitated. To put it plainly, they looked in as arrant a fright as I have seen men look, and they gazed apprehensively at a man who stood in the middle of the bridge, sword in hand. Rupert Hentzau was in his trousers and shirt; the white linen was stained with blood, but his easy, buoyant pose told me that he was himself either not touched at all or merely scratched. There he stood, holding the bridge against them, and daring them to come on; or, rather, bidding them send Black Michael to him; and they, having no firearms, cowered before the desperate man and dared not attack him. They whispered to one another; and in the backmost rank, I saw my friend Johann, leaning against the portal of the door and stanching with a handkerchief the blood which flowed from a wound in his cheek.

By marvellous chance, I was master. The cravens would oppose me no more than they dared attack Rupert. I had but to raise my revolver, and I sent him to his account with his sins on his head. He did not so much as know that I was there. I did nothing—why, I hardly know to this day. I had killed one man stealthily that night, and another by luck rather than skill—perhaps it was that. Again, villain as the man was, I did not relish being one of a crowd against him—perhaps it was that. But stronger than either of these restrained feelings came a curiosity and a fascination which held me spellbound, watching for the outcome of the scene.

"Michael, you dog! Michael! If you can stand, come on!" cried Rupert; and he advanced a step, the group shrinking back a little before him. "Michael, you bastard! Come on!"

The answer to his taunts came in the wild cry of a woman:

"He's dead! My God, he's dead!"

"Dead!" shouted Rupert. "I struck better than I knew!" and he laughed triumphantly. Then he went on: "Down with your weapons there! I'm your master now! Down with them, I say!"

I believe they would have obeyed, but as he spoke came new things. First, there arose a distant sound, as of shouts and knockings from the other side of the chateau. My heart leapt. It must be my men, come by a happy disobedience to seek me. The noise continued, but none of the rest seemed to heed it. Their attention was chained by what now happened before their eyes. The group of servants parted and a woman staggered on to the bridge. Antoinette de Mauban was in a loose white robe, her dark hair streamed over her shoulders, her face was ghastly pale, and her eyes gleamed wildly in the light of the torches. In her shaking hand she held a revolver, and, as she tottered forward, she fired it at Rupert Hentzau. The ball missed him, and struck the wood-work over my head.

"Faith, madame," laughed Rupert, "had your eyes been no more deadly than your shooting, I had not been in this scrape—nor Black Michael in hell—tonight!"

She took no notice of his words. With a wonder-ful effort, she calmed herself till she stood still and rigid. Then very slowly and deliberately she began to raise her arm again, taking most careful aim.

He would be mad to risk it. He must rush on her, chancing the bullet, or retreat towards me. I covered him with my weapon.

He did neither. Before she had got her aim, he bowed in his most graceful fashion, cried "I can't kill where I've kissed," and before she or I could stop him, laid his hand on the parapet of the bridge, and lightly leapt into the moat.

At that very moment I heard a rush of feet, and a voice I knew—Sapt's—cry: "God! it's the duke—dead!" Then I knew that the King needed me no more, and throwing down my revolver, I sprang out on the bridge. There was a cry of wild wonder, "The King!" and then I, like Rupert of Hentzau, sword in hand, vaulted over the parapet, intent on finishing my quarrel with him where I saw his curly head fifteen yards off in the water of the moat.

He swam swiftly and easily. I was weary and half crippled with my wounded arm. I could not gain on him. For a time I made no sound, but as we rounded the corner of the old keep I cried:

"Stop, Rupert, stop!"

I saw him look over his shoulder, but he swam on. He was under the bank now, searching, as I guessed, for a spot that he could climb. I knew there to be none—but there was my rope, which would still be hanging where I had left it. He would come to where it was before I could. Perhaps he would miss it—perhaps he would find it; and if he drew it up after him, he would get a good start of me. I put forth all my remaining strength and pressed on. At last I began to gain on him; for he, occupied with his search, unconsciously slackened his pace.

Ah, he had found it! A low shout of triumph came from him. He laid hold of it and began to haul himself up. I was near enough to hear him mutter: "How the devil comes this here?" I was at the rope, and he, hanging in mid air, saw me, but I could not reach him.

"Hullo! who's here?" he cried in startled tones.

For a moment, I believe, he took me for the King—I dare say I was pale enough to lend colour to the thought; but an instant later he cried:

"Why it's the play-actor! How come you here, man?"

And so saying he gained the bank.

I laid hold of the rope, but I paused. He stood on the bank, sword in hand, and he could cut my head open or spit me through the heart as I came up. I let go the rope.

"Never mind," said I; "but as I am here, I think I'll stay."

He smiled down on me.

"These women are the deuce—" he began; when suddenly the great bell of the Castle started to ring furiously, and a loud shout reached us from the moat.

Rupert smiled again, and waved his hand to me.

"I should like a turn with you, but it's a little too hot!" said he, and he disappeared from above me.

In an instant, without thinking of danger, I laid my hand to the rope. I was up. I saw him thirty yards off, running like a deer towards the shelter of the forest. For once Rupert Hentzau had chosen discretion for his part. I laid my feet to the ground and rushed after him, calling to him to stand. He would not. Unwounded and vigorous, he gained on me at every step; but, forgetting everything in the world except him and my thirst for his blood, I pressed on, and soon the deep shades of the forest of Zenda engulfed us both, pursued and pursuer.

It was three o'clock know, and day was dawning. I was on a long straight grass avenue, and a hundred yards ahead ran young Rupert, his curls waving in the fresh breeze. I was weary and panting; he looked over his shoulder and waved his hand again to me. He was mocking me, for he saw he had the pace of me. I was forced to pause for breath. A moment later, Rupert turned sharply to the right and was lost from my sight.

I thought all was over, and in deep vexation sank on the ground. But I was up again directly, for a scream rang through the forest—a woman's scream. Putting forth the last of my strength, I ran on to the place where he had turned out of my sight, and, turning also, I saw him again. But alas! I could not touch him. He was in the act of lifting a girl down from her horse; doubtless it was her scream that I heard. She looked like a small farmer's or a peasant's daughter, and she carried a basket on her arm. Probably she was on her way to the early market at Zenda. Her horse was a stout, well shaped animal. Master Rupert lifted her down amid her shrieks— the sight of him frightened her; but he treated her gently, laughed, kissed her, and gave her money. Then he jumped on the horse, sitting sideways like a woman; and then he waited for me. I, on my part, waited for him.

Presently he rode towards me, keeping his distance, however. He lifted up his hand, saying:

"What did you in the Castle?"

"I killed three of your friends," said I.

"What! You got to the cells?"

"Yes."

"And the King?"

"He was hurt by Detchard before I killed Detchard, but I pray that he lives."

"You fool!" said Rupert, pleasantly.

"One thing more I did."

"And what's that?"

"I spared your life. I was behind you on the bridge, with a revolver in my hand."

"No? Faith, I was between two fires!"

"Get off your horse," I cried, "and fight like a man."

"Before a lady!" said he, pointing to the girl. "Fie, your Majesty!'"

Then in my rage, hardly knowing what I did, I rushed at him. For a moment he seemed to waver. Then he reined his horse in and stood waiting for me. On I went in my folly. I seized the bridle and I struck at him. He parried and thrust at me. I fell back a pace and rushed at him again; and this time I reached his face and laid his cheek open, and darted back almost before he could strike me. He seemed almost dazed at the fierceness of my attack; otherwise I think he must have killed me. I sank on my knee panting, expecting him to ride at me. And so he would have done, and then and there, I doubt not, one or both of us would have died; but at the moment there came a shout from behind us, and, looking round, I saw, just at the turn of the avenue, a man on a horse. He was riding hard, and he carried a revolver in his hand. It was Fritz von Tar-lenheim, my faithful friend. Rupert saw him, and knew that the game was up. He checked his rush at me and flung his leg over the saddle, but yet for just a moment he waited. Leaning forward, he tossed his hair off his forehead and smiled, and said: "Au revoir, Rudolf Rassendyll!"

Then, with his cheek streaming blood, but his lips laughing and his body swaying with ease and grace, he bowed to me; and he bowed to the farm-girl, who had drawn near in trembling fascination, and he waved his hand to Fritz, who was just within range and let fly a shot at him. The ball came nigh doing its work, for it struck the sword he held, and he dropped the sword with an oath, wringing his fingers and clapped his heels hard on his horse's belly, and rode away at a gallop.

And I watched him go down the long avenue, riding as though he rode for his pleasure and singing as he went, for all there was that gash in his cheek.

Once again he turned to wave his hand, and then the gloom of thickets swallowed him and he was lost from our sight. Thus he vanished—reckless and wary, graceful and graceless, handsome, debonair, vile, and unconquered. And I flung my sword passionately on the ground and cried to Fritz to ride after him. But Fritz stopped his horse, and leapt down and ran to me, and knelt, putting his arm about me. And indeed it was time, for the wound that Detchard had given me was broken forth afresh, and my blood was staining the ground.

"Then give me the horse!" I cried, staggering to my feet and throwing his arms off me. And the strength of my rage carried me so far as where the horse stood, and then I fell prone beside it. And Fritz knelt by me again.

"Fritz!" I said.

"Ay, friend—dear friend!" he said, tender as a woman.

"Is the King alive?"

He took his handkerchief and wiped my lips, and bent and kissed me on the forehead.

"Thanks to the most gallant gentleman that lives," said he softly, "the King is alive!"

The little farm-girl stood by us, weeping for fright and wide-eyed for wonder; for she had seen me at Zenda; and was not I, pallid, dripping, foul, and bloody as I was—yet was not I the King?

And when I heard that the King was alive, I strove to cry "Hurrah!" But I could not speak, and I laid my head back in Fritz's arms and closed my eyes, and I groaned; and then, lest Fritz should do me wrong in his thoughts, I opened my eyes and tried to say "Hurrah!" again. But I could not. And being very tired, and now very cold, I huddled myself close up to Fritz, to get the warmth of him, and shut my eyes again and went to sleep.

The Venturers

[O.HENRY]

Let the story wreck itself on the spreading rails of the *Non Sequitur* Limited, if it will; first you must take your seat in the observation car *"Raison d'être"* for one moment. It is for no longer than to consider a brief essay on the subject—let us call it: "What's Around the Corner."

Omne mundus in duas partes divisum est—men who wear rubbers and pay poll-taxes, and men who discover new continents. There are no more continents to discover; but by the time overshoes are out of date and the poll has developed into an income tax, the other half will be paralleling the canals of Mars with radium railways.

Fortune, Chance, and Adventure are given as synonymous in the dictionaries. To the knowing each has a different meaning. Fortune is a prize to be won. Adventure is the road to it. Chance is what may lurk in the shadows at the roadside. The face of Fortune is radiant and alluring; that of Adventure is flushed and heroic. The face of Chance is the beautiful countenance—perfect because vague and dream-born—that we see in our tea-cups at breakfast while we growl over our chops and toast.

The VENTURER is one who keeps his eye on the hedgerows and wayside groves and meadows while he travels the road to Fortune. That is the difference between him and the Adventurer. Eating the forbidden fruit was the best record ever made by a Venturer. Trying to prove that it happened is the highest work of the Adventuresome. To be either is disturbing to the cosmogony of creation. So, as bracket-sawed and city-directoried citizens, let us light our pipes, chide the children and the cat, arrange ourselves in the willow rocker under the flickering gas jet at the coolest window and scan this little tale of two modern followers of Chance.

"Did you ever hear that story about the man from the West?" asked Billinger, in the little dark-oak room to your left as you penetrate the interior of the Powhatan Club.

"Doubtless," said John Reginald Forster, rising and leaving the room.

Forster got his straw hat (straws will be in and maybe out again long before this is printed) from the checkroom boy, and walked out of the air (as Hamlet says). Billinger was used to having his stories insulted and would not mind. Forster was in his favorite mood and wanted to go away from anywhere. A man, in order to get on good terms with himself, must have his opinions corroborated and his moods matched by some one else. (I had written that "somebody"; but an A. D. T. boy who once took a telegram for me pointed out that I could save money by using the compound word. This is a vice versa case).

Forster's favorite mood was that of greatly desiring to be a follower of Chance. He was a Venturer by nature, but convention, birth, tradition and the narrowing influences of the tribe of Manhattan had denied him full privilege. He had trodden all the main-traveled thoroughfares and many of the side roads that are supposed to relieve the tedium of life. But none had sufficed. The reason was that he knew what was to be found at the end of every street. He knew from experience and logic almost precisely to what end each digression from routine must lead. He found a depressing monotony in all the variations that the music of his sphere had grafted upon the tune of life. He had not learned that, although the world was made round, the circle has been squared, and that its true interest is to be in "What's Around the Corner."

Forster walked abroad aimlessly from the Powhatan, trying not to tax either his judgment or his desire as to what streets he traveled. He would have been glad to lose his way if it were possible; but he had no hope of that. Adventure and Fortune move at your beck and call in the Greater City; but Chance is oriental. She is a veiled lady in a sedan chair, protected by a special traffic squad of dragonians. Crosstown, uptown, and downtown you may move without seeing her.

At the end of an hour's stroll, Forster stood on a corner of a broad, smooth avenue, looking disconsolately across it at a picturesque old hotel softly but brilliantly lit. Disconsolately, because he knew that he must dine; and dining in that hotel was no venture. It was one of his favorite caravansaries, and so silent and swift would be the service and so delicately choice the food, that he regretted the hunger that must be appeased by the "dead perfection" of the place's cuisine. Even the music there seemed to be always playing *da capo*.

Fancy came to him that he would dine at some cheap, even dubious, restaurant lower down in the city, where the erratic chefs from all countries of the world spread their national cookery for the omnivorous American. Something might happen there out of the routine—he might come upon a subject without a predicate, a road without an end, a question without an answer, a cause without an effect, a gulf stream in life's salt ocean. He had not dressed for evening; he wore a dark business suit that would not be questioned even where the waiters served the spaghetti in their shirt sleeves.

So John Reginald Forster began to search his clothes for money; because the more cheaply you dine, the more surely must you pay. All of the thirteen pockets, large and small, of his business suit he explored carefully and found not a penny. His bank book showed a balance of five figures to his credit in the Old Ironsides Trust Company, but—

Forster became aware of a man nearby at his left hand who was really regarding him with some amusement. He looked like any business man of thirty or so, neatly dressed and standing in the attitude of one waiting for a street car. But there was no car line on that avenue. So his proximity and unconcealed curiosity seemed to Forster to partake of the nature of a personal intrusion. But, as he was a consistent seeker after "What's Around the Corner," instead of manifesting resentment he only turned a half-embarrassed smile upon the other's grin of amusement.

"All in?" asked the intruder, drawing nearer.

"Seems so," said Forster. "Now, I thought there was a dollar in—"

"Oh, I know," said the other man, with a laugh. "But there wasn't. I've just been through the same process myself, as I was coming around the corner. I found in an upper vest pocket—I don't know how they got there—exactly two pennies. You know what kind of a dinner exactly two pennies will buy!"

"You haven't dined, then?" asked Forster.

"I have not. But I would like to. Now, I'll make you a proposition. You look like a man who would take up one. Your clothes look neat and respectable. Excuse personalities. I think mine will pass the scrutiny of a head waiter, also. Suppose we go over to that hotel and dine together. We will choose from the menu like millionaires—or, if you prefer, like gentlemen in moderate circumstances dining extravagantly for once. When we have finished we will match with my two pennies to see which of us will stand the brunt of the house's displeasure and vengeance. My name is Ives. I think we have lived in the same station of life—before our money took wings."

"You're on," said Forster, joyfully.

Here was a venture at least within the borders of the mysterious country of Change—anyhow, it promised something better than the stale infestivity of a table *d'hôtel*.

The two were soon seated at a corner table in the hotel dining room. Ives chucked one of his pennies across the table to Forster.

"Match for which of us gives the order," he said.

Forster lost.

Ives laughed and began to name liquids and viands to the waiter with the absorbed but calm deliberation of one who was to the menu born. Forster, listening, gave his admiring approval of the order.

"I am a man," said Ives, during the oysters, "Who has made a lifetime search after the to-be-continued-in-our-next. I am not like the ordinary adventurer who strikes for a coveted prize. Nor yet am I like a gambler who knows he is either to win or lose a certain set stake. What I want is to encounter an adventure to which I can predict no conclusion. It is the breath of existence to me to dare Fate in its blindest manifestations. The world has come to run so much by rote and gravitation that you can enter upon hardly any footpath of chance in which you do not find signboards informing you of what you may expect at its end. I am like the clerk in the Circumlocution Office who always complained bitterly when any one came in to ask information. 'He wanted to know, you know!' was the kick he made to his fellow-clerks. Well, I don't want to know, I don't want to reason, I don't want to guess—I want to bet my hand without seeing it."

"I understand," said Forster delightedly. "I've often wanted the way I feel put into words. You've done it. I want to take chances on what's coming. Suppose we have a bottle of Moselle with the next course."

"Agreed," said Ives. "I'm glad you catch my idea. It will increase the animosity of the house toward the loser. If it does not weary you, we will pursue the theme. Only a few times have I met a true venturer—one who does not ask a schedule and map from Fate when he begins a journey. But, as the world becomes more civilized and wiser, the more difficult it is to come upon an adventure the end of which you cannot foresee. In the Elizabethan days you could assault the watch, wring knockers from doors and have a jolly set-to with the blades in any convenient angle of a wall and 'get away with it.' Nowadays, if you speak disrespectfully to a policeman, all that is left to the most romantic fancy is to conjecture in what particular police station he will land you."

"I know—I know," said Forster, nodding approval.

"I returned to New York to-day," continued Ives, "from a three years' ramble around the globe. Things are not much better abroad than they are at home. The whole world seems to be overrun by conclusions. The only thing that interests me greatly is a premise. I've tried shooting big game in Africa. I know what an express rifle will do at so many yards; and when an elephant or a rhinoceros falls to the bullet, I enjoy it about as much as I did when I was kept in after school to do a sum in long division on the blackboard."

"I know—I know," said Forster.

"There might be something in aeroplanes," went on Ives, reflectively. "I've tried ballooning; but it seems to be merely a cut-and-dried affair of wind and ballast."

"Women," suggested Forster, with a smile.

"Three months ago," said Ives. "I was pottering around in one of the bazaars in Constantinople. I noticed a lady, veiled, of course, but with a pair of especially fine eyes visible, who was examining some amber and pearl ornaments at one of the booths. With her was an attendant—a big Nubian, as black as coal. After a while the attendant drew nearer to me by degrees and slipped a scrap of paper into my hand. I looked at it when I got a chance. On it was scrawled hastily in pencil: 'The arched gate of the Nightingale Garden at nine to-night.' Does that appear to you to be an interesting premise, Mr. Forster?"

"I made inquiries and learned that the Nightingale Garden was the property of an old Turk—a grand vizier, or something of the sort. Of course I prospected for the arched gate and was there at nine. The same Nubian attendant opened the gate promptly on time, and I went inside and sat on a bench by a perfumed fountain with the veiled lady. We had quite an extended chat. She was Myrtle Thompson, a lady journalist, who was writing up the Turkish harems for a Chicago newspaper. She said she noticed the New York cut of my clothes in the bazaar and wondered if I couldn't work something into the metropolitan papers about it."

"I see," said Forster. "I see."

"I've canoed through Canada," said Ives, "down many rapids and over many falls. But I didn't seem to get what I wanted out of it because I knew there were only two possible outcomes—I would either go to the bottom or arrive at the sea level. I've played all games at cards; but the mathematicians have spoiled that sport by computing the percentages. I've made acquaintances on trains, I've answered advertisements, I've rung strange door-bells, I've taken every chance that presented itself; but there has always been the conventional ending—the logical conclusion to the premise."

"I know," repeated Forster. "I've felt it all. But I've had few chances to take my chance at chances. Is there any life so devoid of impossibilities as life in this city? There seems to be a myriad of opportunities for testing the undeterminable; but not one in a thousand fails to land you where you expected it to stop. I wish the subways and street cars disappointed one as seldom."

"The sun has risen," said Ives, "on the Arabian nights. There are no more caliphs. The fisherman's vase is turned to a vacuum bottle, warranted to keep any genie boiling or frozen for forty-eight hours. Life moves by rote. Science has killed adventure. There are no more opportunities such as Columbus and the man who ate the first oyster had. The only certain thing is that there is nothing uncertain."

"Well," said Forster, "my experience has been the limited one of a city man. I haven't seen the world as you have; but it seems that we view it with the same opinion. But, I tell you I am grateful for even this little venture of ours into the borders of the haphazard. There may be at least one breathless moment when the bill for the dinner is presented. Perhaps, after all, the pilgrims who traveled without scrip or purse found a keener taste to life than did the knights of the Round Table who rode abroad with a retinue and King Arthur's certified checks in the lining of their helmets. And now, if you've finished your coffee, suppose we match one of your insufficient coins for the impending blow of Fate. What have I up?"

"Heads," called Ives.

"Heads it is," said Forster, lifting his hand. "I lose. We forgot to agree upon a plan for the winner to escape. I suggest that when the waiter comes you make a remark about telephoning to a friend. I will hold the fort and the dinner check long enough for you to get your hat and be off. I thank you for an evening out of the ordinary, Mr. Ives, and wish we might have others."

"If my memory is not at fault," said Ives, laughing, "the nearest police station is in MacDougal Street. I have enjoyed the dinner, too, let me assure you."

Forster crooked his finger for the waiter. Victor, with a locomotive effort that seemed to owe more to pneumatics than to pedestrianism, glided to the table and laid the card, face downward, by the loser's cup. Forster took it up and added the figures with deliberate care. Ives leaned back comfortably in his chair.

"Escuse me," said Forster; "but I though you were going to ring Grimes about that theatre party for Thursday night. Had you forgotten about it?"

"Oh," said Ives, settling himself more comfortably, "I can do that later on. Get me a glass of water, waiter."

"Want to be in at the death, do you?" asked Forster.

"I hope you don't object," said Ives, pleadingly. "Never in my life have I seen a gentleman arrested in a public restaurant for swindling it out of a dinner."

"All right," said Forster, calmly. "You are entitled to see a Christian die in the arena as your *pousse-caf'e*."

Victor came with the glass of water and remained, with the disengaged air of an inexorable collector.

Forster hesitated for fifteen seconds, and then took a pencil from his pocket and scribbled his name on the dinner check. The waiter bowed and took it away.

"The fact is," said Forster, with a little embarrassed laugh, "I doubt whether I'm what they call a 'game sport,' which means the same as a 'soldier of Fortune.' I'll have to make a confession. I've been dining at this hotel two or three times a week for more than a year. I always sign my checks." And then, with a note of appreciation in his voice: "It was first-rate of you to stay to see me through with it when you knew I had no money, and that you might be scooped in, too."

"I guess I'll confess, too," said Ives, with a grin. "I own the hotel. I don't run it, of course, but I always keep a suite on the third floor for my use when I happen to stray into town."

He called a waiter and said: "Is Mr. Gilmore still behind the desk? All right. Tell him that Mr. Ives is here, and ask him to have my rooms made ready and aired."

"Another venture cut short by the inevitable," said Forster. "Is there a conundrum without an answer in the next number? But let's hold to our subject just for a minute or two, if you will. It isn't often that I meet a man who understands the flaws I pick in existence. I am engaged to be married a month from to-day."

"I reserve comment," said Ives.

"Right; I am going to add to the assertion. I am devotedly fond of the lady; but I can't decide whether to show up at the church or make a sneak for Alaska. It's the same idea, you know, that we were discussing—it does for a fellow as far as possibilities are concerned. Everybody knows the routine—you get a kiss flavored with Ceylon tea after breakfast; you go to the office; you come back home and dress for dinner—theatre twice a week—bills—moping around most evenings trying to make conversation—a little quarrel occasionally—maybe sometimes a big one, and a separation—or else a settling down into a middle-aged contentment, which is worst of all."

"I know," said Ives, nodding wisely.

"It's the dead certainty of the thing," went on Forster, "that keeps me in doubt. There'll nevermore be anything around the corner."

"Nothing after the 'Little Church,'" said Ives. "I know."

"Understand," said Forster, "that I am in no doubt as to my feelings toward the lady. I may say that I love her truly and deeply. But there is something in the current that runs through my veins that cries out against any form of the calculable. I do not know what I want; but I know that I want it. I'm talking like an idiot, I suppose, but I'm sure of what I mean."

"I understand you," said Ives, with a slow smile. "Well, I think I will be going up to my rooms now. If you would dine with me here one evening soon, Mr. Forster, I'd be glad."

"Thursday?" suggested Forster.

"At seven, if it's convenient," answered Ives.

"Seven goes," assented Forster.

At half-past eight Ives got into a cab and was driven to a number in one of the correct West Seventies. His card admitted him to the reception room of an old-fashioned house into which the spirits of Fortune, Chance and Adventure had never dared to enter. On the walls were the Whistler etchings, the steel engravings by Oh-what's-his-name?, the still-life paintings of the grapes and garden truck with the watermelon seeds spilled on the table as natural as life, and the Greuze head. It was a household. There was even brass andirons. On a table was an album, half-morocco, with oxidized-silver protections on the corners of the lids. A clock on the mantel ticked loudly, with a warning click at five minutes to nine. Ives looked at it curiously, remembering a time-piece in his grandmother's home that gave such a warning.

And then down the stairs and into the room came Mary Marsden. She was twenty-four, and I leave her to your imagination. But I must say this much— youth and health and simplicity and courage and greenish-violet eyes are beautiful, and she had all these. She gave Ives her hand with the sweet cordiality of an old friendship.

"You can't think what a pleasure it is," she said, "to have you drop in once every three years or so."

For half an hour they talked. I confess that I cannot repeat the conversation. You will find it in books in the circulating library. When that part of it was over, Mary said:

"And did you find what you wanted while you were abroad?"

"What I wanted?" said Ives.

"Yes. You know you were always queer. Even as a boy you wouldn't play marbles or baseball or any game with rules. You wanted to dive in water where you didn't know whether it was ten inches or ten feet deep. And when you grew up you were just the same. We've often talked about your peculiar ways."

"I suppose I am an incorrigible," said Ives. "I am opposed to the doctrine of predestination, to the rule of three, gravitation, taxation, and everything of the kind. Life has always seemed to me something like a serial story would be if they printed above each instalment a synopsis of succeeding chapters."

Mary laughed merrily.

"Bob Ames told us once," she said, "of a funny thing you did. It was when you and he were on a train in the South, and you got off at a town where you hadn't intended to stop just because the brakeman hung up a sign in the end of the car with the name of the next station on it."

"I remember," said Ives. "That 'next station' has been the thing I've always tried to get away from."

"I know it," said Mary. "And you've been very foolish. I hope you didn't find what you wanted not to find, or get off at the station where there wasn't any, or whatever it was you expected wouldn't happen to you during the three years you've been away."

"There was something I wanted before I went away," said Ives.

Mary looked in his eyes clearly, with a slight, but perfectly sweet smile.

"There was," she said. "You wanted me. And you could have had me, as you very well know."

Without replying, Ives let his gaze wander slowly about the room. There had been no change in it since last he had been in it, three years before. He vividly recalled the thoughts that had been in his mind then. The contents of that room were as fixed in their way, as the everlasting hills. No change would ever come there except the inevitable ones wrought by time and decay. That silver-mounted album would occupy that corner of that table, those pictures would hang on the walls, those chairs be found in their same places every morn and noon and night while the household hung together. The brass andirons were monuments to order and stability. Here and there were relics of a hundred years ago which were still living mementos and would be for many years to come. One going from and coming back to that house would never need to forecast or doubt. He would find what he left, and leave what he found. The veiled lady, Chance, would never lift her hand to the knocker on the outer door.

And before him sat the lady who belonged in the room. Cool and sweet and unchangeable she was. She offered no surprises. If one should pass his life with her, though she might grow white-haired and wrinkled, he would never perceive the change. Three years he had been away from her, and she was still waiting for him as established and constant as the house itself. He was sure that she had once cared for him. It was the knowledge that she would always do so that had driven him away. Thus his thoughts ran.

"I am going to be married soon," said Mary.

On the next Thursday afternoon Forster came hurriedly to Ives' hotel.

"Old man," said he, "we'll have to put that dinner off for a year or so; I'm going abroad. The steamer sails at four. That was a great talk we had the other night, and it decided me. I'm going to knock around the world and get rid of that incubus that has been weighing on both you and me—the terrible dread of knowing what's going to happen. I've done one thing that hurts my conscience a little; but I know it's best for both of us. I've written to the lady to whom I was engaged and explained everything—told her plainly why I was leaving—that the monotony of matrimony would never do for me. Don't you think I was right?"

"It is not for me to say," answered Ives. "Go ahead and shoot elephants if you think it will bring the element of chance into your life. We've got to decide these things for ourselves. But I tell you one thing, Forster, I've found the way. I've found out the biggest hazard in the world—a game of chance that never is concluded, a venture that may end in the highest heaven or the blackest pit. It will keep a man on edge until the clods fall on his coffin, because he will never know—not until his last day, and not then will he know. It is a voyage without a rudder or compass, and you must be captain and crew and keep watch, every day and night, yourself, with no one to relieve you. I have found the VENTURE. Don't bother yourself about leaving Mary Marsden, Forster. I married her yesterday at noon."

In a Cuban Cave

[JULIUS A. PALMER]

Between the Morro Castle at Santiago and Cape Maisi, or the eastern point of the island of Cuba, lie a number of remarkable defiles cut by the sea into this precipitous coast. There is port Escondido, or the Hidden Port, with an entrance of, say one hundred feet, yet by the peculiar contour of the adjacent land a ship may sail close to the mouth of the channel without observing the harbour.

Not twelve hours' sail from Santiago, in the direction of Escondido, may be found that wondrous cave, often mentioned by tourists, which has not been explored because of the belief that no boat which has entered its mouth has been known to return. An adventure of my younger days indicates that there may be more truth than superstition in the tradition.

My sister Bertina and I, being thoroughly acquainted with the regular alternation of land- and sea-breezes on that coast, were able to enjoy together many delightful sails in the course of the years when our parents were residing at Santiago. With the farewell sighing of the morning's land-breeze, we sailed our little skiff down the channel, and gained an offing. We then laid our course alongshore close to the wind with the first puffs of the change, and came back to port with the final breathings of the sea-breeze.

Bertina had suggested from time to time that we should explore the nameless cave.

I shook my head at first, thinking it was a passing whim; but she came back to the proposal day after day.

The result of these entreaties was, that on one of the national holidays of the year 1853 it was agreed that our sail should be to the mouth of the mysterious cave. We passed the frowning bastions of the Morro with a fresh land-breeze, and laid our course alongshore to the eastward. Before the calm interval between the land- and sea-breezes came we were opposite the cavern. Into its mouth we shot our boat and unshipped the mast, though this seemed an unnecessary precaution. A delicious coolness welcomed us into the shade.

The inward draught of the breeze made a perceptible current from the mouth of the cavern to its dark background. I had taken the precaution to bring a bull's-eye lantern, and lighting it, we took in the grapnel, and allowed the boat to drift slowly into the unknown recesses, the bull's-eye pointing ahead like a locomotive light, insuring us against collision with any projection of the rock. There was no sign of danger, however. Though the altitude of the roof grew less as we advanced, its height, for the whole distance before us illuminated by the lantern, exceeded that of the tallest man. The width perceptibly enlarged.

"It is all perfectly fascinating!" cried Bertina, in a rapture.

The waters were dark, smooth and still; I had just spoken of their apparently great depth, when a slight concussion shook our boat.

"We're touching bottom," said Bertina. I at once thrust my paddle down its full length into the water, touching nothing.

"How queer!" said my sister, looking a little grave.

After advancing a few yards farther, another tremor jarred the boat. It was a very peculiar motion, similar to that of a swiftly moving craft when it slips over a bar of soft ooze. Then came a third shock, this time under the stern of the skiff, so that the boat shot ahead as though propelled by a shove or kick. I turned the light of the lantern astern, but saw nothing, though it seemed strange that so light a craft should leave a track so disturbed.

The next vibration and impetus from astern was still more violent. Turning instantly, I brought the rays of the bull's-eye to bear on the wake, and plainly saw, moving here and there on the surface of the water, the fin which rises from the back of the shark.

Not one only, but two three, four—I could not tell how many, since they constantly appeared and disappeared. The fearful truth flashed upon me that we were in one of those sheltered localities on the Caribbean Sea which are selected by sharks for the home of their young. Our boat had disturbed them. It was useless to make any attempt to turn the boat and retreat from the cave. The sharks were now breaking the water in every direction, and with the sweep of their powerful tails they made such a succession of whirlpools and currents that they made the light boat almost unmanageable.

The sharks were evidently attempting to upset us. From the gentle nudge, which first had startled us, the shocks had become so heavy that they seemed like the bumping of a yacht when she passes over a short reach of shoal water with headway enough to enable her to clear one after another of the obstructions. The single chance for us was that the cavern might have an outlet at the farther end.

Bertina was not nervous or alarmed; she did not realise our danger. I availed myself of this coolness on her part. The boat was moving, carried forward apparently by a slight current.

"Lie down flat, forward, as near the bow as you can get," I said, and she obeyed promptly. I took a position astern, with my hand on the tiller. By means of this arrangement I had the boat well trimmed, and although the motion imparted by the sharks was like that given by a short, choppy sea, their striking was not so likely to make her overturn.

Soon, however, a new peril was evident; the channel perceptibly narrowed, and what was still more ominous, the height of the roof quickly lessened. I glanced toward the bow, wondering if it were not best to tell Bertina our danger, when I perceived a faint ray of light. If there were any exit ahead, I thought it might conduct us into a basin where young sharks are nourished, prior to their venture into the deep sea.

There are species of these creatures, the young of which are enclosed at the earliest stage of their existence in small sacks. These are left by the female shark in protected localities until the growth of the infant fish allows it to break the confinement, after which it takes care of itself.

The prow of our boat now grated on the irregularities of the rocky roof. We were still pursued by our foes, who continued to thrust themselves with more or less of energy against the bottom of the boat.

The lantern was eclipsed by something very like sunlight ahead, when the projecting stem of the boat met with an obstruction. For one awful moment I thought that the sharks and the current would swing the boat broadside on to the narrow aperture, which seemed to open into a lighted chamber.

"Put your hand upon the rock, and press the boat downward," I cried to Bertina.

My brave sister saw that this was the critical moment, and without rising stretched upward her hands, and by her skilful pressure guided the prow so that in a few seconds we were moved out into an open lake, the sun beating down upon the glassy water, and the mountains towering above our heads. The sides seemed steep and abrupt, and the basin to have been hewn out of solid rock.

Our enemies did not accompany us farther. With sharp turns and quick flashes, which revealed their ugly under-jaws and long, white bellies, they disappeared under the rocks, leaving, by the swing of their powerful tails, a succession of eddies which soon disappeared. We had escaped the sharks, but seemed imprisoned in the lagoon. Soon, however, I saw that by abandoning our boat we might ascend a portion of the cliffs and probably find our way back to Santiago down the farther slope. Some natural steps to the summit were soon found. They had evidently been used by others, ignorant that the lake communicated with the cavern.

By means of these rocky projections we reached the hilltop, and from thence once more looked forth on the fertile valleys, wooded hill-sides and smiling plains of beautiful Cuba. By good fortune the heat of the day had moderated, and we arrived safely at our house before sunset.

Dutch Courage

[JACK LONDON]

"Just our luck!"

Gus Lafee finished wiping his hands and sullenly threw the towel upon the rocks. His attitude was one of deep dejection. The light seemed gone out of the day and the glory from the golden sun. Even the keen mountain air was devoid of relish, and the early morning no longer yielded its customary zest.

"Just our luck!" Gus repeated, this time avowedly for the edification of another young fellow who was busily engaged in sousing his head in the water of the lake.

"What are you grumbling about, anyway?" Hazard Van Dorn lifted a soap-rimmed face questioningly. His eyes were shut. "What's our luck?"

"Look there!" Gus threw a moody glance skyward. "Some duffer's got ahead of us. We've been scooped, that's all!"

Hazard opened his eyes, and caught a fleeting glimpse of a white flag waving arrogantly on the edge of a wall of rock nearly a mile above his head. Then his eyes closed with a snap, and his face wrinkled spasmodically. Gus threw him the towel, and uncommiseratingly watched him wipe out the offending soap. He felt too blue himself to take stock in trivialities.

Hazard groaned.

"Does it hurt much?" Gus queried, coldly, without interest, as if it were no more than his duty to ask after the welfare of his comrade.

"I guess it does," responded the suffering one.

"Soap's pretty strong, eh? Noticed it myself."

"'Tisn't the soap. It's—it's that!" He opened his reddened eyes and pointed toward the innocent white little flag. "That's what hurts."

Gus Lafee did not reply, but turned away to start the fire and begin cooking breakfast. His disappointment and grief were too deep for anything but silence, and Hazard, who felt likewise, never opened his mouth as he fed the horses, nor once laid his head against their arching necks or passed caressing fingers through their manes. The two boys were blind, also, to the manifold glories of Mirror Lake which reposed at their very feet. Nine times, had they chosen to move along its margin the short distance of a hundred yards, could they have seen the sunrise repeated; nine times, from behind as many successive peaks, could they have seen the great orb rear his blazing rim; and nine times, had they but looked into the waters of the lake, could they have seen the phenomena reflected faithfully and vividly. But all the Titanic grandeur of the scene was lost to them. They had been robbed of the chief pleasure of their trip to Yosemite Valley. They had been frustrated in their long-cherished design upon Half Dome, and hence were rendered disconsolate and blind to the beauties and the wonders of the place.

Half Dome rears its ice-scarred head fully five thousand feet above the level floor of Yosemite Valley. In the name itself of this great rock lies an accurate and complete description. Nothing more nor less is it than a cyclopean, rounded dome, split in half as cleanly as an apple that is divided by a knife. It is, perhaps, quite needless to state that but one half remains, hence its name, the other half having been carried away by the great ice-river in the stormy time of the Glacial Period. In that dim day one of those frigid rivers gouged a mighty channel from out the solid rock. This channel today is Yosemite Valley. But to return to the Half Dome. On its northeastern side, by circuitous trails and stiff climbing, one may gain the Saddle. Against the slope of the Dome the Saddle leans like a gigantic slab, and from the top of this slab, one thousand feet in length, curves the great circle to the summit of the Dome. A few degrees too steep for unaided climbing, these one thousand feet defied for years the adventurous spirits who fixed yearning eyes upon the crest above.

One day, a couple of clear-headed mountaineers had proceeded to insert iron eye-bolts into holes which they drilled into the rock every few feet apart. But when they found themselves three hundred feet above the Saddle, clinging like flies to the precarious wall with on either hand a yawning abyss, their nerves failed them and they abandoned the enterprise. So it remained for an indomitable Scotchman, one George Anderson, finally to achieve the feat. Beginning where they had left off, drilling and climbing for a week, he had at last set foot upon that awful summit and gazed down into the depths where Mirror Lake reposed, nearly a mile beneath.

In the years which followed, many bold men took advantage of the huge rope ladder which he had put in place; but one winter ladder, cables and all were carried away by the snow and ice. True, most of the eye-bolts, twisted and bent, remained. But few men had since essayed the hazardous undertaking, and of those few more than one gave up his life on the treacherous heights, and not one succeeded.

But Gus Lafee and Hazard Van Dorn had left the smiling valley-land of California and journeyed into the high Sierras, intent on the great adventure. And thus it was that their disappointment was deep and grievous when they awoke on this morning to receive the forestalling message of the little white flag.

"Camped at the foot of the Saddle last night and went up at the first peep of day," Hazard ventured, long after the silent breakfast had been tucked away and the dishes washed.

Gus nodded. It was not in the nature of things that a youth's spirits should long remain at low ebb, and his tongue was beginning to loosen.

"Guess he's down by now, lying in camp and feeling as big as Alexander," the other went on. "And I don't blame him, either; only I wish it were we."

"You can be sure he's down," Gus spoke up at last. "It's mighty warm on that naked rock with the sun beating down on it at this time of year. That was our plan, you know, to go up early and come down early. And any man, sensible enough to get to the top, is bound to have sense enough to do it before the rock gets hot and his hands sweaty."

"And you can be sure he didn't take his shoes with him." Hazard rolled over on his back and lazily regarded the speck of flag fluttering briskly on the sheer edge of the precipice. "Say!" He sat up with a start. "What's that?"

A metallic ray of light flashed out from the summit of Half Dome, then a second and a third. The heads of both boys were craned backward on the instant, agog with excitement.

"What a duffer!" Gus cried. "Why didn't he come down when it was cool?"

Hazard shook his head slowly, as if the question were too deep for immediate answer and they had better defer judgment.

The flashes continued, and as the boys soon noted, at irregular intervals of duration and disappearance. Now they were long, now short; and again they came and went with great rapidity, or ceased altogether for several moments at a time.

"I have it!" Hazard's face lighted up with the coming of understanding. "I have it! That fellow up there is trying to talk to us. He's flashing the sunlight down to us on a pocket-mirror—dot, dash; dot dash; don't you see?"

The light also began to break in Gus's face. "Ah, I know! It's what they do in war-time—signaling. They call it heliographing, don't they? Same thing as telegraphing, only it's done without wires. And they use the same dots and dashes, too."

"Yes, the Morse alphabet. Wish I knew it."

"Same here. He surely must have something to say to us, or he wouldn't be kicking up all that rumpus."

Still the flashes came and went persistently, till Gus exclaimed: "That chap's in trouble, that's what's the matter with him! Most likely he's hurt himself or something or other."

"Go on!" Hazard scouted.

Gus got out the shotgun and fired both barrels three times in rapid succession. A perfect flutter of flashes came back before the echoes had ceased their antics. So unmistakable was the message that even doubting Hazard was convinced that the man who had forestalled them stood in some grave danger.

"Quick, Gus," he cried, "and pack! I'll see to the horses. Our trip hasn't come to nothing, after all. We've got to go right up Half Dome and rescue him. Where's the map? How do we get to the Saddle?"

"Taking the horse-trail below the Vernal Falls," Gus read from the guidebook, "one mile of brisk traveling brings the tourist to the world-famed Nevada Falls. Close by, rising up in all its pomp and glory, the Cap of Liberty stands guard—"

"Skip all that!" Hazard impatiently interrupted. "The trail's what we want."

"Oh, here it is! 'Following the trail up the side of the fall will bring you to the forks. The left one leads to Little Yosemite Valley, Cloud's Rest, and other points.'"

"Hold on; that'll do! I've got it on the map now," again interrupted Hazard. "From the Cloud's Rest trail a dotted line leads off to Half Dome. That shows the trail's abandoned. We'll have to look sharp to find it. It's a day's journey."

"And to think of all that traveling, when right here we're at the bottom of the Dome!" Gus complained, staring up wistfully at the goal.

"That's because this is Yosemite, and all the more reason for us to hurry. Come on! Be lively, now!"

Well used as they were to trail life, but few minutes sufficed to see the camp equipage on the backs of the packhorses and the boys in the saddle. In the late twilight of that evening they hobbled their animals in a tiny mountain meadow, and cooked coffee and bacon for themselves at the very base of the Saddle. Here, also, before they turned into their blankets, they found the camp of the unlucky stranger who was destined to spend the night on the naked roof of the Dome.

Dawn was brightening into day when the panting lads threw themselves down at the summit of the Saddle and began taking off their shoes. Looking down from the great height, they seemed perched upon the ridge-pole of the world, and even the snow-crowned Sierra peaks seemed beneath them. Directly below, on the one hand, lay Little Yosemite Valley, half a mile deep; on the other hand, Big Yosemite, a mile. Already the sun's rays were striking about the adventurers, but the darkness of night still shrouded the two great gulfs into which they peered. And above them, bathed in the full day, rose only the majestic curve of the Dome.

"What's that for?" Gus asked, pointing to a leather-shielded flask which Hazard was securely fastening in his shirt pocket.

"Dutch courage, of course," was the reply. "We'll need all our nerve in this undertaking, and a little bit more, and," he tapped the flask significantly, "here's the little bit more."

"Good idea," Gus commented.

How they had ever come possessed of this erroneous idea, it would be hard to discover; but they were young yet, and there remained for them many uncut pages of life. Believers, also, in the efficacy of whisky as a remedy for snake-bite, they had brought with them a fair supply of medicine-chest liquor. As yet they had not touched it.

"Have some before we start?" Hazard asked.

Gus looked into the gulf and shook his head. "Better wait till we get up higher and the climbing is more ticklish."

Some seventy feet above them projected the first eye-bolt. The winter accumulations of ice had twisted and bent it down till it did not stand more than a bare inch and a half above the rock—a most difficult object to lasso at such a distance. Time and again Hazard coiled his lariat in true cowboy fashion and made the cast, and time and again was he baffled by the elusive peg. Nor could Gus do better. Taking advantage of inequalities in the surface, they scrambled twenty feet up the Dome and found they could rest in a shallow crevice. The cleft side of the Dome was so near that they could look over its edge from the crevice and gaze down the smooth, vertical wall for nearly two thousand feet. It was yet too dark down below for them to see farther.

The peg was now fifty feet away, but the path they must cover to get to it was quite smooth, and ran at an inclination of nearly fifty degrees. It seemed impossible, in that intervening space, to find a resting-place. Either the climber must keep going up, or he must slide down; he could not stop. But just here rose the danger. The Dome was sphere-shaped, and if he should begin to slide, his course would be, not to the point from which he had started and where the Saddle would catch him, but off to the south toward Little Yosemite. This meant a plunge of half a mile.

"I'll try it," Gus said simply.

They knotted the two lariats together, so that they had over a hundred feet of rope between them; and then each boy tied an end to his waist.

"If I slide," Gus cautioned, "come in on the slack and brace yourself. If you don't, you'll follow me, that's all!"

"Ay, ay!" was the confident response. "Better take a nip before you start?"

Gus glanced at the proffered bottle. He knew himself and of what he was capable. "Wait till I make the peg and you join me. All ready?"

"Ay."

He struck out like a cat, on all fours, clawing energetically as he urged his upward progress, his comrade paying out the rope carefully. At first his speed was good, but gradually it dwindled. Now he was fifteen feet from the peg, now ten, now eight—but going, oh, so slowly! Hazard, looking up from his crevice, felt a contempt for him and disappointment in him. It did look easy. Now Gus was five feet away, and after a painful effort, four feet. But when only a yard intervened, he came to a standstill—not exactly a standstill, for, like a squirrel in a wheel, he maintained his position on the face of the Dome by the most desperate clawing.

He had failed, that was evident. The question now was, how to save himself. With a sudden, catlike movement he whirled over on his back, caught his heel in a tiny, saucer-shaped depression and sat up. Then his courage failed him. Day had at last penetrated to the floor of the valley, and he was appalled at the frightful distance.

"Go ahead and make it!" Hazard ordered; but Gus merely shook his head.

"Then come down!"

Again he shook his head. This was his ordeal, to sit, nerveless and insecure, on the brink of the precipice. But Hazard, lying safely in his crevice, now had to face his own ordeal, but one of a different nature. When Gus began to slide—as he soon must—would he, Hazard, be able to take in the slack and then meet the shock as the other tautened the rope and darted toward the plunge? It seemed doubtful. And there he lay, apparently safe, but in reality harnessed to death. Then rose the temptation. Why not cast off the rope about his waist? He would be safe at all events. It was a simple way out of the difficulty. There was no need that two should perish.

But it was impossible for such temptation to over-come his pride of race, and his own pride in himself and in his honor. So the rope remained about him.

"Come down!" he ordered; but Gus seemed to have become petrified.

"Come down," he threatened, "or I'll drag you down!" He pulled on the rope to show he was in earnest.

"Don't you dare!" Gus articulated through his clenched teeth.

"Sure I will, if you don't come!" Again he jerked the rope.

With a despairing gurgle Gus started, doing his best to work sideways from the plunge. Hazard, every sense on the alert, almost exulting in his per-fect coolness, took in the slack with deft rapidity. Then, as the rope began to tighten, he braced him-self. The shock drew him half out of the crevice; but he held firm and served as the center of the circle, while Gus, with the rope as a radius, described the circumference and ended up on the extreme south-ern edge of the Saddle. A few moments later Hazard was offering him the flask.

"Take some yourself," Gus said.

"No; you. I don't need it."

"And I'm past needing it." Evidently Gus was dubious of the bottle and its contents.

Hazard put it away in his pocket. "Are you game," he asked, "or are you going to give it up?"

"Never!" Gus protested. "I am game. No Lafee ever showed the white feather yet. And if I did lose my grit up there, it was only for the moment—sort of like seasickness. I'm all right now, and I'm going to the top."

"Good!" encouraged Hazard. "You lie in the crevice this time, and I'll show you how easy it is."

But Gus refused. He held that it was easier for him to try again, arguing that it was less difficult for his one hundred and sixteen pounds to cling to the smooth rock than for Hazard's one hundred and sixty-five; also that it was easier for one hundred and sixty-five pounds to bring a sliding one hundred and sixteen to a stop than vice versa. And further, that he had the bene-fit of his previous experience. Hazard saw the justice of this, although it was with great reluctance that he gave in.

Success vindicated Gus's contention. The second time, just as it seemed as if his slide would be repeated, he made a last supreme effort and gripped the coveted peg. By means of the rope, Hazard quickly joined him. The next peg was nearly sixty feet away; but for nearly half that distance the base of some glacier in the forgotten past had ground a shal-low furrow. Taking advantage of this, it was easy for Gus to lasso the eye-bolt. And it seemed, as was really the case, that the hardest part of the task was over. True, the curve steepened to nearly sixty degrees above them, but a comparatively unbroken line of eye-bolts, six feet apart, awaited the lads. They no longer had even to use the lasso. Standing on one peg it was child's play to throw the bight of the rope over the next and to draw themselves up to it.

A bronzed and bearded man met them at the top and gripped their hands in hearty fellowship.

"Talk about your Mont Blancs!" he exclaimed, pausing in the midst of greeting them to survey the mighty panorama. "But there's nothing on all the earth, nor over it, nor under it, to compare with this!" Then he recollected himself and thanked them for coming to his aid. No, he was not hurt or injured in any way. Simply because of his own carelessness, just as he had arrived at the top the previous day, he had dropped his climbing rope. Of course it was impossible to descend without it. Did they understand heliographing? No? That was strange! How did they—

"Oh, we knew something was the matter," Gus interrupted, "from the way you flashed when we fired off the shotgun."

"Find it pretty cold last night without blankets?" Hazard queried.

"I should say so. I've hardly thawed out yet."

"Have some of this." Hazard shoved the flask over to him.

The stranger regarded him quite seriously for a moment, then said,

"My dear fellow, do you see that row of pegs? Since it is my honest intention to climb down them very shortly, I am forced to decline. No, I don't think I'll have any, though I thank you just the same."

Hazard glanced at Gus and then put the flask back in his pocket. But when they pulled the doubled rope through the last eye-bolt and set foot on the Saddle, he again drew out the bottle.

"Now that we're down, we don't need it," he remarked, pithily. "And I've about come to the conclusion that there isn't very much in Dutch courage, after all." He gazed up the great curve of the Dome. "Look at what we've done without it!"

Several seconds thereafter a party of tourists, gathered at the margin of Mirror Lake, were astounded at the unwonted phenomenon of a whisky flask descending upon them like a comet out of a clear sky; and all the way back to the hotel they marveled greatly at the wonders of nature, especially meteorites.

A War Correspondent's Kit

[RICHARD HARDING DAVIS]

I am going to try to describe some kits and outfits
I have seen used in different parts of the world by
travellers and explorers, and in different campaigns by army officers and war correspondents.
Among the articles, the reader may learn of some new
thing which, when next he goes hunting, fishing, or
exploring, he can adapt to his own uses. That is my
hope, but I am sceptical. I have seldom met the man
who would allow any one else to select his kit, or who
would admit that any other kit was better than the
one he himself had packed. It is a very delicate question. The same article that one declares is the most
essential to his comfort, is the very first thing that
another will throw into the trail. A man's outfit is a
matter which seems to touch his private honor. I have
heard veterans sitting around a camp-fire proclaim the
superiority of their kits with a jealousy, loyalty, and

enthusiasm they would not exhibit for the flesh of their flesh and the bone of their bone. On a campaign, you may attack a man's courage, the flag he serves, the newspaper for which he works, his intelligence, or his camp manners, and he will ignore you; but if you criticise his patent water-bottle he will fall upon you with both fists. So, in recommending any article for an outfit, one needs to be careful. An outfit lends itself to dispute, because the selection of its component parts is not an exact science. It should be, but it is not. A doctor on his daily rounds can carry in a compact little satchel almost everything he is liable to need; a carpenter can stow away in one box all the tools of his trade. But an outfit is not selected on any recognized principles. It seems to be a question entirely of temperament. As the man said when his friends asked him how he made his famous cocktail, "It depends on my mood." The truth is that each man in selecting his outfit generally follows the lines of least resistance. With one, the pleasure he derives from his morning bath outweighs the fact that for the rest of the day he must carry a rubber bathtub. Another man is hearty, tough, and inured to an out-of-door life. He can sleep on a pile of coal or standing on his head, and he naturally scorns to carry a bed. But another man, should he sleep all night on the ground, the next day would be of no use to himself, his regiment, or his newspaper. So he carries a folding cot and the more fortunate one of tougher fibre laughs at him. Another man says that the only way to campaign is to travel "light," and sets forth with rain-coat and field-glasses. He honestly thinks that he travels light because his intelligence tells him it is the better way; but, as a matter of fact, he does so because he is lazy. Throughout the entire campaign he borrows from his friends, and with that camaraderie and unselfishness that never comes to the surface so strongly as when men are thrown together in camp, they lend him whatever he needs. When the war is over, he is the man who goes about saying: "Some of those fellows carried enough stuff to fill a moving van. Now, look what I did. I made the entire campaign on a tooth-brush."

As a matter of fact, I have a sneaking admiration for the man who dares to borrow. His really is the part of wisdom. But at times he may lose himself in places where he can neither a borrower nor a lender be, and there are men so tenderly constituted that they cannot keep another man hungry while they use his coffee-pot. So it is well to take a few things with you—if only to lend them to the men who travel "light."

On hunting and campaigning trips the climate, the means of transport, and the chance along the road of obtaining food and fodder vary so greatly that it is not possible to map out an outfit which would serve equally well for each of them. What on one journey was your most precious possession on the next is a useless nuisance. On two trips I have packed a tent weighing, with the stakes, fifty pounds, which, as we slept in huts, I never once had occasion to open; while on other trips in countries that promised to be more or less settled, I had to always live under canvas, and sometimes broke camp twice a day.

In one war, in which I worked for an English paper, we travelled like major-generals. When that war started few thought it would last over six weeks, and many of the officers regarded it in the light of a picnic. In consequence, they mobilized as they never would have done had they foreseen what was to come, and the mess contractor grew rich furnishing, not only champagne, which in campaigns in fever countries has saved the life of many a good man, but cases of even port and burgundy, which never greatly helped any one. Later these mess supplies were turned over to the field-hospitals, but at the start every one travelled with more than he needed and more than the regulations allowed, and each correspondent was advised that if he represented a first-class paper and wished to "save his face" he had better travel in state. Those who did not, found the staff and censor less easy of access, and the means of obtaining information more difficult. But it was a nuisance. If, when a man halted at your tent, you could not stand him whiskey and sparklet soda, Egyptian cigarettes, compressed soup, canned meats, and marmalade, your paper was suspected of trying to do it "on the cheap," and not only of being mean, but, as this was a popular war, unpatriotic. When the army stripped down to work all this was discontinued, but at the start I believe there were carried with that column as many tins of tan-leather dressing as there were rifles. On that march my own outfit was as unwieldy as a gypsy's caravan. It consisted of an enormous cart, two oxen, three Basuto ponies, one Australian horse, three servants, and four hundred pounds of supplies and baggage. When it moved across the plain it looked as large as a Fall River boat. Later, when I joined the opposing army, and was not expected to maintain the dignity of a great London daily, I carried all my belongings strapped to my back, or to the back of my one pony, and I was quite as comfortable, clean, and content as I had been with the private car and the circus tent.

Throughout the Greek war, as there were no horses to be had for love or money, we walked, and I learned then that when one has to carry his own kit the number of things he can do without is extraordinary. While I marched with the army, offering my kingdom for a horse, I carried my outfit in saddle-bags thrown over my shoulder. And I think it must have been a good outfit, for I never bought anything to add to it or threw anything away. I submit that as a fair test of a kit.

Further on, should any reader care to know how for several months one may keep going with an outfit he can pack in two saddle-bags, I will give a list of the articles which in three campaigns I carried in mine.

Personally, I am for travelling "light," but at the very start one is confronted with the fact that what one man calls light to another savors of luxury. I call fifty pounds light; in Japan we each were allowed the officer's allowance of sixty-six pounds. Lord Wolseley, in his "Pocketbook," cuts down the officer's kit to forty pounds, while "Nessmut," of the Forest and Stream, claims that for a hunting trip, all one wants does not weigh over twenty-six pounds. It is very largely a question of compromise. You cannot eat your cake and have it. You cannot, under a tropical sun, throw away your blanket and when the night dew falls wrap it around you. And if, after a day of hard climbing or riding, you want to drop into a folding chair, to make room for it in your carry-all you must give up many other lesser things.

By travelling light I do not mean any lighter than the necessity demands. If there is transport at hand, a man is foolish not to avail himself of it. He is always foolish if he does not make things as easy for himself as possible. The tenderfoot will not agree with this. With him there is no idea so fixed, and no idea so absurd, as that to be comfortable is to be effeminate. He believes that "roughing it" is synonymous with hardship, and in season and out of season he plays the Spartan. Any man who suffers discomforts he can avoid because he fears his comrades will think he cannot suffer hardships is an idiot. You often hear it said of a man that "he can rough it with the best of them." Any one can do that. The man I want for a "bunkie" is the one who can be comfortable while the best of them are roughing it. The old soldier knows that it is his duty to keep himself fit, so that he can perform his work, whether his work is scouting for forage or scouting for men, but you will often hear the volunteer captain say: "Now, boys, don't forget we're roughing it; and don't expect to be comfortable." As a rule, the only reason his men are uncomfortable is because he does not know how to make them otherwise; or because he thinks, on a campaign, to endure unnecessary hardship is the mark of a soldier.

In the Cuban campaign the day the American forces landed at Siboney a major-general of volunteers took up his head-quarters in the house from which the Spanish commandant had just fled, and on the veranda of which Caspar Whitney and myself had found two hammocks and made ourselves at home. The Spaniard who had been left to guard the house courteously offered the major-general his choice of three bedrooms. They all were on the first floor and opened upon the veranda, and to the general's staff a tent could have been no easier of access. Obviously, it was the duty of the general to keep himself in good physical condition, to obtain as much sleep as possible, and to rest his great brain and his limbs cramped with ten days on shipboard. But in a tone of stern reproof he said, "No; I am campaigning now, and I have given up all luxuries." And with that he stretched a poncho on the hard boards of the veranda, where, while just a few feet from him the three beds and white mosquito nets gleamed incitingly, he tossed and turned. Besides being a silly spectacle, the sight of an old gentleman lying wide awake on his shoulder-blades was disturbing, and as the hours dragged on we repeatedly offered him our hammocks. But he fretfully persisted in his determination to be uncomfortable. And he was. The feelings of his unhappy staff, several of whom were officers of the regular army, who had to follow the example of their chief, were toward morning hardly loyal. Later, at the very moment the army moved up to the battle of San Juan this same major-general was relieved of his command on account of illness. Had he sensibly taken care of himself, when the moment came when he was needed, he would have been able to better serve his brigade and his country. In contrast to this pose is the conduct of the veteran hunter, or old soldier. When he gets into camp his first thought, after he has cared for his horse, is for his own comfort. He does not wolf down a cold supper and then spread his blanket wherever he happens to be standing. He knows that, especially at night, it is unfair to ask his stomach to digest cold rations. He knows that the warmth of his body is needed to help him to sleep soundly, not to fight chunks of canned meat. So, no matter how sleepy he may be, he takes the time to build a fire and boil a cup of tea or coffee. Its warmth aids digestion and saves his stomach from working overtime. Nor will he act on the theory that he is "so tired he can sleep anywhere." For a few hours the man who does that may sleep the sleep of exhaustion. But before day breaks he will feel under him the roots and stones, and when he awakes he is stiff, sore and unrefreshed. Ten minutes spent in digging holes for hips and shoulder-blades, in collecting grass and branches to spread beneath his blanket, and leaves to stuff in his boots for a pillow, will give him a whole night of comfort and start him well and fit on the next day's tramp. If you have watched an old sergeant, one of the Indian fighters, of which there are now too few left in the army, when he goes into camp, you will see him build a bunk and possibly a shelter of boughs just as though for the rest of his life he intended to dwell in that particular spot. Down in the Garcia campaign along the Rio Grande I said to one of them: "Why do you go to all that trouble? We break camp at daybreak." He said: "Do we? Well, maybe you know that, and maybe the captain knows that, but I don't know it. And so long as I don't know it, I am going to be just as snug as though I was halted here for a month." In camping, that was one of my first and best lessons—to make your surroundings healthy and comfortable. The temptation always is to say, "Oh, it is for only one night, and I am too tired." The next day you say the same thing, "We'll move tomorrow. What's the use?" But the fishing or shooting around the camp proves good, or it comes on to storm, and for maybe a week you do not move, and for a week you suffer discomforts. An hour of work put in at the beginning would have turned it into a week of ease.

When there is transport of even one pack-horse, one of the best helps toward making camp quickly is a combination of panniers and bed used for many years by E. F. Knight, the *Times* war correspondent, who lost an arm at Gras Pan. It consists of two leather trunks, which by day carry your belongings slung on either side of the pack-animal, and by night act as uprights for your bed. The bed is made of canvas stretched on two poles which rest on the two trunks. For travelling in upper India this arrangement is used almost universally. Mr. Knight obtained his during the Chitral campaign, and since then has used it in every war. He had it with Kuroki's army during this last campaign in Manchuria.

A more compact form of valise and bed combined is the "carry-all," or any of the many makes of sleeping-bags, which during the day carry the kit and at night when spread upon the ground serve for a bed. The one once most used by Englishmen was

Lord Wolseley's "valise and sleeping-bag." It was complicated by a number of strings, and required as much lacing as a dozen pairs of boots. It has been greatly improved by a new sleeping-bag with straps, and flaps that tuck in at the ends. But the obvious disadvantage of all sleeping-bags is that in rain and mud you are virtually lying on the hard ground, at the mercy of tarantula and fever.

The carry-all is, nevertheless, to my mind, the most nearly perfect way in which to pack a kit. I have tried the trunk, valise, and sleeping-bag, and vastly prefer it to them all. My carry-all differs only from the sleeping-bag in that, instead of lining it so that it may be used as a bed, I carry in its pocket a folding cot. By omitting the extra lining for the bed, I save almost the weight of the cot. The folding cot I pack is the Gold Medal Bed, made in this country, but which you can purchase almost any-where. I once carried one from Chicago to Cape Town to find on arriving I could buy the bed there at exactly the same price I had paid for it in America. I also found them in Tokio, where imitations of them were being made by the ingenious and disin-genuous Japanese. They are light in weight, strong, and comfortable, and are undoubtedly the best camp-bed made. When at your elevation of six inches above the ground you look down from one of them upon a comrade in a sleeping-bag with rivulets of rain and a tide of muddy water rising above him, your satisfaction, as you fall asleep, is worth the weight of the bed in gold.

My carry-all is of canvas with a back of waterproof. It is made up of three strips six and a half feet long. The two outer strips are each two feet three inches wide, the middle strip four feet. At one end of the middle strip is a deep pocket of heavy canvas with a flap that can be fastened by two straps. When the kit has been packed in this pocket, the two side strips are folded over it and the middle strip and the whole is rolled up and buckled by two heavy straps on the waterproof side. It is impossible for any article to fall out or for the rain to soak in. I have a smaller carry-all made on the same plan, but on a tiny scale, in which to carry small articles and a change of clothing. It goes into the pocket after the bed, chair, and the heavier articles are packed away. When the bag is rolled up they are on the outside of and form a protection to the articles of lighter weight.

The only objection to the carry-all is that it is an awkward bundle to pack. It is difficult to balance it on the back of an animal, but when you are taking a tent with you or carrying your provisions, it can be slung on one side of the pack saddle to offset their weight on the other.

I use the carry-all when I am travelling "heavy." By that I mean when it is possible to obtain pack-animal or cart. When travelling light and bivouacking by night without a pack-horse, bed, or tent, I use the saddle-bags, already described. These can be slung over the back of the horse you ride, or if you walk, carried over your shoulder. I carried them in this latter way in Greece, in the Transvaal, and Cuba during the rebellion, and later with our own army.

The list of articles I find most useful when travelling where it is possible to obtain transport, or, as we may call it, travelling heavy, are the following:

A tent, seven by ten feet, with fly, jointed poles, tent-pins, a heavy mallet. I recommend a tent open at both ends with a window cut in one end. The window, when that end is laced and the other open, furnishes a draught of air. The window should be covered with a flap which, in case of rain, can be tied down over it with tapes. A great convenience in a tent is a pocket sewn inside of each wall, for boots, books, and such small articles. The pocket should not be filled with anything so heavy as to cause the walls to sag. Another convenience with a tent is a leather strap stretched from pole to pole, upon which to hang clothes, and another is a strap to be buckled around the front tent-pole, and which is studded with projecting hooks for your lantern, water-bottle, and field-glasses. This latter can be bought ready-made at any military outfitter's.

Many men object to the wooden tent-pin on account of its tendency to split, and carry pins made of iron. With these, an inch below the head of the pin is a projecting barb which holds the tent rope.

When the pin is being driven in, the barb is out of reach of the mallet. Any blacksmith can beat out such pins, and if you can afford the extra weight, they are better than those of ash. Also, if you can afford the weight, it is well to carry a strip of water-proof or oilcloth for the floor of the tent to keep out dampness. All these things appertaining to the tent should be rolled up in it, and the tent itself carried in a light-weight receptacle, with a running noose like a sailor's kit-bag.

The carry-all has already been described. Of its contents, I consider first in importance the folding bed.

And second in importance I would place a folding chair. Many men scoff at a chair as a cumbersome luxury. But after a hard day on foot or in the saddle, when you sit on the ground with your back to a rock and your hands locked across your knees to keep yourself from sliding, or on a box with no rest for your spinal column, you begin to think a chair is not a luxury, but a necessity. During the Cuban campaign, for a time I was a member of General Sumner's mess. The general owned a folding chair, and whenever his back was turned every one would make a rush to get into it. One time we were discussing what, in the light of our experience of that campaign, we would take with us on our next, and all agreed, Colonel Howze, Captain Andrews, and Major Harmon, that if one could only take one article it would be a chair. I carried one in Manchuria, but it was of no use to me, as the other correspondents occupied it, relieving each other like sentries on guard duty. I had to pin a sign on it, reading, "Don't sit on me," but no one ever saw the sign. Once, in order to rest in my own chair, I weakly established a precedent by giving George Lynch a cigar to allow me to sit down (on that march there was a mess contractor who supplied us even with cigars, and occasionally with food), and after that, whenever a man wanted to smoke, he would commandeer my chair, and unless bribed refused to budge. This seems to argue the popularity of the contractor's cigars rather than that of the chair, but, nevertheless, I submit that on a campaign the article second in importance for rest, comfort, and content is a chair. The best I know is one invented by Major Elliott of the British army. I have an Elliott chair that I have used four years, not only when camping out, but in my writing-room at home. It is an arm-chair, and is as comfortable as any made. The objections to it are its weight, that it packs bulkily, and takes down into too many pieces. Even with these disadvantages it is the best chair. It can be purchased at the Army and Navy and Anglo-Indian stores in London. A chair of lighter weight and one-fourth the bulk is the Willisden chair, of green canvas and thin iron supports. It breaks in only two pieces, and is very comfortable.

Sir Harry Johnson, in his advice to explorers, makes a great point of their packing a chair. But he recommends one known as the "Wellington," which is a cane-bottomed affair, heavy and cumbersome. Dr. Harford, the instructor in outfit for the Royal Geographical Society, recommends a steamer-chair, because it can be used on shipboard and "can be easily carried afterward." If there be anything less easy to carry than a deck-chair I have not met it. One might as soon think of packing a folding stepladder. But if he has the transport, the man who packs any reasonably light folding chair will not regret it.

As a rule, a cooking kit is built like every other cooking kit in that the utensils for cooking are carried in the same pot that is used for boiling the water, and the top of the pot turns itself into a frying-pan. For eight years I always have used the same kind of cooking kit, so I cannot speak of others with knowledge; but I have always looked with envious eyes at the Preston cooking kit and water-bottle. Why it has not already been adopted by every army I do not understand, for in no army have I seen a kit as compact or as light, or one that combines as many useful articles and takes up as little room. It is the invention of Captain Guy H. Preston, Thirteenth Cavalry, and can be purchased at any military outfitter's.

The cooking kit I carry is, or was, in use in the German army. It is made of aluminum, weighs about as much as a cigarette-case, and takes up as little room as would a high hat. It is a frying-pan and coffee-pot combined. From the Germans it has been borrowed by the Japanese, and one smaller than mine, but of the same pattern, is part of the equipment of each Japanese soldier. On a day's march there are three things a man must carry: his water-bottle, his food, which, with the soldier, is generally carried in a haversack, and his cooking kit. Preston has succeeded most ingeniously in combining the water-bottle and the cooking kit, and I believe by cutting his water-bottle in half, he can make room in his coffee-pot for the food. If he will do this, he will solve the problem of carrying water, food, and the utensils for cooking the food and for boiling the water in one receptacle, which can be carried from the shoulder by a single strap. The alteration I have made for my own use in Captain Preston's water-bottle enables me to carry in the coffee-pot one day's rations of bacon, coffee, and biscuit.

In Tokio, before leaving for Manchuria, General Fukushima asked me to bring my entire outfit to the office of the General Staff. I spread it out on the floor, and with unerring accuracy he selected from it the three articles of greatest value. They were the Gold Medal cot, the Elliott chair, and Preston's water-bottle. He asked if he could borrow these, and, understanding that he wanted to copy them for his own use, and supposing that if he used them, he would, of course, make some restitution to the officers who had invented them, I foolishly loaned them to him. Later, he issued them in numbers to the General Staff. As I felt, in a manner, responsible, I wrote to the Secretary of War, saying I was sure the Japanese army did not wish to benefit by these inventions without making some acknowledgment or return to the inventors. But the Japanese War Office could not see the point I tried to make, and the General Staff wrote a letter in reply asking why I had not directed my communication to General Fukushima, as it was not the Secretary of War, but he, who had taken the articles. The fact that they were being issued without any return being made, did not interest them. They passed cheerfully over the fact that the articles had been stolen, and were indignant, not because I had accused a Japanese general of pilfering, but because I had accused the wrong general. The letter was so insolent that I went to the General Staff Office and explained that the officer who wrote it must withdraw it, and apologize for it. Both of which things he did. In case the gentlemen whose inventions were "borrowed" might, if they wished, take further steps in the matter, I sent the documents in the case, with the exception of the letter which was withdrawn, to the chief of the General Staff in the United States and in England.

In importance after the bed, cooking kit, and chair, I would place these articles:

Two collapsible water-buckets of rubber or canvas. Two collapsible brass lanterns, with extra isinglass sides. Two boxes of sick-room candles. One dozen boxes of safety matches. One axe. The best I have seen is the Marble Safety Axe, made at Gladstone, Mich. You can carry it in your hip-pocket, and you can cut down a tree with it. One medicine case containing quinine, calomel, and Sun Cholera Mixture in tablets. Toilet-case for razors, tooth-powder, brushes, and paper. Folding bathtub of rubber in rubber case. These are manufactured to fold into a space little larger than a cigar-box. Two towels old, and soft. Three cakes of soap. One Jaeger blanket. One mosquito head-bag. One extra pair of shoes, old and comfortable. One extra pair of riding-breeches. One extra pair of gaiters. The former regulation army gaiter of canvas, laced, rolls up in a small compass and weighs but little. One flannel shirt. Gray shows the least dust. Two pairs of drawers. For riding, the best are those of silk. Two undershirts, balbriggan or woollen. Three pairs of woollen socks. Two linen handkerchiefs, large enough, if needed, to tie around the throat and protect the back of the neck. One pair of pajamas, woollen, not linen. One housewife. Two briarwood pipes. Six bags of smoking tobacco; Durham or Seal of North Carolina pack easily. One pad of writing paper. One fountain pen, SELF-FILLING. One bottle of ink, with screw top, held tight by a spring. One dozen linen envelopes. Stamps, wrapped in oil-silk with mucilage side next to the silk. One stick sealing-wax. In tropical countries mucilage on the flap of envelopes sticks to everything except the envelope. One dozen elastic bands of the largest size. In packing they help to compress articles like clothing into the smallest possible compass and in many other ways will be found very useful. One pack of playing-cards. Books. One revolver and six cartridges.

The reason for most of these articles is obvious. Some of them may need a word of recommendation. I place the water-buckets first in the list for the reason that I have found them one of my most valuable assets. With one, as soon as you halt, instead of waiting for your turn at the well or water-hole, you can carry water to your horse, and one of them once filled and set in the shelter of the tent, later saves you many steps. It also can be used as a nose-bag, and to carry fodder. I recommend the brass folding lantern, because those I have tried of tin or aluminum have invariably broken. A lantern is an absolute necessity. When before daylight you break camp, or hurry out in a wind storm to struggle with flying tent-pegs, or when at night you wish to read or play cards, a lantern with a stout frame and steady light is indispensable. The original cost of the sick-room candles is more than that of ordinary candles, but they burn longer, are brighter, and take up much less room. To protect them and the matches from dampness, or the sun, it is well to carry them in a rubber sponge-bag. Any one who has forgotten to pack a towel will not need to be advised to take two. An old sergeant of Troop G, Third Cavalry, once told me that if he had to throw away everything he carried in his roll but one article, he would save his towel. And he was not a particularly fastidious sergeant either, but he preferred a damp towel in his roll to damp clothes on his back. Every man knows the dreary halts in camp when the rain pours outside, or the regiment is held in reserve. For times like these a pack of cards or a book is worth carrying, even if it weighs as much as the plates from which it was printed. At present it is easy to obtain all of the modern classics in volumes small enough to go into the coat-pocket. In Japan, before starting for China, we divided up among the correspondents Thomas Nelson & Sons' and Doubleday, Page & Co.'s pocket editions of Dickens, Thackeray, and Lever, and as most of our time in Manchuria was spent locked up in compounds, they proved a great blessing.

In the list I have included a revolver, following out the old saying that "You may not need it for a long time, but when you do need it, you want it damned quick." Except to impress guides and mule-drivers, it is not an essential article. In six campaigns I have carried one, and never used it, nor needed it but once, and then while I was dodging behind the foremast it lay under tons of luggage in the hold. The number of cartridges I have limited to six, on the theory that if in six shots you haven't hit the other fellow, he will have hit you, and you will not require another six.

This, I think, completes the list of articles that on different expeditions I either have found of use, or have seen render good service to some one else. But the really wise man will pack none of the things enumerated in this article. For the larger his kit, the less benefit he will have of it. It will all be taken from him. And accordingly my final advice is to go forth empty-handed, naked and unashamed, and borrow from your friends. I have never tried that method of collecting an outfit, but I have never seen it fail, and of all travellers the man who borrows is the wisest.

The Road Home

❦

[PETER COLLINSON]

"You're a fool to pass it up! You'll get just as much credit and reward for taking back proof of my death as you will for taking me back. And I got papers and stuff buried back near the Yunnan border that you can have to back up your story; and you needn't be afraid that I'll ever show up to spoil your play."

The gaunt man in faded khaki frowned with patient annoyance and looked away from the blood-shot brown eyes in front of him, over the teak side of the jahaz to where the wrinkled snout of a muggar broke the surface of the river. When the small crocodile submerged again, Hagedorn's gray eyes came back to the pleading ones before him, and he spoke wearily, as one who has been answering the same arguments again and again.

"I can't do it, Barnes. I left New York two years ago to get you, and for two years I've been in this damned country here and in Yunnan—hunting you. I promised my people I'd stay until I found you, and I kept my word. Lord! man," with a touch of exasperation, "after all I've gone through you don't expect me to throw them down now—now that the job's as good as done!"

The dark man in the garb of a native smiled an oily, ingratiating smile and brushed away his captor's words with a wave of his hand.

"I ain't offering you a dinky coupla thousand dollars; I'm offering you your pick out of one of the richest gem beds in Asia—a bed that was hidden by the Mran-ma when the British jumped the country. Come back up there with me and I'll show you rubies and sapphires and topazes that'll knock your eye out. All I'm asking you is to go back up there with me and take a look at 'em. If you don't like 'em you'll still have me to take back to New York."

Hagedorn shook his head slowly.

"You're going back to New York with me. Maybe man-hunting isn't the nicest trade in the world but it's all the trade I've got, and this jewel bed of yours sounds phoney to me. I can't blame you for not wanting to go back—but just the same I'm taking you."

Barnes glared at the detective disgustedly.

"You're a fine chump! And it's costing me and you thousands of dollars! Hell!"

He spat over the side insultingly—native-like—and settled himself back on his corner of the split-bamboo mat.

Hagedorn was looking past the lateen sail, down the river—the beginning of the route to New York—along which a miasmal breeze was carrying the fifty-foot boat with surprising speed. Four more days and they would be aboard a steamer for Rangoon; then another steamer to Calcutta, and in the end, one to New York—home, after two years!

Two years through unknown country, pursuing what until the very day of the capture had never been more than a vague shadow. Through Yunnan and Burma, combing wilderness with microscopic thoroughness—a game of hide-and-seek up the rivers, over the hills and through the jungles—sometimes a year, sometimes two months and then six behind his quarry. And now successfully home! Betty would be fifteen—quite a lady.

Barnes edged forward and resumed his pleading, with a whine creeping into his voice.

"Say, Hagedorn, why don't you listen to reason? There ain't no sense in us losing all that money just for something that happened over two years ago. I didn't mean to kill that guy, anyway. You know how it is; I was a kid and wild and foolish—but I wasn't mean—and I got in with a bunch. Why, I thought of that hold-up as a lark when we planned it! And then that messenger yelled and I guess I was excited, and my gun went off the first thing I knew. I didn't go to kill him; and it won't do him no good to take me back and hang me for it. The express company didn't lose no money. What do they want to hound me like this for? I been trying to live it down."

The gaunt detective answered quietly enough but what kindness there had been in his dry voice before was gone now.

"I know—the old story! And the bruises on the Burmese woman you were living with sure show that there's nothing mean about you. Cut it, Barnes, and make up your mind to face it—you and I are going back to New York."

"The hell we are!"

Barnes got slowly to his feet and backed away a step.

"I'd just as leave—"

Hagedorn's automatic came out a split second too late; his prisoner was over the side and swimming toward the bank. The detective caught up his rifle from the deck behind him and sprang to the rail. Barnes' head showed for a moment and then went down again, to appear again twenty feet nearer shore. Upstream the man in the boat saw the blunt, wrinkled noses of three muggars, moving toward the shore at a tangent that would intercept the fugitive. He leaned against the teak rail and summed up the situation.

"Looks like I'm not going to take him back alive after all—but my job's done. I can shoot him when he shows again, or I can let him alone and the muggars will get him."

Then the sudden but logical instinct to side with the member of his own species against enemies from another wiped out all other considerations, and sent his rifle to his shoulder to throw a shower of bullets into the muggars.

Barnes clambered up the bank of the river, waved his hand over his head without looking back, and plunged into the jungle.

Hagedorn turned to the bearded owner of the jahaz, who had come to his side, and addressed him in his broken Burmese.

"Put me ashore—yu nga apau mye—and wait— thaing—until I bring him back—thu yughe."

The captain wagged his black beard protestingly.

"Mahok! In the jungle here, sahib, a man is as a lei. Twenty men might find him in a week, or a month, it may take five years. I cannot wait that long."

The gaunt white man gnawed at his lower lip and looked down the river—the road to New York.

"Two years," he said aloud to himself, "it took to find him when he didn't know I was hunting for him. Now—Oh, hell! It may take five years. I wonder about them jewels of his."

He turned to the boatman.

"I go after him. You wait three hours," pointing over head, "until noon—ne apomha. If I am not back then do not wait—malotu thaing, thwa. Thi?"

The captain nodded.

"Hokhe!"

For five hours the captain kept the jahaz at anchor, and then, when the shadows of the trees on the west bank were creeping out into the river, he ordered the latten sail hoisted, and the teak craft vanished around a bend in the river.

Leiningen Versus the Ants

[CARL STEPHENSON]

"Unless they alter their course and there's no reason why they should, they'll reach your plantation in two days at the latest."

Leiningen sucked placidly at a cigar about the size of a corncob and for a few seconds gazed without answering at the agitated District Commissioner. Then he took the cigar from his lips, and leaned slightly forward. With his bristling grey hair, bulky nose, and lucid eyes, he had the look of an aging and shabby eagle.

"Decent of you," he murmured, "paddling all this way just to give me the tip. But you're pulling my leg of course when you say I must do a bunk. Why, even a herd of saurians couldn't drive me from this plantation of mine."

The Brazilian official threw up lean and lanky arms and clawed the air with wildly distended fingers.

"Leiningen!" he shouted. "You're insane! They're not creatures you can fight—they're an elemental— an 'act of God!' Ten miles long, two miles wide— ants, nothing but ants! And every single one of them a fiend from hell; before you can spit three times they'll eat a full-grown buffalo to the bones. I tell you if you don't clear out at once there'll be nothing left of you but a skeleton picked as clean as your own plantation."

Leiningen grinned. "Act of God, my eye! Anyway, I'm not an old woman; I'm not going to run for it just because an elemental's on the way. And don't think I'm the kind of fathead who tries to fend off lightning with his fists either. I use my intelligence, old man. With me, the brain isn't a second blindgut; I know what it's there for. When I began this model farm and plantation three years ago, I took into account all that could conceivably happen to it. And now I'm ready for anything and everything— including your ants."

The Brazilian rose heavily to his feet. "I've done my best," he gasped. "Your obstinacy endangers not only yourself, but the lives of your four hundred workers. You don't know these ants!"

Leiningen accompanied him down to the river, where the Government launch was moored. The vessel cast off. As it moved downstream, the exclamation mark neared the rail and began waving its arms frantically. Long after the launch had disappeared round the bend, Leiningen thought he could still hear that dimming imploring voice, "You don't know them, I tell you! You don't know them!"

But the reported enemy was by no means unfamiliar to the planter. Before he started work on his settlement, he had lived long enough in the country to see for himself the fearful devastations sometimes wrought by these ravenous insects in their campaigns for food. But since then he had planned measures of defence accordingly, and these, he was convinced, were in every way adequate to withstand the approaching peril.

Moreover, during his three years as a planter, Leiningen had met and defeated drought, flood, plague and all other "acts of God" which had come against him—unlike his fellow-settlers in the district, who had made little or no resistance. This unbroken success he attributed solely to the observance of his lifelong motto: The human brain needs only to become fully aware of its powers to conquer even the elements. Dullards reeled senselessly and aimlessly into the abyss; cranks, however brilliant, lost their heads when circumstances suddenly altered or accelerated and ran into stone walls, sluggards drifted with the current until they were caught in whirlpools and dragged under. But such disasters, Leiningen contended, merely strengthened his argument that intelligence, directed aright, invariably makes man the master of his fate.

Yes, Leiningen had always known how to grapple with life. Even here, in this Brazilian wilderness, his brain had triumphed over every difficulty and danger it had so far encountered. First he had vanquished primal forces by cunning and organization, then he had enlisted the resources of modern science to increase miraculously the yield of his plantation. And now he was sure he would prove more than a match for the "irresistible" ants.

That same evening, however, Leiningen assembled his workers. He had no intention of waiting till the news reached their ears from other sources. Most of them had been born in the district; the cry "The ants are coming!" was to them an imperative signal for instant, panic-stricken flight, a spring for life itself. But so great was the Indians' trust in Leiningen, in Leiningen's word, and in Leiningen's wisdom, that they received his curt tidings, and his orders for the imminent struggle, with the calmness with which they were given. They waited, unafraid, alert, as if for the beginning of a new game or hunt which he had just described to them. The ants were indeed mighty, but not so mighty as the boss. Let them come!

They came at noon the second day. Their approach was announced by the wild unrest of the horses, scarcely controllable now either in stall or under rider, scenting from afar a vapor instinct with horror.

It was announced by a stampede of animals, timid and savage, hurtling past each other; jaguars and pumas flashing by nimble stags of the pampas, bulky tapirs, no longer hunters, themselves hunted, outpacing fleet kinkajous, maddened herds of cattle, heads lowered, nostrils snorting, rushing through tribes of loping monkeys, chattering in a dementia of terror; then followed the creeping and springing denizens of bush and steppe, big and little rodents, snakes, and lizards.

Pell-mell the rabble swarmed down the hill to the plantation, scattered right and left before the barrier of the water-filled ditch, then sped onwards to the river, where, again hindered, they fled along its bank out of sight.

This water-filled ditch was one of the defence measures which Leiningen had long since prepared against the advent of the ants. It encompassed three sides of the plantation like a huge horseshoe. Twelve feet across, but not very deep, when dry it could hardly be described as an obstacle to either man or beast. But the ends of the "horseshoe" ran into the river which formed the northern boundary, and fourth side, of the plantation. And at the end nearer the house and outbuildings in the middle of the plantation, Leiningen had constructed a dam by means of which water from the river could be diverted into the ditch.

So now, by opening the dam, he was able to fling an imposing girdle of water, a huge quadrilateral with the river as its base, completely around the plantation, like the moat encircling a medieval city. Unless the ants were clever enough to build rafts, they had no hope of reaching the plantation, Leiningen concluded.

The twelve-foot water ditch seemed to afford in itself all the security needed. But while awaiting the arrival of the ants, Leiningen made a further improvement. The western section of the ditch ran along the edge of a tamarind wood, and the branches of some great trees reached over the water. Leiningen now had them lopped so that ants could not descend from them within the "moat."

The women and children, then the herds of cattle, were escorted by peons on rafts over the river, to remain on the other side in absolute safety until the plunderers had departed. Leiningen gave this instruction, not because he believed the non-combatants were in any danger, but in order to avoid hampering the efficiency of the defenders. "Critical situations first become crises," he explained to his men, "when oxen or women get excited."

Finally, he made a careful inspection of the "inner moat"—a smaller ditch lined with concrete, which extended around the hill on which stood the ranch house, barns, stables and other buildings. Into this concrete ditch emptied the inflow pipes from three great petrol tanks. If by some miracle the ants managed to cross the water and reached the plantation,

this "rampart of petrol," would be an absolutely
impassable protection for the besieged and their
dwellings and stock. Such, at least, was Leiningen's
opinion.

He stationed his men at irregular distances along
the water ditch, the first line of defence. Then he lay
down in his hammock and puffed drowsily away at
his pipe until a peon came with the report that the
ants had been observed far away in the South.

Leiningen mounted his horse, which at the feel of
its master seemed to forget its uneasiness, and rode
leisurely in the direction of the threatening offensive. The southern stretch of ditch—the upper side
of the quadrilateral—was nearly three miles long;
from its center one could survey the entire country-
side. This was destined to be the scene of the out-
break of war between Leiningen's brain and twenty
square miles of life-destroying ants.

It was a sight one could never forget. Over the
range of hills, as far as eye could see, crept a darkening hem, ever longer and broader, until the shadow
spread across the slope from east to west, then downwards, downwards, uncannily swift, and all the green
herbage of that wide vista was being mown as by a
giant sickle, leaving only the vast moving shadow,
extending, deepening, and moving rapidly nearer.

When Leiningen's men, behind their barrier of
water, perceived the approach of the long-expected
foe, they gave vent to their suspense in screams and

imprecations. But as the distance began to lessen between the "sons of hell" and the water ditch, they relapsed into silence. Before the advance of that awe-inspiring throng, their belief in the powers of the boss began to steadily dwindle.

Even Leiningen himself, who had ridden up just in time to restore their loss of heart by a display of unshakable calm, even he could not free himself from a qualm of malaise. Yonder were thousands of millions of voracious jaws bearing down upon him and only a suddenly insignificant, narrow ditch lay between him and his men and being gnawed to the bones "before you can spit three times."

Hadn't this brain for once taken on more than it could manage? If the blighters decided to rush the ditch, fill it to the brim with their corpses, there'd still be more than enough to destroy every trace of that cranium of his. The planter's chin jutted; they hadn't got him yet, and he'd see to it they never would. While he could think at all, he'd flout both death and the devil.

The hostile army was approaching in perfect formation; no human battalions, however well-drilled, could ever hope to rival the precision of that advance. Along a front that moved forward as uniformly as a straight line, the ants drew nearer and nearer to the water ditch. Then, when they learned through their scouts the nature of the obstacle, the two outlying wings of the army detached themselves from the main body and marched down the western and eastern sides of the ditch.

This surrounding maneuver took rather more than an hour to accomplish; no doubt the ants expected that at some point they would find a crossing.

During this outflanking movement by the wings, the army on the center and southern front remained still. The besieged were therefore able to contemplate at their leisure the thumb-long, reddish black, long-legged insects; some of the Indians believed they could see, too, intent on them, the brilliant, cold eyes, and the razor-edged mandibles, of this host of infinity.

It is not easy for the average person to imagine that an animal, not to mention an insect, can think. But now both the European brain of Leiningen and the primitive brains of the Indians began to stir with the unpleasant foreboding that inside every single one of that deluge of insects dwelt a thought. And that thought was: Ditch or no ditch, we'll get to your flesh!

Not until four o'clock did the wings reach the "horseshoe" ends of the ditch, only to find these ran into the great river. Through some kind of secret telegraphy, the report must then have flashed very swiftly indeed along the entire enemy line. And Leiningen, riding—no longer casually—along his side of the ditch, noticed by energetic and widespread movements of troops that for some unknown reason the news of the check had its greatest effect on the southern front, where the main army was massed. Perhaps the failure to find a way over the ditch was persuading the ants to withdraw from the plantation in search of spoils more easily attainable.

An immense flood of ants, about a hundred yards in width, was pouring in a glimmering-black cataract down the far slope of the ditch. Many thousands were already drowning in the sluggish creeping flow, but they were followed by troop after troop, who clambered over their sinking comrades, and then themselves served as dying bridges to the reserves hurrying on in their rear.

Shoals of ants were being carried away by the current into the middle of the ditch, where gradually they broke asunder and then, exhausted by their struggles, vanished below the surface. Nevertheless, the wavering, floundering hundred-yard front was remorselessly if slowly advancing towards the besieged on the other bank. Leiningen had been wrong when he supposed the enemy would first have to fill the ditch with their bodies before they could cross; instead, they merely needed to act as steppingstones, as they swam and sank, to the hordes ever pressing onwards from behind.

Near Leiningen a few mounted herdsmen awaited his orders. He sent one to the weir—the river must be dammed more strongly to increase the speed and power of the water coursing through the ditch.

A second peon was dispatched to the outhouses to bring spades and petrol sprinklers. A third rode away to summon to the zone of the offensive all the men, except the observation posts, on the near-by sections of the ditch, which were not yet actively threatened.

The ants were getting across far more quickly than Leiningen would have deemed possible. Impelled by the mighty cascade behind them, they struggled nearer and nearer to the inner bank. The momentum of the attack was so great that neither the tardy flow of the stream nor its downward pull could exert its proper force; and into the gap left by every submerging insect, hastened forward a dozen more.

When reinforcements reached Leiningen, the invaders were halfway over. The planter had to admit to himself that it was only by a stroke of luck for him that the ants were attempting the crossing on a relatively short front: had they assaulted simultaneously along the entire length of the ditch, the outlook for the defenders would have been black indeed.

Even as it was, it could hardly be described as rosy, though the planter seemed quite unaware that death in a gruesome form was drawing closer and closer. As the war between his brain and the "act of God" reached its climax, the very shadow of annihilation began to pale to Leiningen, who now felt like a champion in a new Olympic game, a gigantic and thrilling contest, from which he was determined to emerge victor. Such, indeed, was his aura of confidence that the Indians forgot their stupefied fear of the peril only a yard or two away; under the planter's supervision, they began fervidly digging up to the edge of the bank and throwing clods of earth and spadefuls of sand into the midst of the hostile fleet.

The petrol sprinklers, hitherto used to destroy pests and blights on the plantation, were also brought into action. Streams of evil-reeking oil now soared and fell over an enemy already in disorder through the bombardment of earth and sand.

The ants responded to these vigorous and successful measures of defence by further developments of their offensive. Entire clumps of huddling insects began to roll down the opposite bank into the water. At the same time, Leiningen noticed that the ants were now attacking along an ever-widening front. As the numbers both of his men and his petrol sprinklers were severely limited, this rapid extension of the line of battle was becoming an overwhelming danger.

To add to his difficulties, the very clods of earth they flung into that black floating carpet often whirled fragments toward the defenders' side, and here and there dark ribbons were already mounting the inner bank. True, wherever a man saw these they could still be driven back into the water by spadefuls of earth or jets of petrol. But the file of defenders was too sparse and scattered to hold off at all points these landing parties, and though the peons toiled like madmen, their plight became momentarily more perilous.

One man struck with his spade at an enemy clump, did not draw it back quickly enough from the water; in a trice the wooden shaft swarmed with upward scurrying insects. With a curse, he dropped the spade into the ditch; too late, they were already on his body. They lost no time; wherever they encountered bare flesh they bit deeply; a few, bigger than the rest, carried in their hind-quarters a sting which injected a burning and paralyzing venom. Screaming, frantic with pain, the peon danced and twirled like a dervish.

Realizing that another such casualty, yes, perhaps this alone, might plunge his men into confusion and destroy their morale, Leiningen roared in a bellow louder than the yells of the victim: "Into the petrol, idiot! Douse your paws in the petrol!" The dervish ceased his pirouette as if transfixed, then tore off his shirt and plunged his arm and the ants hanging to it up to the shoulder in one of the large open tins of petrol. But even then the fierce mandibles did not slacken; another peon had to help him squash and detach each separate insect.

Distracted by the episode, some defenders had turned away from the ditch. And now cries of fury, a thudding of spades, and a wild trampling to and fro, showed that the ants had made full use of the interval, though luckily only a few had managed to get across. The men set to work again desperately with the barrage of earth and sand. Meanwhile an old Indian, who acted as medicine-man to the plantation workers, gave the bitten peon a drink he had prepared some hours before, which, he claimed, possessed the virtue of dissolving and weakening ants' venom.

Leiningen surveyed his position. A dispassionate observer would have estimated the odds against him at a thousand to one. But then such an on-looker would have reckoned only by what he saw—the advance of myriad battalions of ants against the futile efforts of a few defenders—and not by the unseen activity that can go on in a man's brain.

For Leiningen had not erred when he decided he would fight elemental with elemental. The water in the ditch was beginning to rise; the stronger damming of the river was making itself apparent.

Visibly the swiftness and power of the masses of water increased, swirling into quicker and quicker movement its living black surface, dispersing its pattern, carrying away more and more of it on the hastening current.

Victory had been snatched from the very jaws of defeat. With a hysterical shout of joy, the peons feverishly intensified their bombardment of earth clods and sand.

And now the wide cataract down the opposite bank was thinning and ceasing, as if the ants were becoming aware that they could not attain their aim. They were scurrying back up the slope to safety.

All the troops so far hurled into the ditch had been sacrificed in vain. Drowned and floundering insects eddied in thousands along the flow, while Indians running on the bank destroyed every swimmer that reached the side.

Not until the ditch curved towards the east did the scattered ranks assemble again in a coherent mass. And now, exhausted and half-numbed, they were in no condition to ascend the bank. Fusillades of clods drove them round the bend towards the mouth of the ditch and then into the river, wherein they vanished without leaving a trace.

The news ran swiftly along the entire chain of outposts, and soon a long scattered line of laughing men could be seen hastening along the ditch towards the scene of victory.

For once they seemed to have lost all their native reserve, for it was in wild abandon now they celebrated the triumph—as if there were no longer thousands of millions of merciless, cold and hungry eyes watching them from the opposite bank, watching and waiting.

The sun sank behind the rim of the tamarind wood and twilight deepened into night. It was not only hoped but expected that the ants would remain quiet until dawn. But to defeat any forlorn attempt at a crossing, the flow of water through the ditch was powerfully increased by opening the dam still further.

In spite of this impregnable barrier, Leiningen was not yet altogether convinced that the ants would not venture another surprise attack. He ordered his men to camp along the bank overnight. He also detailed parties of them to patrol the ditch in two of his motor cars and ceaselessly to illuminate the surface of the water with headlights and electric torches.

After having taken all the precautions he deemed necessary, the farmer ate his supper with considerable appetite and went to bed. His slumbers were in no wise disturbed by the memory of the waiting, live, twenty square miles.

Dawn found a thoroughly refreshed and active Leiningen riding along the edge of the ditch. The planter saw before him a motionless and unaltered throng of besiegers. He studied the wide belt of water between them and the plantation, and for a moment almost regretted that the fight had ended so soon and so simply. In the comforting, matter-of-fact light of morning, it seemed to him now that the ants hadn't the ghost of a chance to cross the ditch. Even if they plunged headlong into it on all three fronts at once, the force of the now powerful current would inevitably sweep them away. He had got quite a thrill out of the fight—a pity it was already over.

He rode along the eastern and southern sections of the ditch and found everything in order. He reached the western section, opposite the tamarind wood, and here, contrary to the other battle fronts, he found the enemy very busy indeed. The trunks and branches of the trees and the creepers of the lianas, on the far bank of the ditch, fairly swarmed with industrious insects. But instead of eating the leaves there and then, they were merely gnawing through the stalks, so that a thick green shower fell steadily to the ground.

No doubt they were victualing columns sent out to obtain provender for the rest of the army. The discovery did not surprise Leiningen. He did not need to be told that ants are intelligent, that certain species even use others as milch cows, watchdogs and slaves. He was well aware of their power of adaptation, their sense of discipline, their marvelous talent for organization.

His belief that a foray to supply the army was in progress was strengthened when he saw the leaves that fell to the ground being dragged to the troops waiting outside the wood. Then all at once he realized the aim that rain of green was intended to serve.

Each single leaf, pulled or pushed by dozens of toiling insects, was borne straight to the edge of the ditch. Even as Macbeth watched the approach of Birnam Wood in the hands of his enemies, Leiningen saw the tamarind wood move nearer and nearer in the mandibles of the ants. Unlike the fey Scot, however, he did not lose his nerve; no witches had prophesied his doom, and if they had he would have slept just as soundly. All the same, he was forced to admit to himself that the situation was far more ominous than that of the day before.

He had thought it impossible for the ants to build rafts for themselves—well, here they were, coming in thousands, more than enough to bridge the ditch. Leaves after leaves rustled down the slope into the water, where the current drew them away from the bank and carried them into midstream. And every single leaf carried several ants. This time the farmer did not trust to the alacrity of his messengers. He galloped away, leaning from his saddle and yelling orders as he rushed past outpost after outpost: "Bring petrol pumps to the southwest front! Issue spades to every man along the line facing the wood!" And arrived at the eastern and southern sections, he dispatched every man except the observation posts to the menaced west.

Then, as he rode past the stretch where the ants had failed to cross the day before, he witnessed a brief but impressive scene. Down the slope of the distant hill there came towards him a singular being, writhing rather than running, an animal-like blackened statue with shapeless head and four quivering feet that knuckled under almost ceaselessly. When the creature reached the far bank of the ditch and collapsed opposite Leiningen, he recognized it as a pampas stag, covered over and over with ants.

It had strayed near the zone of the army. As usual, they had attacked its eyes first. Blinded, it had reeled in the madness of hideous torment straight into the ranks of its persecutors, and now the beast swayed to and fro in its death agony.

With a shot from his rifle Leiningen put it out of its misery. Then he pulled out his watch. He hadn't a second to lose, but for life itself he could not have denied his curiosity the satisfaction of knowing how long the ants would take—for personal reasons, so to speak. After six minutes the white polished bones alone remained. That's how he himself would look before you can—Leiningen spat once, and put spurs to his horse.

The sporting zest with which the excitement of the novel contest had inspired him the day before had now vanished; in its place was a cold and violent purpose. He would send these vermin back to the hell where they belonged, somehow, anyhow. Yes, but how was indeed the question; as things stood at present it looked as if the devils would raze him and his men from the earth instead. He had under-estimated the might of the enemy; he really would have to bestir himself if he hoped to outwit them.

The biggest danger now, he decided, was the point where the western section of the ditch curved southwards. And arrived there, he found his worst expectations justified. The very power of the current had huddled the leaves and their crews of ants so close together at the bend that the bridge was almost ready.

True, streams of petrol and clumps of earth still prevented a landing. But the number of floating leaves was increasing ever more swiftly. It could not be long now before a stretch of water a mile in length was decked by a green pontoon over which the ants could rush in millions.

Leiningen galloped to the weir. The damming of the river was controlled by a wheel on its bank. The planter ordered the man at the wheel first to lower the water in the ditch almost to vanishing point, next to wait a moment, then suddenly to let the river in again. This maneuver of lowering and raising the surface, of decreasing then increasing the flow of water through the ditch was to be repeated over and over again until further notice.

This tactic was at first successful. The water in the ditch sank, and with it the film of leaves. The green fleet nearly reached the bed and the troops on the far bank swarmed down the slope to it. Then a violent flow of water at the original depth raced through the ditch, overwhelming leaves and ants, and sweeping them along.

This intermittent rapid flushing prevented just in time the almost completed fording of the ditch. But it also flung here and there squads of the enemy vanguard simultaneously up the inner bank. These seemed to know their duty only too well, and lost no time accomplishing it. The air rang with the curses of bitten Indians. They had removed their shirts and pants to detect the quicker the upwards-hastening insects; when they saw one, they crushed it; and fortunately the onslaught as yet was only by skirmishers. Again and again, the water sank and rose, carrying leaves and drowned ants away with it. It lowered once more nearly to its bed; but this time the exhausted defenders waited in vain for the flush of destruction. Leiningen sensed disaster; something must have gone wrong with the machinery of the dam. Then a sweating peon tore up to him—

"They're over!"

While the besieged were concentrating upon the defence of the stretch opposite the wood, the seem-ingly unaffected line beyond the wood had become the theatre of decisive action. Here the defenders' front was sparse and scattered; everyone who could be spared had hurried away to the south.

Just as the man at the weir had lowered the water almost to the bed of the ditch, the ants on a wide front began another attempt at a direct crossing like that of the preceding day. Into the emptied bed poured an irresistible throng. Rushing across the ditch, they attained the inner bank before the slow-witted Indians fully grasped the situation. Their fran-tic screams dumfounded the man at the weir. Before he could direct the river anew into the safeguarding bed he saw himself surrounded by raging ants. He ran like the others, ran for his life.

When Leiningen heard this, he knew the plantation was doomed. He wasted no time bemoaning the inevitable. For as long as there was the slightest chance of success, he had stood his ground, and now any further resistance was both useless and dangerous. He fired three revolver shots into the air—the prearranged signal for his men to retreat instantly within the "inner moat." Then he rode towards the ranch house.

This was two miles from the point of invasion. There was therefore time enough to prepare the second line of defence against the advent of the ants. Of the three great petrol cisterns near the house, one had already been half emptied by the constant withdrawals needed for the pumps during the fight at the water ditch. The remaining petrol in it was now drawn off through underground pipes into the concrete trench which encircled the ranch house and its outbuildings.

And there, drifting in twos and threes, Leiningen's men reached him. Most of them were obviously trying to preserve an air of calm and indifference, belied, however, by their restless glances and knitted brows. One could see their belief in a favorable outcome of the struggle was already considerably shaken.

The planter called his peons around him.

"Well, lads," he began, "we've lost the first round. But we'll smash the beggars yet, don't you worry. Anyone who thinks otherwise can draw his pay here and now and push off. There are rafts enough to spare on the river and plenty of time still to reach 'em."

Not a man stirred.

Leiningen acknowledged his silent vote of confidence with a laugh that was half a grunt. "That's the stuff, lads. Too bad if you'd missed the rest of the show, eh? Well, the fun won't start till morning. Once these blighters turn tail, there'll be plenty of work for everyone and higher wages all round. And now run along and get something to eat; you've earned it all right."

In the excitement of the fight the greater part of the day had passed without the men once pausing to snatch a bite. Now that the ants were for the time being out of sight, and the "wall of petrol" gave a stronger feeling of security, hungry stomachs began to assert their claims.

The bridges over the concrete ditch were removed. Here and there solitary ants had reached the ditch; they gazed at the petrol meditatively, then scurried back again. Apparently they had little interest at the moment for what lay beyond the evil-reeking barrier; the abundant spoils of the plantation were the main attraction. Soon the trees, shrubs and beds for miles around were hulled with ants zealously gobbling the yield of long weary months of strenuous toil.

As twilight began to fall, a cordon of ants marched around the petrol trench, but as yet made no move towards its brink. Leiningen posted sentries with headlights and electric torches, then withdrew to his office, and began to reckon up his losses. He estimated these as large, but, in comparison with his bank balance, by no means unbearable. He worked out in some detail a scheme of intensive cultivation which would enable him, before very long, to more than compensate himself for the damage now being wrought to his crops. It was with a contented mind that he finally betook himself to bed where he slept deeply until dawn, undisturbed by any thought that next day little more might be left of him than a glistening skeleton.

He rose with the sun and went out on the flat roof of his house. And a scene like one from Dante lay around him; for miles in every direction there was nothing but a black, glittering multitude, a multitude of rested, sated, but none the less voracious ants: yes, look as far as one might, one could see nothing but that rustling black throng, except in the north, where the great river drew a boundary they could not hope to pass. But even the high stone breakwater, along the bank of the river, which Leiningen had built as a defence against inundations, was, like the paths, the shorn trees and shrubs, the ground itself, black with ants.

So their greed was not glutted in razing that vast plantation? Not by a long shot; they were all the more eager now on a rich and certain booty—four hundred men, numerous horses, and bursting granaries.

At first it seemed that the petrol trench would serve its purpose. The besiegers sensed the peril of swimming it, and made no move to plunge blindly over its brink. Instead they devised a better maneuver; they began to collect shreds of bark, twigs and dried leaves and dropped these into the petrol. Everything green, which could have been similarly used, had long since been eaten. After a time, though, a long procession could be seen bringing from the west the tamarind leaves used as rafts the day before.

Since the petrol, unlike the water in the outer ditch, was perfectly still, the refuse stayed where it was thrown. It was several hours before the ants succeeded in covering an appreciable part of the surface. At length, however, they were ready to proceed to a direct attack.

Their storm troops swarmed down the concrete side, scrambled over the supporting surface of twigs and leaves, and impelled these over the few remaining streaks of open petrol until they reached the other side. Then they began to climb up this to make straight for the helpless garrison.

During the entire offensive, the planter sat peacefully, watching them with interest, but not stirring a muscle. Moreover, he had ordered his men not to disturb in any way whatever the advancing horde. So they squatted listlessly along the bank of the ditch and waited for a sign from the boss. The petrol was now covered with ants. A few had climbed the inner concrete wall and were scurrying towards the defenders.

"Everyone back from the ditch!" roared Leiningen. The men rushed away, without the slightest idea of his plan. He stooped forward and cautiously dropped into the ditch a stone which split the floating carpet and its living freight, to reveal a gleaming patch of petrol. A match spurted, sank down to the oily surface—Leiningen sprang back; in a flash a towering rampart of fire encompassed the garrison.

This spectacular and instant repulse threw the Indians into ecstasy. They applauded, yelled and stamped, like children at a pantomime. Had it not been for the awe in which they held the boss, they would infallibly have carried him shoulder high.

It was some time before the petrol burned down to the bed of the ditch, and the wall of smoke and flame began to lower. The ants had retreated in a wide circle from the devastation, and innumerable charred fragments along the outer bank showed that the flames had spread from the holocaust in the ditch well into the ranks beyond, where they had wrought havoc far and wide.

Yet the perseverance of the ants was by no means broken; indeed, each setback seemed only to whet it. The concrete cooled, the flicker of the dying flames wavered and vanished, petrol from the second tank poured into the trench—and the ants marched forward anew to the attack.

The foregoing scene repeated itself in every detail, except that on this occasion less time was needed to bridge the ditch, for the petrol was now already filmed by a layer of ash. Once again they withdrew; once again petrol flowed into the ditch. Would the creatures never learn that their self-sacrifice was utterly senseless? It really was senseless, wasn't it? Yes, of course it was senseless—provided the defenders had an unlimited supply of petrol.

When Leiningen reached this stage of reasoning, he felt for the first time since the arrival of the ants that his confidence was deserting him. His skin began to creep; he loosened his collar. Once the devils were over the trench there wasn't a chance in hell for him and his men. God, what a prospect, to be eaten alive like that!

For the third time the flames immolated the attacking troops, and burned down to extinction. Yet the ants were coming on again as if nothing had happened. And meanwhile Leiningen had made a discovery that chilled him to the bone—petrol was no longer flowing into the ditch. Something must be blocking the outflow pipe of the third and last cistern—a snake or a dead rat? Whatever it was, the ants could be held off no longer, unless petrol could by some method be let from the cistern into the ditch.

Then Leiningen remembered that in an outhouse nearby were two old disused fire engines. Spry as never before in their lives, the peons dragged them out of the shed, connected their pumps to the cistern, uncoiled and laid the hose. They were just in time to aim a stream of petrol at a column of ants that had already crossed and drive them back down the incline into the ditch. Once more an oily girdle surrounded the garrison, once more it was possible to hold the position—for the moment.

It was obvious, however, that this last resource meant only the postponement of defeat and death. A few of the peons fell on their knees and began to pray; others, shrieking insanely, fired their revolvers at the black, advancing masses, as if they felt their despair was pitiful enough to sway fate itself to mercy.

At length, two of the men's nerves broke: Leiningen saw a naked Indian leap over the north side of the petrol trench, quickly followed by a second. They sprinted with incredible speed towards the river. But their fleetness did not save them; long before they could attain the rafts, the enemy covered their bodies from head to foot.

In the agony of their torment, both sprang blindly into the wide river, where enemies no less sinister awaited them. Wild screams of mortal anguish informed the breathless onlookers that crocodiles and sword-toothed piranhas were no less ravenous than ants, and even nimbler in reaching their prey.

In spite of this bloody warning, more and more men showed they were making up their minds to run the blockade. Anything, even a fight midstream against alligators, seemed better than powerlessly waiting for death to come and slowly consume their living bodies.

Leiningen flogged his brain till it reeled. Was there nothing on earth could sweep this devil's spawn back into the hell from which it came?

Then out of the inferno of his bewilderment rose a terrifying inspiration. Yes, one hope remained, and one alone. It might be possible to dam the great river completely, so that its waters would fill not only the water ditch but overflow into the entire gigantic "saucer" of land in which lay the plantation.

The far bank of the river was too high for the waters to escape that way. The stone breakwater ran between the river and the plantation; its only gaps occurred where the "horseshoe" ends of the water ditch passed into the river. So its waters would not only be forced to inundate into the plantation, they would also be held there by the breakwater until they rose to its own high level. In half an hour, perhaps even earlier, the plantation and its hostile army of occupation would be flooded.

The ranch house and outbuildings stood upon rising ground. Their foundations were higher than the breakwater, so the flood would not reach them. And any remaining ants trying to ascend the slope could be repulsed by petrol.

It was possible—yes, if one could only get to the dam! A distance of nearly two miles lay between the ranch house and the weir—two miles of ants. Those two peons had managed only a fifth of that distance at the cost of their lives. Was there an Indian daring enough after that to run the gauntlet five times as far? Hardly likely; and if there were, his prospect of getting back was almost nil.

No, there was only one thing for it, he'd have to make the attempt himself; he might just as well be running as sitting still, anyway, when the ants finally got him. Besides, there was a bit of a chance. Perhaps the ants weren't so almighty after all; perhaps he had allowed the mass suggestion of that evil black throng to hypnotize him, just as a snake fascinates and over-powers.

The ants were building their bridges. Leiningen got up on a chair. "Hey, lads, listen to me!" he cried. Slowly and listlessly, from all sides of the trench, the men began to shuffle towards him, the apathy of death already stamped on their faces.

"Listen, lads!" he shouted. "You're frightened of those beggars, but you're a damn sight more fright-ened of me, and I'm proud of you. There's still a chance to save our lives—by flooding the plantation from the river. Now one of you might manage to get as far as the weir—but he'd never come back.

Well, I'm not going to let you try it; if I did I'd be worse than one of those ants. No, I called the tune, and now I'm going to pay the piper.

"The moment I'm over the ditch, set fire to the petrol. That'll allow time for the flood to do the trick. Then all you have to do is wait here all snug and quiet till I'm back. Yes, I'm coming back, trust me"—he grinned—"when I've finished my slimming-cure."

He pulled on high leather boots, drew heavy gauntlets over his hands, and stuffed the spaces between breeches and boots, gauntlets and arms, shirt and neck, with rags soaked in petrol. With close-fitting mosquito goggles he shielded his eyes, knowing too well the ants' dodge of first robbing their victim of sight. Finally, he plugged his nostrils and ears with cotton-wool, and let the peons drench his clothes with petrol.

He was about to set off, when the old Indian medicine man came up to him; he had a wondrous salve, he said, prepared from a species of chafer whose odor was intolerable to ants. Yes, this odor protected these chafers from the attacks of even the most murderous ants. The Indian smeared the boss' boots, his gauntlets, and his face over and over with the extract.

Leiningen then remembered the paralyzing effect of ants' venom, and the Indian gave him a gourd full of the medicine he had administered to the bitten peon at the water ditch. The planter drank it down without noticing its bitter taste; his mind was already at the weir.

He started off towards the northwest corner of the trench. With a bound he was over—and among the ants.

The beleaguered garrison had no opportunity to watch Leiningen's race against death. The ants were climbing the inner bank again—the lurid ring of petrol blazed aloft. For the fourth time that day the reflection from the fire shone on the sweating faces of the imprisoned men, and on the reddish-black cuirasses of their oppressors. The red and blue, dark-edged flames leaped vividly now, celebrating what? The funeral pyre of the four hundred, or of the hosts of destruction? Leiningen ran. He ran in long, equal strides, with only one thought, one sensation, in his being—he must get through. He dodged all trees and shrubs; except for the split seconds his soles touched the ground the ants should have no opportunity to alight on him. That they would get to him soon, despite the salve on his boots, the petrol in his clothes, he realized only too well, but he knew even more surely that he must, and that he would, get to the weir.

Apparently the salve was some use after all; not until he reached halfway did he feel ants under his clothes, and a few on his face. Mechanically, in his stride, he struck at them, scarcely conscious of their bites. He saw he was drawing appreciably nearer the weir—the distance grew less and less—sank to five hundred—three—two—one hundred yards.

Then he was at the weir and gripping the ant-hulled wheel. Hardly had he seized it when a horde of infuriated ants flowed over his hands, arms and shoulders. He started the wheel—before it turned once on its axis the swarm covered his face. Leiningen strained like a madman, his lips pressed tight; if he opened them to draw breath. . . .

He turned and turned; slowly the dam lowered until it reached the bed of the river. Already the water was overflowing the ditch. Another minute, and the river was pouring through the nearby gap in the breakwater. The flooding of the plantation had begun.

Leiningen let go the wheel. Now, for the first time, he realized he was coated from head to foot with a layer of ants. In spite of the petrol his clothes were full of them, several had got to his body or were clinging to his face. Now that he had completed his task, he felt the smart raging over his flesh from the bites of sawing and piercing insects.

Frantic with pain, he almost plunged into the river. To be ripped and splashed to shreds by piranhas? Already he was running the return journey, knocking ants from his gloves and jacket, brushing them from his bloodied face, squashing them to death under his clothes.

One of the creatures bit him just below the rim of his goggles; he managed to tear it away, but the agony of the bite and its etching acid drilled into the eye nerves; he saw now through circles of fire into a milky mist, then he ran for a time almost blinded, knowing that if he once tripped and fell. . . . The old Indian's brew didn't seem much good; it weakened the poison a bit, but didn't get rid of it. His heart pounded as if it would burst; blood roared in his ears; a giant's fist battered his lungs.

Then he could see again, but the burning girdle of petrol appeared infinitely far away; he could not last half that distance. Swift-changing pictures flashed through his head, episodes in his life, while in another part of his brain a cool and impartial onlooker informed this ant-blurred, gasping, exhausted bundle named Leiningen that such a rushing panorama of scenes from one's past is seen only in the moment before death.

A stone in the path . . . too weak to avoid it . . . the planter stumbled and collapsed. He tried to rise . . . he must be pinned under a rock . . . it was impossible . . . the slightest movement was impossible. . . .

Then all at once he saw, starkly clear and huge, and, right before his eyes, furred with ants, towering and swaying in its death agony, the pampas stag. In six minutes—gnawed to the bones. God, he couldn't die like that! And something outside him seemed to drag him to his feet. He tottered. He began to stagger forward again.

Through the blazing ring hurtled an apparition which, as soon as it reached the ground on the inner side, fell full length and did not move. Leiningen, at the moment he made that leap through the flames, lost consciousness for the first time in his life. As he lay there, with glazing eyes and lacerated face, he appeared a man returned from the grave. The peons rushed to him, stripped off his clothes, tore away the ants from a body that seemed almost one open wound; in some places the bones were showing. They carried him into the ranch house.

As the curtain of flames lowered, one could see in place of the illimitable host of ants an extensive vista of water. The thwarted river had swept over the plantation, carrying with it the entire army. The water had collected and mounted in the great "saucer," while the ants had in vain attempted to reach the hill on which stood the ranch house. The girdle of flames held them back.

And so imprisoned between water and fire, they had been delivered into the annihilation that was their god. And near the farther mouth of the water ditch, where the stone mole had its second gap, the ocean swept the lost battalions into the river, to vanish forever.

The ring of fire dwindled as the water mounted to the petrol trench, and quenched the dimming flames. The inundation rose higher and higher: because its outflow was impeded by the timber and underbrush it had carried along with it, its surface required some time to reach the top of the high stone breakwater and discharge over it the rest of the shattered army.

It swelled over ant-stippled shrubs and bushes, until it washed against the foot of the knoll whereon the besieged had taken refuge. For a while an alluvial of ants tried again and again to attain this dry land, only to be repulsed by streams of petrol back into the merciless flood.

Leiningen lay on his bed, his body swathed from head to foot in bandages. With fomentations and salves, they had managed to stop the bleeding, and had dressed his many wounds. Now they thronged around him, one question in every face. Would he recover? "He won't die," said the old man who had bandaged him, "if he doesn't want to."

The planter opened his eyes. "Everything in order?" he asked.

"They're gone," said his nurse. "To hell." He held out to his master a gourd full of a powerful sleeping draught. Leiningen gulped it down.

"I told you I'd come back," he murmured, "even if I am a bit streamlined." He grinned and shut his eyes. He slept.

Sources

"Jonah," from the *King James Bible.*

"Book XII," from *The Odyssey* by Homer, translated by Samuel Butler, 1900.

"Shipwreck," from *Sufferings in Africa,* by Captain James Riley, 1817.

"Ice Again," from *Two Years before the Mast,* by Richard Henry Dana, 1840.

"The First Lowering," from *Moby Dick,* by Herman Melville, 1851.

"The Pirate Crew Set Sail," from *The Adventures of Tom Sawyer,* by Mark Twain, 1876.

"In Which a Conversation Takes Place Which Seems Likely to Cost Phileas Fogg Dear," from *Around the World in Eighty Days,* by Jules Verne, 1873.

"Among the Crocodiles," from *Fifty-Two Stories of Animal Life and Adventure,* by H. Hervey, 1903.

"Wild-Fowling Adventures," from *Far Away and Long Ago,* by W. H. Hudson, 1918.

"How the Brigadier Slew the Fox," from *The Adventures of Gerard,* by Arthur Conan Doyle, 1903.

"Hunting Musk-Oxen Near the Pole," from *Fifty-Two Stories of Animal Life and Adventure,* by Lieutenant R. E. Perry, USN, 1903.

"Youth," by Joseph Conrad, 1903.

"The Strange Days That Came to Jimmie Friday," by Frederic Remington, 1896.

"Lion-Hunting," from *Fifty-Two Stories of Animal Life and Adventure,* by Alfred H. Miles, 1903.

"The Forcing of the Trap," from *The Prisoner of Zenda,* by Anthony Hope, 1894.

"The Venturers," from *Strictly Business: More Stories of the Four Million,* by O'Henry, 1910.

"In a Cuban Cave," from *Fifty-Two Stories of Animal Life and Adventure,* by Julius A. Palmer, 1903.

"Dutch Courage," from *Dutch Courage and Other Stories,* by Jack London, 1922.

"A War Correspondent's Kit," from *Notes of a War Correspondent* by Richard Harding Davis, 1911.

"The Road Home," by Peter Collinson (Dashiell Hammett), 1922.

"Leiningen Versus the Ants," by Carl Stephenson, 1938.